The Psychology
of
Private Events

Contributors to This Volume

Louis J. J. Bruno
Joseph R. Cautela
Ralph F. Hefferline
Alfred Jacobs
Frederick H. Kanfer
Karel Lambert
Hayne W. Reese
Lewis B. Sachs
Milton Wolpin

The Psychology of Private Events

PERSPECTIVES ON COVERT RESPONSE SYSTEMS

Edited by

ALFRED JACOBS
AND LEWIS B. SACHS

West Virginia University
Morgantown, West Virginia

1971

ACADEMIC PRESS
New York and London

ACADEMIC PRESS, INC.
111 Fifth Avenue, New York, New York 10003

United Kingdom Edition published by
ACADEMIC PRESS, INC. (LONDON) LTD.
Berkeley Square House, London W1X 6BA

LIBRARY OF CONGRESS CATALOG CARD NUMBER: 73-162936

PRINTED IN THE UNITED STATES OF AMERICA

Contents

List of Contributors

Numbers in parentheses indicate the pages on which the authors' contributions begin.

LOUIS J. J. BRUNO (163), Electropsychology Laboratory, Columbia University, New York, New York

JOSEPH R. CAUTELA (109), Boston College, Boston, Massachusetts

RALPH F. HEFFERLINE (163), Electropsychology Laboratory, Columbia University, New York, New York

ALFRED JACOBS (1, 77, 131), West Virginia University, Morgantown, West Virginia

FREDERICK H. KANFER (39), University of Cincinnati, Cincinnati, Ohio

KAREL LAMBERT (7), University of California, Irvine, California

HAYNE W. REESE[1] (17), Department of Human Development, University of Kansas, Lawrence, Kansas

LEWIS B. SACHS (1, 61), West Virginia University, Morgantown, West Virginia

MILTON WOLPIN (77), University of Southern California, Los Angeles, California

[1] *Present affiliation*: West Virginia University, Morgantown, West Virginia.

Preface

The study of thoughts, feelings, images has suffered from many years of scientific neglect. Now, psychologists are returning to the old, important, and unsolved issues which were first raised in the early years of psychology as a science. Armed with new and more effective techniques and methodologies, psychologists are providing the long sought answers. The purpose of this book is to provide the recently accumulated evidence that the assessment and manipulation of such private events facilitates the prediction and control of human behavior.

The individual contributions represent a variety of approaches to theorizing and research into private events, and to the clinical applications or potential applications which have been generated by such study. The authors have addressed themselves in creative and ingenious ways to such diverse topics as creating resistance to temptation; developing feelings of attraction to appropriate sex objects; training people to experience less pain; and having mental hospital patients practice being happier.

We believe the book will be of primary interest to students and teachers of psychology, particularly those interested in behaviorally oriented clinical research and practice. Other professionals and teachers in the social sciences may also find it useful to become aware of the newer trends in psychology.

In conclusion, the editors would like to express again their appreciation to the contributors for their cooperativeness as well as the excellence of their contributions, and to the colleagues, students, and other staff at West Virginia University for their many forms of assistance.

The Psychology
of
Private Events

Private Events

Alfred Jacobs and Lewis B. Sachs
West Virginia University
Morgantown, West Virginia

This book provides evidence that the scientific investigation of such events as thoughts, feelings, and images is not only possible, but also useful. Most historians date the beginnings of psychology from Wilhelm Wundt's attempt to study mental states by developing a "chemistry of the mind"—an approach that led to a very sterile and unproductive 30 years. The rejection of the structuralist school took a number of forms. The Gestalt psychologists and the functionalists rejected analysis into parts, and, with it, part of the scientific method in psychology. The psychoanalytic movements, with their focus on treatments, found it necessary to invent their own mental concepts, and, perhaps by mutual consent, a full commitment never developed between the psychoanalytic movements and the mainstream of American research and behavior-oriented psychology. Behaviorism, led by Watson, rejected the introspective method, and tried to develop a black-box psychology that ignored the existence of internal events and processes.

Today, much serious research in psychology is directed toward understanding a type of treatment, systematic desensitization, which begins by instructing the phobic patient to imagine himself approaching a feared object and questions him whether or not he can see the image clearly. Today, behaviorists ask people to chart the number of times they smoke and have patients record their feelings or smoking urges as well. Today may also be the time for psychology to try to evaluate the usefulness and effectiveness of mental concepts. The fact is that for the past decade and at an ever increasing rate, psychologists have become more concerned with classes of covert responses.

Much evidence for the possibility and usefulness of studying covert responses has accumulated from the expectancy research [for example, the experimental bias studies by Rosenthal (1966) and the subject bias or demand characteristics studies by Orne (1962)]. In addition, psychologists such as Bandura (1969) have demonstrated the effect of cognitive or symbolic processes on the outcome of symptomatic treatment and the evidence from such placebo research as that done by Frank (1961) suggests that attitudes, expectancies, and thoughts make an impressive contribution to the effectiveness of traditional treatments.

A number of different kinds of developments have contributed to the relevance of the present return to the study of private events. Clearly, one development is the improved technology which we possess over the 1870s. The computer, which is now available to all of us, makes possible a complex analysis of response classes in a number of minutes instead of days or weeks. As a matter of fact, the methodology inherent in factor analysis was not available to the structuralists. The computer is also beginning to be of use in the analysis of verbal data, the content of which heretofore was so complex as to deter attempts to study it. Such verbal behavior is often part of the definition for covert responses in humans. The greater accessibility to ordinary psychologists of polygraphs and simple, reasonably sturdy devices for the recording of internal states also has contributed to our increased ability to mount an attack on the study of internal processes.

Also, it is of no small importance that more than half of us represented in this volume are, as well as scientists, applied psychologists and social engineers. We feel a need to change behavior that is socially ineffective but we also like things that we can count, measure and study. All of us have a commitment to research. As we leave our laboratories to work with real problems, as perhaps also happened in the case of the schools of psychology that sprung up around the turn of the century, we have found it necessary and useful to put something inside the "black box" and to conceptualize the presence of covert responses.

We believe it is far-fetched at this time for psychologists to deny that people think, that as you read this page you are not thinking about it, evaluating it, etc. We believe that it is unscientific to deny, *a priori,* that covert responses are by their nature unable to be studied, or do not behave in lawful ways. In fact, the evidence that you will read in this book gives further support to the proposition that covert events operate as if they are amenable to some of the same learning processes and manipulations as other classes of responses; that is to say that thoughts and feelings may be shaped, reinforced, or extinguished. Although the nature of many classes of covert responses will always render them private, manipulation of their frequency or probability has observable consequences for covert behavior, and a potential source of validation is thereby provided. The probability of occurrence of covert responses can be controlled (and probably has been for years) by various kinds of social institutions. The social and personal implications are important and perhaps even frightening.

We believe that covert responses can be reliably operationally specified. For example, when we specify the stimulus situation—that is, evoking the set—try to imagine a snake and specifying some verbal response "I can picture a snake" or "I can't do it," we are being operational. We are not being unscientific or sliding into some mystic realm of parapsychology. We believe that such data are available and potentially useful for prediction. In the pages to follow, we hope to convince you, if necessary, that not only do you think, imagine, and feel, but that these are also useful, legitimate, and scientifically respectable areas for research. We also have tried to represent various samples of approaches, models, research, and theorizing about the nature of various kinds of private events or covert responses.

The first chapter, by Karel Lambert, a philosopher of science, attempts to deal with various philosophical positions taken by the psychologists in their attempts to deal with words like 'belief' and 'expectation' with relationship to psychological explanation. Lambert points out that all attempts to reduce intentional expressions eventually run afoul of one philosophical dilemma or another. However, Lambert concludes on a somewhat optimistic note by suggesting that explanations by causal law may not necessarily be regarded as the unique kind of explanation in the science of behavior.

The second chapter, by Hayne Reese, addresses itself to covert verbal and nonverbal mediation. Reese presents different models for mediation, attention, and set. He then shows how these models can be used to generate different predictions about research as well as have differential goodness of fit to completed mediational process research results.

The chapter on mood and affect, by Jacobs, suggests that positive and negative affects may constitute a large number of classes of covert events. He concludes that positive and negative affect are not one simple bipolar dimension, but that positive affects are probably generated by rewarding states of affairs and negative affects by rewarding aversive states. He suggests that psychology has devoted an extraordinary amount of attention to negative affects and practically none to positive affects. He shows that having mental hospital patients practice feeling happy causes them to be happier and more energetic after the practice has ceased, and that verbal reports of affect generally appear to have much potential utility in the study of psychopathology and treatment.

In contrast to the historical view of hypnosis as a stable characteristic of the individual, Sachs presents data demonstrating the modifiable nature of hypnotic phenomena. He accomplished changes in hypnotic behaviors by the development of training techniques for the alteration of sensations and images. The reduction of pain was one of the most important changes made possible by this training.

Kanfer's paper is addressed to a study of self-regulatory behavior by which a person maintains his own behavior in the absence of immediate environmental support or feedback. He points out that such behavior is important and that it is ordinarily considered the mark of a socialized person. Kanfer describes models for self-monitoring, self-reinforcement, and self control and describes the recent research in this area

Jacobs and Wolpin describe their research suggesting that increases in reported fear during systematic desensitization treatments do not necessarily sensitize the subject so that he is more likely to avoid fearful objects. The authors report that the literature suggests that neither the absence of fear during visualization, relaxation, nor the use of a graduated hierarchy are essential components to the success of systematic desensitization, but rather that a large part of the success of desensitization is clearly attributable to the expectations of success of treatment by its recipient.

Cautela's paper describes his successes with covert conditioning, and the manner in which he treats alcoholics by covert sensitization, a process in which the patient is trained to follow urges to drink by aversive thoughts Cautela has also employed covert reinforcement in which the frequency of desirable overt responses is increased by training the *S*s to follow desirable responses by a reinforcing stimulus presented in the imagination. In covert negative reinforcement which may be particularly useful with depressives Cautela uses the escape from a negative or aversive covert image as an effective reinforcement

Hefferline and Bruno describe their work in training electromyographic impulses. They show that *S*s can learn, with practice, to fire individual muscle groups, even in complex patterns. The authors have trained muscular responses, of which the *S*s were unaware to become the conditioned stimulus for overt responses even while the *S* remains unaware of the occurrence of the nonverbalizable muscular response. This process can be used to induce artificially generated hallucinations in *S*s.

References

Bandura, A. *Principles of behavior modification.* New York: Holt, 1969.
Frank, J. D. *Persuasion and Healing: A comparative study of psychotherapy.* Baltimore: Johns Hopkins Press, 1961.

Orne, M. T. On the social psychology of the psychological experiment: With particular reference to demand characteristics and their implications. *American Psychologist,* 1962, **17**, 776-783.

Rosenthal, R. *Experimenter effects in behavioral research.* New York: Appleton-Century-Crofts, 1966.

Explanation and Intention

Karel Lambert
University of California
Irvine, California

At the beginning of a symposium similar in character to the present one, B. F. Skinner "spoke of his feelings of loneliness" and of his search among the other speakers for a friendly face. His initial hopes that Sigmund Koch might have been his man were dashed by Koch's passionate and polemical rejection of radical behaviorism. However, unexpected support came from—of all places—a philosopher, Norman Malcolm. Skinner took so much comfort from Malcolm's critical, but enormously sympathetic remarks on radical behaviorism, that his feelings of desertion and loneliness were partially allayed. So the originators of the present symposium, having carefully examined the previous literature on psychology symposia and in the hope of allaying possible feelings of desertion and loneliness, invited a philosopher to the present gathering. Thus, my presence is certainly testimony to the humanity of the directors of this symposium; whether it also reflects their predictive skills remains to be seen.

My topic of concern is the place of intention in the explanation of behavior. Philosophers have been vitally interested in this problem during this century, and a good deal of this interest has been stimulated by the remarks of 20th century psychologists. Indeed, the influence of behavioral scientists on philosophers is clear, if not always direct or well advertised in the scientific community. Examples are easy to elicit. Behavioristic psychologists, for example, have certainly influenced contemporary philosophers like Rudolf Carnap and W. V. Quine, and the physiologizing of Donald Hebb has had a strong effect on materialistic philosophers like David Armstrong and J. C. C. Smart.

Words like 'belief' and 'expectation' have loomed large in psychological explanation, especially among that group of theoretical psychologists called cognitive psychologists. Further, even among noncognitive psychologists, they represent an important intermediate step in the reduction (or replacement) of teleological explanation to (or by) behavioral explanation. Skinner (1966), for example, is very explicit about the intermediate character of beliefs, expectations and their ilk in the replacement of teleological explanation by behavioral explanation.

Teleological—or goal—explantions are very common in everyday life. To the question, why did the rat turn right in the T maze? a common reply might be: *in order to* get to the food. The goal in the explanation of the rat's behavior is, to use a Tolmanism, the-getting-to-the-food. Now the-getting-to-the-food occurs later than the behavior it explains. However, a canon of scientific explanation is that the explaining event must not occur after the occurrence of the event to be explained. Most psychologists regard the temporally consequent character of the explaining event as the essential characteristic of teleological explanations (Taylor, 1964).[1] So given the fact that science shuns final causes, it is clear that teleological explanations are inadequate explanations from a scientific point of view.

Nevertheless, the explanatory force in our common-sense, teleological explanations of human behavior has been strongly felt. Accordingly many philosophers and psychologists have attempted to recast teleological explanations in a form acceptable to the scientist. For example, to the question: Why did Rat A turn right in the T maze? the recasted explanation might take the following form: because (1) Rat A demands food, and because (2) Rat A expects that if he turns right in the T maze he will get to food, and finally because (3) whenever something that is demanded strongly enough is such that some response is expected to result in obtaining the demanded object then the response will be performed. In the recast explanation, the reference to future goals has been replaced by antecedent demands and expectations.

There is much to complain about in this reduction of teleological explanations to explanations in terms of antecedent demands and expectations. To

[1] It is debatable that this is the correct way to characterize teleological explanations. For example, Taylor (1964) rejects this way of characterizing "teleological explanation." However, I am not concerned with what is, in fact, the correct way to characterize "teleological explanation" but rather with the way psychologists tend to characterize them.

begin with, Rat A's taking a right turn in the T maze is not inferable from the antecedent demands and expectations alone. What would be needed would be another condition, namely, (4) that Rat A demands to get to the food strongly enough. For without this added premise, we could not utilize the generalization relating demands and expectations mentioned previously to explain the rat's right turning behavior in the T maze. However, given that all scientific explanation involves essential reference to law, it would follow that without (4), the conjunction of Rat A's demand to get to the food and his expectation that if he turned right in a T maze he would get to the food, would be insufficient to explain his right turning behavior in the T maze.

What sort of a premise in an explanation is a premise of the sort: Rat A demands to get to the food *strongly enough*? How else can one measure the strength of Rat A's demand to get to food other than by looking to see whether he in fact goes to the food? This is circular: we attribute a demand to the rat and say it caused him to act in a certain way when our only evidence for attributing the demand and making the causal claim was the fact that he ran to the food. Equally, the purported law relating demand and expectation is suspect. It verges on a definitional truth to say that when someone wants to do something strongly enough he will do it. The phrase "strongly enough" ensures against counterexamples.

On the other hand, if we do not ensure against counterexamples in this way, (4) is obviously false. We are all aware of cases where some organism has a demand for something and expects that a certain course of action will satisfy that demand, but still does not take that course of action. Accordingly, we are faced with a dilemma in the proposed reduction of teleological explanation to intentional explanation. The dilemma is this: laws formulated in terms of demand, expectation, and so on are either true *ex vi terminorum* or they are false. On the one hand, if they are true by meanings above, they have no explanatory force because they are unfalsifiable. On the other hand, if they are false, they have no explanatory force because they are not really laws.

Finally above these difficulties in our proposed reduction, there is the objection—one hears more from psychologists than from philosophers—that we have done away with future causes only at the expense of unacceptable, antecedent mental causes. To many psychologists, this move has seemed about as helpful as replacing the local witch doctor by a chiropractor.[2]

At this point, it will perhaps be useful to distinguish between two varieties of behaviorism. I shall call them *reductionistic behaviorism* and *replacement behaviorism*.

---

[2] History shows, I think, the inaccuracy of the recent assertion of Farber (1968) that ". . . no one these days denies the existence of mental events." To say that there are beliefs is not to say that there are mental events; the existence of beliefs does not necessarily commit one to a world containing mental events.

There are two kinds of reductionistic behaviorism In the first kind, the scientific vocabulary contains both intentional expressions like 'expects', 'desires', 'hopes', and so on, and nonintentional expressions like 'runs,' 'touches,' 'is red,' and so on. In this version of reductionistic behaviorism, intentional expressions are reduced by definitions (or by other techniques like, for example, Carnap's technique or reduction sentences) to words or phrases that purport to describe behavior and/or purely physical events.

The second version of reductionistic behaviorism does not contain intentional expressions in its theoretical vocabulary. Reduction, in this version of behaviorism, takes place by *paraphrasing* from the ordinary language into scientific language. That is, expressions like 'expects', or more accurately contexts containing expressions like 'expects', are paraphrased into sentences in the purified scientific vocabulary. Psychological exponents of this particular variety of behaviorism are those in the Hullian tradition and at times the Skinnerian (Skinner, 1953). Various philosophers, including Russell, at particular moments, have espoused this weaker version of reductionistic behaviorism.

In psychology, the difference between the two varieties of reductionistic behaviorism probably stems from different opinions about the ontological commitment of languages containing intentional expressions. Generally, psychologists who are reductionistic behaviorists of the second kind believe that if a language contains intentional expressions then that language is committed to nonphysical events. Nevertheless, they admit the explanatory force of explanations couched in intentional language, but deny that the explanatory power of same requires appeal to nonphysical or mental inner-states. Accordingly, they believe that the features of our common-sense intentional explanations that make them explanatory can be expressed in a language devoid of expressions suggesting the existence of nonphysical entities.

A much more radical version of behaviorism is what I shall call *replacement behaviorism.* Replacement behaviorism, like the second kind of reductionistic behaviorism, does not contain any intentional expressions in its theoretical vocabulary. Indeed, it contains no intentional expressions in either its theoretical *or* its nontheoretical vocabulary. On the other hand, it offers no nonintentional paraphrases of sentences or contexts containing intentional expressions like 'expects' and 'demands'. Rather, it provides *substitutes* for our common-sense intentional explanations; that is, the replacement behaviorist claims only to be able to give a nonintentional explanation of that piece of behavior explained in intentional terms. Replacement behaviorists are much less sanguine than reductionistic behaviorists of the second kind about the ontological commitment of paraphrased intentional explanations. In general, they believe that commitment to nonphysical entities cannot be avoided even in the second version of reductionistic behaviorism.

Reductionistic behaviorism, in either the first (strong) or second (weaker) variety, can be interpreted as a response to the dilemma engendered by intentional explanation. For my purposes, I do not think it makes much difference whether this response is couched in the language of the strong or the weak reductionist behaviorist.

The philosophical counterparts of the response I am about to describe are Gilbert Ryle and Rudolf Carnap. According to Ryle and Carnap, expressions like 'expects', 'desires', 'hopes', and so on are best construed as a *disposition to behave in a certain way under certain circumstances*. The psychologist most clearly identified with this manner of treating intentional expressions is Edward Tolman. Employing Carnap's technique of bilateral reduction sentences, in a paper co-authored by Ritchie and Kalish, Tolman (1946) gives the following reduction sentence for the disposition term 'expects':

When we assert that a rat expects food at location L, what we assert is that *if* (1) he is deprived of food, (2) he has been trained on path P, (3) he is now put on path P, (4) path P is now blocked, and (5) there are other paths which lead away from path P or which point directly to location L, *then* he will run down the path which points directly to location L. When we assert that he does *not* expect food at location L, what we assert is that, under the same conditions, he will *not* run directly down the path which leads to location L [p. 15].

The point in giving this sort of reduction for intentional expressions is that it now provides for the possibility of formulating nontrivial laws in a purely behavioral vocabulary, and thus it avoids the dilemma resulting from the reduction of teleological explanation to intentional explanation explained earlier. For if we now substitute the reducing words for words like 'expects' in laws containing the latter, what we obtain, so it is claimed, is a nontrivial, true generalization couched in purely behavioral terms. Accordingly, the resulting explanation of a piece of behavior such as the rat's turning right in the T maze, is legitimatized from the scientific point of view.

However, there are serious difficulties in reductionistic behaviorism. For one, difficulties arise in the attempt to reconstrue intentional expressions in a purely behavioral vocabulary. Consider Tolman's reduction of 'expectation'. There are a variety of circumstances under which, given the stated conditions, the rat will not run down the path; for example, when a cat suddenly crosses it, and yet in which we surely would not conclude that the rat did not expect food at location L. On the other hand, were we to insist that Tolman's reduction of 'expectation' be adopted as it stand, then it would be equally clear that the meaning of this expression would have to be altered rather radically. Philosophers like Chisholm (1957) have urged that every attempt to dispense with intentional expressions inevitably employs one of them. For example, to rule out the influence of the cat crossing the path on the rat's behavior, we must assume that the rat is motivated solely by the *demand* for food. By doing this, however, now we are explaining 'expectation' in terms of 'demand', a purely intentional expression.

Finally, there is the objection voiced by materialistic philosophers like Armstrong (1968) who point out that reductionistic behaviorism fails to satisfy our original objective: namely, to reduce teleological explanation to causal explanation. In doing away with intentional inner states in terms of dispositions, we have also done away with antecedent *causal* states, for dispositions are not causes!

I have just suggested that materialistic philosophers are discontent with the reductionistic behaviorist's analysis of explanations in terms of expectations, demands, and so on because the sort of explanations that are the products of that analysis are not causal in character. Now many psychologists who call themselves behaviorists are, in my opinion, really materialists. A materialist, like a behaviorist of the reductionistic variety exemplified by early Tolman, cheerfully admits intentional expressions into the scientific vocabulary. In contrast, however, he does not believe that it is possible to give definitions or reduction sentences of intentional expressions in nonintentional terms. The reason is not that intentional expressions purport to refer to mysterious mental entities, but rather that there are features of the logic of expressions such as 'belief', 'expectation', 'desire', etc., that cannot be captured by an analysis of such expressions in terms of words or phrases purporting to describe purely physical events or behavior. For example, the statement, "Rat A touched the card with his nose," which contains the nonintentional word 'touches', logically implies, "There is something that Rat A touches," but it does not follow that if Rat A believes in round squares, there is something that he believes in.

The materialist holds that words like 'expectation' are constituents of phrases like 'having an expectation' and these denote certain physiological states, for example, states of the central nervous system. To put it another way, having an expectation is correlated or identified with certain physiological states of the central nervous system. Any psychologist who includes such expressions as 'belief', 'desire', etc. in his scientific vocabulary, and who says that ultimately phrases like 'having a belief' are to be identified with physiological states of one sort or another, is a materialist. This is true even of those psychologists who say that physiologizing in the present state of the psychology of learning and motivation is precipitous.

Materialist philosophers like Armstrong and Smart hold that the correlation or identification of, say, having an expectation with a certain state of the central nervous system, is a purely factual one; it is not a matter of meaning. It is like the relation of identity in the statement, "Tully is identical with Cicero" and not like identity in "Two is identical with one plus one." They also maintain that the states of the central nervous system can be connected in a lawlike way with behavior. Now the possibility of neurophysiological causal laws certainly seems reasonable enough, although, as of this date, rather remote. Accordingly, the materialist holds that explanation in terms of having expectations, having desires, etc. are ultimately causal in virtue of the *fact* that these entities can be identified with physical states of the body. It is not surprising, therefore, to find materialist philosophers of the present generation supporting many of their claims by appeal to those psychologists who seek to explain learning and motivation on the basis of physiological models—Hebb, for example.

Let me recapitulate. How does a materialistic philosopher rid himself of teleological explanation, that is, of explanation in terms of future causes? Consider the lowly thermostat. It seems to offer a paradigm case of purposive behavior, and one can certainly explain its behavior teleologically. For example, to the question, "Why did the thermostat activate the furnace?" the reply might be "*In order to* maintain the temperature of the room." On the other hand, the activating behavior of the thermostat can be explained in causal, and even in mechanical, terms. Now the materialist argues that both kinds of explanations are explanations of one and the same state of affairs; there is no incompatibility between them, although one cannot be analyzed or defined in terms of the other. To be sure, the causal explanation of the behavior of the thermostat contains no intentional expressions; one does not ordinarily ascribe desires and beliefs to thermostats. Yet, materialists argue, there is no important difference between the purposive behavior of homing rockets, for example, and the purposive behavior of human beings, even though explanation of the behavior of human beings often does take place in terms of intentional expressions. There is nothing inconsistent here, says the materialist, because beliefs, desires, etc. are just different ways of describing certain physiological states that are causally related to behavior.

There is no denying the attractive quality of materialism's way out of the dilemma associated with explanations in terms of expectations, demands, etc. Still, there are some rather strong objections it must face.

A famous principle of logic tells us that if a given property is true of A but not of B, then A is not identical with B. Now, as we saw earlier, having an expectation, for example, does not stand in a nontrivial relation to behavior. In other words, having an expectation cannot stand in lawlike relations to behavior. On the other hand, physiological states of the central nervous system are just the sort of property which can stand in lawlike relations to behavior. So it would seem to follow from our logical principle, that having an expectation cannot be identified with certain states of the central nervous system. In general, the cogency of the materialist's way out of the dilemma produced by the reduction of teleological explanation to explanations in terms of alleged intentional states depends on an ancient metaphysical issue, namely, the relation of mind to body. Now it may be disappointing to be told this, but it serves to remind one that although problems in the philosophy of science arise in rather well-defined contexts, they can, and frequently do, lead one into extremely difficult metaphysical questions.

The final way out of the dilemma occasioned by intentional explanations that I shall consider is the way out proposed by the replacement behaviorist. Recall, please, two features of replacement behaviorism mentioned earlier; a methodological feature and a motivational feature. Methodologically, the replacement behaviorist adopts a vocabulary of terms that specifically excludes intentional expressions. The motivational basis behind this move is, as I said before, the direct result of the replacement behaviorist's belief that it is impossible to escape the positing of inner *mental* states if such terms are included in the scientific vocabulary.

According to the replacement behaviorist, one must give up the attempt to find a way out of the dilemma associated with intentional explanations by attempting to find a satisfactory analysis of intentional expressions. Indeed, the replacement behaviorist accepts the dilemma associated with intentional expressions at face value. About the only thing the replacement behaviorist accepts in the present program for ridding oneself of teleological explanations is the move to replace explanations in terms of future causes by intentional explanations. To this extent, he approves of the attempt to supply intermediate, intentional explanations for teleological ones; for intentional explanations at least purport to be explanations in terms of antecedent inner states.

The novel feature of replacement behaviorism consists in this: For most explanations couched in intentional terms, the replacement behaviorist provides a substitute or replacement explanation not containing such terms. No attempt is made to *analyze* expressions like 'expectation' and 'desire' in other terms, or to *identify* what 'having an expectation', 'having a desire', etc. purport to describe with physiological states. Rather, one begins with certain notions as primitive—perhaps not even widely used now in the description of human behavior—and stakes his case on, for example, the eventual success in controlling and predicting behavior. The whole idea behind this program is to get along *without* intentional explanations.

The most notable exponent of replacement behaviorism in philosophy is Quine. His attitude is roughly this: The language of intention is autonomous; it does not reduce. According to Quine (1960), this shows either the indispensibility of the intentional and therefore the importance of an autonomous science of intention or it shows that the intentional idiom is baseless and that the science of intention is empty. His attitude is the latter; it is my impression that this attitude is now also shared in psychology by Skinner (1966).

There are two important objections to this program, however. First, there are good reasons to believe that a vocabulary adequate to at least the *description* of behavior cannot avoid the intentional (C. Taylor, 1964). Second, explanations of the sort offered by Skinner, though surely explanations in terms of antecedent events, are not causal explanations. That is to say, explanations of the sort offered by Skinner do not support contrafactual statements. For example, to explain Rat A's present bar-pressing response in terms of the antecedent circumstance that whenever that response has occurred in the past, food has followed is not to give an explanation of the present occurrence of the response in terms of a cause. The expression "whenever a barpressing has occurred in the past food has followed" does not denote anything like a causal situation except perhaps in the purely Humean sense of 'causal', a point which Skinner has recently acknowledged. Skinner (1966) writes:

Pressing a lever is not a natural or unconditioned way of getting food. The response produces food only in the sense that food follows it—a Humean version of causality [p. 14].

Earlier he compares this situation with the classical conditioning situation, noting in the latter that "the salivation elicited by the conditional stimulus did not produce the food which followed (p. 13)." In other words, the sense of 'produce' in the bar-pressing situation is Pickwickian; hence, it would be strange to say that bar pressing caused the occurrence of food, in the sense of producing food. If we think of the Skinner-box situation, what this means is that the truth of the bar-pressing–food generalization does not support the truth of the conditional: If the pencil in my hand were a bar in a Skinner box it would yield food if pressed. This is the formal counterpart of the metaphorical notion of cause as something *producing* something else.

What observations can be made on the basis of the foregoing account of the reduction of teleological explanation to intentional explanation? The following three points have emerged. First, it is highly dubious that the intentional reduces. Second, if explanations in terms of words like 'expects', 'believes', and so on are admitted into the class of scientific explanations, then what many regard as *the* essential feature of scientific explanation—appeal to law—will have to be abandoned. Third, barring a justification of materialism, any explanation in terms of antecedent states or events that purports to capture the force of, or to be an adequate substitute for, a given teleological explanation would seem bound to be noncausal. I, for one, do not find a ground for pessimism here. Explanation by causal law has been shaken in physics, and I do not see why it must be regarded as the unique kind of explanation in the science of behavior.

References

Armstrong, D. *A materialist theory of mind.* New York: Humanities Press, 1968.
Chisholm, R. *Perceiving: A philosophical study.* Ithaca, New York: Cornell Univ. Press, 1957.

Farber, I. E. *In* M. Brodbeck (ed.), *Philosophy of the social sciences.* New York: Macmillan, 1968. P.149.

Quine, W. V. *Word and object.* New York: Wiley, 1960. P. 221.

Skinner, B. F. *Science and human behavior.* New York: Macmillan, 1953.

Skinner, B. F. Operant behavior. In W. K. Honig (Ed.), *Operant behavior: Areas of research and application.* Century Psychology Series. New York: Appleton-Century-Crofts, 1966. Pp. 12-32.

Taylor, C. *The explanation of behavior.* New York: Humanities Press, 1964.

Tolman, E. C., Ritchie, B. F., & Kalish, D. Studies in spatial learning: I. Orientation and the shortcut. *Journal of Experimental Psychology,* 1946, **1,** 13-24.

The Study of Covert Verbal and Nonverbal Mediation

Hayne W. Reese [1, 2]

University of Kansas
Lawrence, Kansas

Introduction

Mediation

The concept of mediation has a history dating back at least to John Locke (Goss, 1961a). It has been given numerous different formal definitions, but Goss's (1961b) definition is both useful and clear:

A temporal sequence of stimulus–response events in which a mediating response and stimulus may be distinguished can be represented as

$$S_{\text{Initiating}} - R_{\text{Mediating}} \sim S_{\text{Mediating}} - R_{\text{Terminating}}. \cdots$$

[1] This paper was written while the author's work was supported, in part, by Grant OEC 3-7-070706-3118 from the U.S. Office of Education to the Kansas Center for Research in Early Childhood Education.

[2] *Present affiliation:* West Virginia University, Morgantown, West Virginia.

Ideally, two criteria must be met in order for responses and the stimuli they produce to be considered mediating responses and stimuli. The first criterion is the observation of or grounds for inferring the occurrence of one or more responses subsequent to the initiating stimulus and before the terminating response. The second criterion is the demonstration that such temporally intermediate responses and stimuli have actual or potential facilitative or inhibitory effects on one or more measures of the occurrence and strength of the terminating response [Footnote 3, pp. 249–250].

The definition is not without problems, however, and three of these seem to be critical. Two of these relate to the functional nature of the mediating mechanism, and one to its structural nature. By its functional nature, I mean its assumed timing and its assumed effect: the assumed temporal appearance of the mechanism after the initiating stimulus and before the terminal response and the assumed effect of the mechanism on the terminal response.

The problem with applying the timing criterion is that the relative time at which the mechanism actually appears cannot be known if the mechanism is unobservable—which usually means when it is covert. Most of the interesting mediators seem to be covert, and, therefore, the application of the criterion is often a serious problem.

The problem with the criterion of affecting the terminal response was created by Goss when he said that the effect on the terminal response could be "potential." Thus, it is possible to meet this criterion even when the mechanism has no effect on a terminal response, provided it can be argued that the mechanism "potentially" could affect this response.

The "structural" problem is that Goss specified not only the functional nature of the mechanism—and, as just seen, he specified it somewhat loosely—but he also specified its structural nature as a response (together with the stimulation produced by the response). If it is a response in the usual sense of a pattern of muscular movements, then it presumably develops according to the laws of learning and is dependent on drive level and the other variables that influence response strength. However, if "response" is to be understood in a broad sense, to include neural and glandular processes, then perhaps the laws of neurophysiological functioning are more applicable. Also, if "response" is given even broader meaning, to incorporate attention and set, then it is not at all clear what set of laws should be referred to in making predictions.

On the assumption that this broadest meaning of "response" is appropriate, a wide variety of mechanisms that are structurally distinguishable fit the functional criteria of mediators, including not only such obvious mediators as words, but also attentional mechanisms and sets. None of these would be ruled out by the definition, but I think it is a mistake to treat all of them as mediators. I think it is important to distinguish among them, and to emphasize their distinctiveness by not placing them under the one rubric of "mediation." I intend to show briefly that although they all have the general functional nature specified for mediators in Goss's definition, they have other functions that are more important.

Mediation, Attention, and Set. It is convenient to illustrate the different functions of mediation, attention, and set by referring to models that represent these functions. As Lachman (1960) noted, however, it is important to make it clear that presenting such models is not the same as presenting theoretical analyses. These models are supposed to represent phenomena (or sets of phenomena), and to show how the relevant theory is to be applied. It is not asserted that the model *describes* the phenomenon, or more generally, that it describes reality; rather, it is asserted that the phenomenon—or reality—behaves *as if* the model were descriptive. That is, the model functions as a metaphor (see Reese & Overton, 1970).

What I propose to do in this section is present models; I shall make no more than passing reference to specific theories, and then only to clarify points pertaining to the models.

First, for comparison, consider the familiar single-stage stimulus-response model (see Fig. 1A). The symbol S in this model represents the initial stimulus, R represents the terminal response, and the arrow means "elicits" or "arouses."

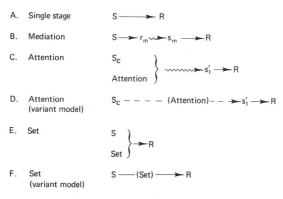

Fig. 1. Single-stage model and "mediation" models.

The essential point of this model is that nothing intervenes between the stimulus and the response. Let me digress briefly to repeat the earlier caveat. It is not asserted that there is no organism, nor that the organism is empty, nor that external stimuli produce responses. It is asserted that the behavior of organisms can be *represented* by this empty-organism model. The accompanying theory might well specify that the stimuli in question are not external to the organism but are produced within the organism by the action of external stimuli on sensory receptors (e.g., Hull, 1943, pp. 32-33). To argue that the model is an inadequate description of the way organisms behave is to reveal a lack of understanding of the nature of such models; the model cannot be an inadequate *description*, because it is not a description but a representation or metaphor. A given model may be a useless way to represent reality, but the demonstration that that is so depends on how well the theory associated with it works, among other things (see Reese & Overton, 1970).

To continue with the models, consider Goss's mediation model (Fig. 1B), where r_m symbolizes a mediating response (lower case to indicate that it is covert, upper case if it is overt), s_m symbolizes an internal stimulus, the wavy line means "unconditionally produces," and *S, R,* and the arrow have the same meanings as in the single-stage model. Note that both responses—the mediating response and the terminal response—are depicted as being elicited by a specific stimulus; the mediating response is elicited by the initial stimulus *S*, and the terminal response is elicited specifically by the internal stimulus s_m. This is an important aspect of the mediation model, as will be seen when the attention and set models are considered.

The next model is the attentional model (Fig. 1C). In this model, S_c is a stimulus complex composed of several elements, including S_1', which is a value (represented by the prime) on a particular dimension (represented by the subscript). "Attention" in the model is a mechanism described in various ways in various theories, but its full description is part of the theory and not part of the model. For purposes of constructing the model, it is necessary only to describe it as a mechanism in whose presence the initial stimulus complex S_c produces within the organism an unobservable stimulus s_1' related to the element S_1'. The other symbols have the same meanings as in the first two models. Here the terminal response is elicited by an internal cue produced by a specific value on a specific stimulus dimension, and that cue is produced by the filtering action of attention on the initial stimulus complex.

A major difference between this attentional model and the mediation model is that here the intervening mechanism acts on a range of stimulus complexes and produces a cue that depends on a corresponding value of an element in the stimulus complex. This cue cannot be produced by the intervening mechanism—attention—when the corresponding element is absent from the stimulus complex. Another way to represent this is shown in the next model (Fig. 1D), where all of the old symbols have the same meanings as before, and the new symbol—the broken line with intervening parentheses—means "is acted upon by (the mechanism in parentheses) to produce. . . ." That is, this model says that the stimulus complex is acted upon by attention to produce the internal cue.

The effect of set is shown in the next model (Fig. 1E). The terminal response is elicited by the initial stimulus only if "Set" is present, or is elicited more vigorously if "Set" is present. Another way to represent this is shown in Fig. 1F, where the solid line broken by parentheses means "elicits if (the mechanism in parentheses) is present."

The single-stage and set models both show the terminal response as elicited by the initial stimulus. They differ from each other in the influence of an intermediary in the latter model, and they differ from the mediation and attention models in that the latter two models show the terminal response as elicited not by the initial stimulus, but by another stimulus. The mediation and attention models differ from each other in that the effective stimulus in the mediation model is invariably produced by the mediating response r_m whatever elicits r_m, while the effective stimulus in the attention model is produced by the initial stimulus complex through the action of the intervening mechanism. Thus, attention differs from r_m in that attention produces no characteristic cue of its own; it only filters S_c to allow S_c to produce a characteristic cue.

Perhaps it is worthwhile to illustrate all this with other forms of the models, to show that the model differences do not depend on the details of model construction. Figure 2 shows all the models in a different form. In all of the models, S_c is the initial, external stimulus and R is the terminal response. There

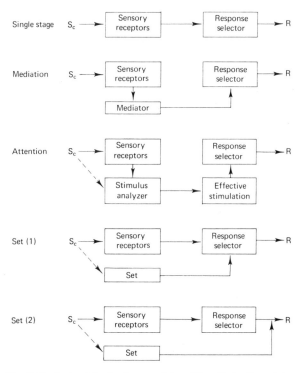

Fig. 2. Variants of single-stage model and "mediation" models.

are sensory receptors that receive input from S_c, and there is a response selector that produces the physical terminal response. In the single-stage model, there are no other components. In the mediation model, a mediator determines response selection. In the attention model, the stimulus analyzer determines the effective stimulation, which in turn determines response selection. The dotted line in the attention model indicates that the nature of the stimulus analyzer may depend on the nature of the initial stimulus complex. This feature is included because it is present in some theories, such as Zeaman and House's (1963), although it may not be included in all attention theories. In the set models, set may be aroused by the situation (as shown by the dotted line), but however it is aroused it always affects not the stimulus, but the response. It affects the response either through an effect on response selection (first set model) or through an effect on the implementation of the response already selected (second set model).

Just how the arrows are supposed to work is a theoretical problem, and not relevant to the issues under consideration here.

Example. O'Connor and Hermelin (1959) trained imbeciles on a two-stimulus discrimination problem with simultaneous presentation of stimuli differing in size and position, with size the relevant dimension. Subjects in a verbalization group verbalized the size names during training, and *S*s in a control group did not. The verbalization group learned the discrimination more rapidly than the control group. This result is predictable if single-stage theory is applied for the control group and mediation theory or attention theory is applied for the verbalization group (see Reese, 1968, p. 266). A set theory might also be used. For example, verbalization might make the task more interesting. If this results in closer attention to the task, or greater cooperativeness, or a more appropriate *Aufgabe,* the set model is applicable and responding should be facilitated. The attention model could be used in accounting for this effect, provided attention means facilitation of the registering of stimuli, either peripherally—by preparing the sensorium for sensory reception, for example—or centrally as in Sokolov's (1960) neuronal model of the orientation reaction. Note, however, that this kind of attention would be nonselective, and thus different from the selective attentional mechanism which the attention models in Figs. 1 and 2 were designed to represent. Alternatively, verbalization may somehow optimize motivation, making it not so strong that it would be predicted to interfere with acquisition of a nondominant habit nor so weak that responsiveness would be too low (see Longstreth, 1970). This effect would clearly fit the second set model in Fig. 2. However, the problem with these "set" interpretations is that there seems to be no particularly good reason to assume that verbalization has effects like these.

After each *S* in the experiment reached the learning criterion, he was given a reversal task; that is, the size dimension remained relevant, but the other size became positive. The verbalization group required more trials to learn the reversal than the control group. This result can be explained by again assuming single-stage learning in the control group, and by assuming both single-stage learning and mediation in the verbalization group. The control group would need to inhibit the response to the old positive stimulus and disinhibit the response to the old negative stimulus. The verbalization group would have to go through these processes *and* would have to inhibit the response to the old correct mediator and disinhibit the response to the old incorrect mediator (or inhibit both mediators). The verbalization group therefore would have more to learn in the reversal phase, and therefore should learn the reversal more slowly than the control group.

Attention theory does not predict this outcome, because according to attention theory, the reversal should be learned more rapidly by *S*s who are attending to the relevant dimension, as the *S*s in the verbalization group presumably would be (see Eimas, 1970; Reese, 1968, pp. 266-267). A set interpretation could work. For example, it might be that motivation is now strong enough in the verbalization group to interfere with performance since the now incorrect response (the previously correct response) is too dominant.

To summarize, the combined results of the two phases can be explained by assuming single-stage learning in nonverbalizing imbeciles and by assuming in verbalizing imbeciles either both single-stage learning and mediation or single-stage learning and a set effect. This example is instructive because it shows, first, that the data often permit a choice to be made among theories that generate relatively precise predictions (the single-stage, mediation, and attention theories), but, second, that less precise theories (such as theories of set) often cannot be eliminated as possibilities. I shall return to this point later in the section on controls.

Potential Mediators

The kinds of mechanisms that have been identified as mediators can all be classified as responses, provided "response" is loosely defined. They include verbal responses, gestures, and images. Jeffrey's (1953) study included both verbal and gestural mediators, but the study is too complex to be summarized briefly. Simpler examples of verbal-mediation studies include the series conducted by Spiker and Norcross, in which children learned names for two stimuli in a pretraining phase and then learned a discriminative-choice response to one of them in a subsequent phase (Norcross & Spiker, 1957; Spiker & Norcross, 1962). This research has been reviewed in detail elsewhere (Jeffrey, 1970, pp. 230-233). An example of gestural mediation is Jeffrey's (1958) study of left–right discrimination. The stimuli were stick figures pointing to the left or to the right. Experimental *S*s learned a button-pressing discriminative response to the stimuli, then learned to associate different names with the stimuli. Control *S*s were given only the name-learning task. The experimental *S*s were more successful than the control *S*s in the name-learning task, and Jeffrey observed that some children in the experimental group gave attenuated versions of the button-pressing response—lifting a shoulder or looking at the appropriate button—before responding verbally in the name-learning task. (See Jeffrey, 1970, for details of controls in these and similar studies.)

Imaginal mediators are studied with two general kinds of procedure: Either the experimenter instructs the *S*s to form images, or uses specially constructed stimulus materials designed to enhance or retard spontaneous image-formation. For example, in a paired-associates study with fifth-grade children, Spiker (1960) instructed the experimental *S*s to use imaginal mnemonics by telling them that it was a trick that would help them learn the list and then describing an interaction between the stimulus and response members of each pair. For the pair "cake–boat," the *S* "was instructed to visualize a 'cake-boat', that is a boat made of cake [p. 81]." Control *S*s were not given these instructions. An example of the second technique is Reese's (1965) paired-associates study, in which an "imagery" group was shown pictures of interactions between the stimulus and response items and a control group was shown the items as separate, isolated elements.

There has been relatively little research with gestural and imaginal mediators, and I shall have nothing more to say in this paper about the gestural ones. I shall consider the imaginal mediators in some detail, however, along with verbal mediators.

Rationale for Study of Covert Mediators

Logical Operations Involved

Unobservable processes might actually occur, but an observer can never be certain that they did. The best he can do is to make an inference about their occurrence, but such an inference must have a clearly demonstrated basis in order to be convincing. There are only two possible observational bases for the inference, one on the stimulus side and one on the response side. Thus, it might be asserted that since a particular stimulus occurred, a particular mediating response must have occurred, or that since a particular terminal response occurred, a particular mediating response must have occurred. Such assertions must in turn be justified, and the only way to justify them is by reference to a theory. Consider my paired-associates study mentioned above: The "theory" says that if a *S* remembers the materials presented—that is, if he has a memory image of the materials—he will have a single image including both the stimulus and the response items if he was in the imagery group, and will have separate images of the stimulus and response items if he was in the control group. The theory predicts that the kind of imagery in the experimental group will facilitate performance. If it is inferred that the requisite kind of imagery occurred in the experimental group, on the ground that they experienced a particular kind of stimulus input, and not in the control group, then the data test the prediction that this kind of imagery facilitates paired-associates learning. However, if the

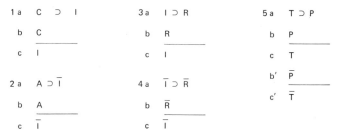

Fig. 3. Illustration of logical bases for inferences about mediation.

o'ccurrence of facilitation is used as a basis for inferring the occurrence of imagery, the data test the prediction that the stimulus materials produce this kind of imagery.

When the occurrence of the mediating response is inferred on the basis of the stimulus materials used, the inference is deductive. When the occurrence of the mediating response is inferred on the basis of the observed responses, the inference is not deductive (see Beck, 1950). Figure 3 lists the logical operations.

Statement 1 in the figure represents the deductive process. The first phrase (1a) is a major premise, the second (1b) is a premise stating the occurrence of the antecedent condition required, and the third (1c) is the conclusion deduced from these premises. For example, let C refer to the presentation of concrete, high-imagery noun pairs in a paired-associates task and let I refer to the occurrence of imagery depicting a pair. Then the statement is: If concrete, high-imagery nouns are used in a paired-associates task, then imagery depicting the pairs is aroused; such noun pairs are used in this experiment; therefore, such imagery is aroused.

Statement 2 is also deduction, and is intended to refer to a control condition. For example, let A refer to the presentation of abstract, low-imagery nouns. Then the statement is: If abstract, low-imagery nouns are used, then imagery will not be aroused; and such nouns are used; therefore, imagery is not aroused.

Statement 3 represents a logical fallacy. Here, R refers to improved retention. To argue that I is true from the premises given is to commit the fallacy of affirming the consequent. The correct argument is that the evidence (*R* observed) is consistent with the inference that *I* occurred.

The fourth statement is the same type and refers to a control condition. The major premises in the third and fourth statements together assert that the observable consequent, *R*, is dependent only upon *I*.

The last statement is the one actually used, and includes elements of all of the others. Here, *T* represents all of the preceding "a" premises conjoined by "and," and hence is some kind of theoretical statement; and *P* symbolizes the prediction that the experimental group (given condition *C*) will be superior to the control group (given condition *A*). The conclusion (5c) is an inference; but note that only if the prediction is not verified (5b′)—yielding the conclusion that the theory is (at least in part) false (5c′)—is the inference deductive.

Controls

Controls serve a variety of purposes which can be divided into two classes: Controls for "baseline" evaluation and controls for "theoretical" evaluation.

Baseline Evaluation. In the example in Fig. 3, the *A* condition is included to provide a baseline for evaluation of the effects of the *C* condition. To be an adequate control of this sort, it is necessary that the control condition include nothing that influences behavior that is not also included in the experimental condition, that is, that it differ from the experimental condition only with respect to the critical variable supposedly being manipulated—in this case *I*—and with respect to other variables that have no influence on the behavior to be observed. In the example, this requirement is not necessarily satisfied, because abstract nouns (*A*) can differ from concrete nouns (*C*) in many ways that would confirm *P* (5b) even if all or part of *I* (5a) were false.

Theoretical Evaluation. To *prove* that the theory (*T*) is true is impossible; to *support* it requires not only the appropriate outcome (*P*), but also assurance that *if I then R* is not itself a deduction. For example, it must not be true that *if C then I*, *if I then S*, and *if S then R*, because in that case *if I then R* is a deduction and not *I* but *S* is causal. It must also be assumed that *if C then R* is not a statement about direct cause, because then the statements about *I* would be irrelevant. If *C* and *A* are given and *P* is observed, it could be inferred that *C* and *A* are causal, but that might be a false-cause fallacy, confusing condition for cause. The problem is to explain why it is true that *if C then R* and *if A then not R*, that is, to advance a theoretical causal chain from *C* and *A* to *R* and *not-R*. Thus, in order for the confirmation of *P* to provide convincing support for the conclusion that *T* is true, it must be shown that no alternative mechanism (*S*) could produce *P*, and that *I* must be the mechanism that mediates between *C* and *R*. The theory, then, is crucial in providing the premises that generate *P*, and also in determining the needed controls for theoretical evaluation. (Compare Kendler & Kendler, 1969.)

Actually, not all of a relevant theory need be formalized, and in this sense there are "levels" of theories. At the lowest level is the folklore or commonsense of a science suggesting certain controls (this is the level of "dubitanda" in Pepper's 1942 system). For example, although there has been no precise analysis of "performance sets" (see Reese, 1970b), it is known that controls for their effects are sometimes needed, and it is known how to implement these controls. In a comparison of experimental and control conditions, where the experimental condition involves some kind of pretraining, it should be automatic to include placebo pretraining in the control condition to take care of the possible effects of warm-up and other irrelevant sources of transfer.

Consider a study in which experimental *S*s learn verbal labels for stimuli in a pretraining task, and all *S*s are given a transfer task requiring discrimination learning with these stimuli. Possible sources of facilitation in the discrimination learning task include:

(a) mediation of instrumental responses by the words;

(b) mediation of attentional responses to specific *attributes* of the stimuli by the words;

(c) mediation of an attentional response to a stimulus *dimension* by the words;

(d) acquisition of attentional responses to stimulus *attributes* during the word learning;

(e) acquisition of an attentional response to a stimulus *dimension* during the course of word learning;

(f) acquisition of a discrimination set of some kind during the course of word learning;

(g) warm-up during the course of word learning;

(h) acquired distinctiveness of cues (see Reese, 1962);

(i) stimulus familiarization (reduction of novelty) during word learning; and probably others.

To compare a group pretrained to label the stimuli with a control group given no pretraining of any kind, and to conclude from observing superior transfer-task performance in the first group that the instrumental responses were mediated by the words, is to ignore all the other possible sources of facilitation. Such a conclusion from such a study would be unconvincing. Controls are needed for each possible source of transfer.

Use of Reports of Subjects

Verbal Reports. In classical psychology, introspective reports were taken as direct evidence about the occurrence of conscious contents. If the *S* said he had a "feeling of relation," for example, it was assumed that he actually experienced this content. As is now well known, however, the reports of *S*s are not properly interpreted in this way. The proper report by the experimenter is not (in this case) that the *S* had a feeling of relation, but that he *said* he had a feeling of relation. It is important to distinguish between the report of the *S* and the report of the scientist. The *S* may report seeing something, and the scientist then reports that the *S* said he saw it—not that the *S* actually saw it. However, when the scientist reports seeing something, that report is taken to be factual, that is, the scientist's report is not a verbal response but a statement of fact (see Spence, 1948).

In many studies of mediation, *S*s are questioned about the processes by which they remembered the responses (e.g., Bugelski, 1968; Paivio, Yuille, & Smythe, 1966). Bugelski questioned *S*s who reported using imagery, and found that by and large these *S*s were quite resistant to suggestions by the experimenter as to the contents of their images. In addition, the *S*s reported a wealth of detail that could be considered irrelevant. Bugelski (1968) concluded, "The refusal to accept suggestions coupled with the excess of detail suggests that *S*s were doing more than talking to themselves. They were describing phenomenal experiences that they had no difficulty in labeling as images [p. 332]." Note that he correctly refrained from using the reports as direct evidence for the occurrence of imagery, and used them only to bolster the conclusion that imagery occurred. The logical argument might run like this: "If a subject uses imagery, he should report using it. This subject reported using it. Therefore he did use it." Symbolically, *if I then R, and R, therefore I,* which is clearly the fallacy of affirming the consequent, but is also clearly appropriate inference. In the example in Fig. 3, it would be required that more *S*s in the experimental group report imagery than in the control group. Confirming this expectation supports the inference about imagery in the experimental (*C*) condition. Note, however, that here too one needs controls to establish a baseline and to rule out alternative interpretations of the occurrence of the reports. Suppose, for example, that the experimenter rather naively asks the *S*s point-blank whether they pictured the items in their minds. The *S*s in the experimental condition presumably remember at least some of the materials, and because the materials were concrete might then realize that images could have been used and consequently falsely report that they were used. The *S*s in the control condition might realize that images would be difficult to use with abstract words, and, therefore, honestly report that they were not used. This differential falsification could be especially a problem when the experimental and control conditions differ only with respect to whether *S*s are instructed to use imagery.

Paivio and Yuille (1967) trained one group of college students on a paired-associates task with concrete words, and another group with abstract words. Half of each of these groups was instructed to use imagery and the other half was instructed to use verbal mnemonics. It was found that the nature of the list had a bigger effect on performance than did the instructions, and also had a bigger effect on reported imagery. It would presumably be very difficult to form images for the abstract list (Bugelski, 1970, disagrees), and it would presumably be easier to form images than verbal mnemonics for the concrete list. If so, then the data suggest that college students tend to adopt the strategy that is best suited for the material rather than to follow instructions slavishly. This in turn suggests that the initial instructions may have less effect on the retrospective reports than might be expected.

Verbal reports can also have another utility. Bugelski (1968) studied proactive and retroactive interference in an imagery study, and found relatively little interference of either kind. Some *S*s reported that they remembered the new responses in the successive lists by "building" images. That is, these *S*s reported that they formed some particular image for a given List-1 pair, and that they then incorporated the List 2 and subsequent responses into this original image. This observation suggests further research in which the building of images is manipulated experimentally by varying the materials presented (e.g., to facilitate it for one group and not to facilitate it for another group) or is manipulated by differential instructions. However, it also raises a theoretical problem (actually, it only compounds the problem; the problem arises initially because of the wealth of apparently irrelevant detail reported to be present in images). The problem is: Why is there not massive interference from the complex image built up? How does the *S* know which part is the correct response? Palermo (1970) has suggested that this kind of problem calls into question the appropriateness of any current behavioristic analysis of imagery, and has suggested that a nonbehavioristic approach may be more fruitful. I suspect that he is right (Reese, 1970a), but many of the findings that he sees as anomolous need further verification in order to become devastating.

Nonverbal Reports. One other kind of "report" by the *S* is possible, that being nonverbal report. Nonverbal reports are properly interpreted in exactly the same way as verbal reports, that is as behaviors which, if predicted and observed, support the theory that predicted them. From this point of view, the button-pushing response in a discrimination task can be a nonverbal "report" about the occurrence of a mediator. Similarly, self-report of free-operant behaviors by punching a counter is a nonverbal report that supports the inference that the behaviors occurred, but does not prove that they did. Another example is provided by a study by Flavell, Beach, and Chinsky (1966). They gave preschool children a memory task while an observer who had been trained to lip-read watched the children's lip movements. It was found that a deficiency in the production of lip movements that could be "read" as the names of the objects to be remembered was associated with a deficiency in performance on the memory task. The experimenters interpreted this result as indicating a production deficiency—a failure to mediate because of a failure of the mediators to be produced. Note, however, that if the lip movements are assumed to be mediated, rather than being the mediators or as being perfectly correlated with the mediators, then the study provides no definitive evidence about production deficiency. Figure 4 illustrates the problem. Part A shows the data. Part B shows the interpretation of A1, assuming either that R_{lip} is the mediator or is mediated by some other response, r_m. Part C shows Flavell's interpretation of A2, and Part D shows two other possible interpretations of A2. In Flavell's interpretation, no mediator is produced. In the first alternative, the mediator is produced but fails (for some reason) to mediate anything. In the second

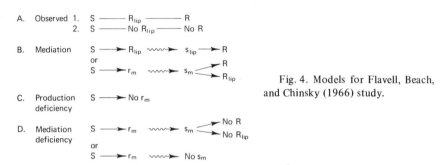

Fig. 4. Models for Flavell, Beach, and Chinsky (1966) study.

alternative, the mediating response is produced, but it fails to produce the internal stimulus that would ordinarily elicit the further responses. (Actually, in this particular study, retrospective verbal reports were also obtained, and were generally consistent with Flavell's interpretation rather than with the ones in Part D.)

By extension, it should be clear that electromyograms of laryngeal responses obtained during thinking, or electromyograms obtained from arm muscles during thinking about throwing a baseball prove nothing about the locus of the mediators—or more grandly, the locus of the vehicles of thought. The electromyograms could be produced not by mediating responses, but by mediated responses. However, note that while no knowledge is gained about the locus of the mediator, it can be established (with proper controls) that mediation is occurring *somewhere*.

Analysis of Sample Study

As an example, consider a verbal-mediation study by Reese (1966). The study dealt with transposition in the intermediate-size problem. The training stimuli were presented until the *S* met a learning criterion, then the *S* was given one-step and three-step transposition tests (with order counterbalanced across Ss). There were two experimental groups and one control group. All Ss were given standard instructions and they all were tested for transposition under identical conditions, with all responses reinforced. The groups differed in the verbalizations by the experimenter during training. For all groups, the experimenter verbally reinforced correct responses (which were also reinforced by delivery of raisins). The control group received no other verbalizations during training. For one experimental group, the experimenter said before each response, "It is not under the big one or the little one" (reversing the order of the size names at random). The Ss in the other experimental group were told before each response, "It is under the medium one." (The word "medium" was used in order to avoid the possible confusion by Ss of "middle-sized" with "middle," which could refer to spatial position rather than to position on the size dimension.) As already noted, these verbalizations were given during training, but not during testing.

The experimental groups did not differ from each other in performance, but met the training criterion significantly more rapidly than the control group and transposed significantly more than the control group. Both results are consistent with the assumption that mediation occurred in the experimental groups and not in the control group. However, all three groups exhibited the distance effect in transposition, that is, they transposed less on the three-step test than on the one-step test. This result is not consistent with mediation theory. The distance effect in the control Ss can be explained without reference to mediation (see Reese, 1968, Chapter 8), but the distance effect in the experimental groups poses a problem for mediation theory. Figure 5 shows the situation for the

Fig. 5. Model of experimental groups in Reese (1966) study.

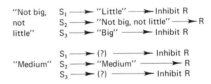

experimental Ss during training. If the Ss continue to emit the verbal responses appropriately during the test, then "medium" and "not big, not little" should mediate transposition responses on both tests, the three-step as well as the one-step test, and no gradient should appear. However, if on the three-step test the sizes are so different from the sizes used during training that these labels are not emitted (i.e., if the labels are not transposed), then the theoretical prediction is complicated, but in any case less transposition is predicted at three steps than at one step and no more is predicted at three steps than in the control group. One could assume that the response at three steps was mediated in some of the experimental Ss and not in others, but the scores were not bimodally distributed, thus contradicting this interpretation.

Figure 6 shows the possible predictions from mediation theory. The solid line shows the predicted performance of Ss who mediate in both tests; the dotted line shows the predicted performance of Ss who mediate at one step and fail to mediate at three steps; and the broken line shows the predicted performance of Ss who mediate in neither test. The broken line is also the prediction for control Ss, and, therefore, the data appear to be inconsistent with mediation theory (the obtained curves were parallel, and dropped in all three groups).

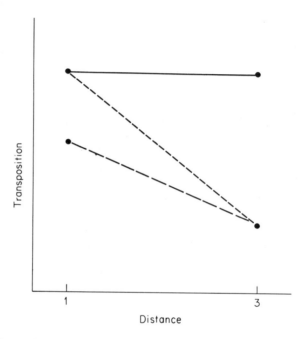

Fig. 6. The predictions of mediation theory for Reese (1966) study. Solid line, mediation at both distances; dotted line, mediation at one step and no mediation at three steps; broken line, no mediation at either distance.

Another possibility is that the mediation model is not applicable, but an attention model is. There are four possible attention models; in two, the attentional response is directed to absolute stimulus attributes; and in the other two it is directed to relational cues (relative sizes). In one model in each of these pairs, the attentional response is mediated by the size names, and in the other model in each pair it is conditioned to the initial stimulus complex (S_c).

Attention to such absolute attributes as position, size, brightness, and so on, can explain the training data but not the test data. Response to attributes during the tests would result in more absolute responses, not more transposition responses. Therefore, it does not matter whether the attentional response is assumed to be mediated or conditioned, because in neither case does the model work.

The other attention models work better. Assume that the verbalization of the sizes by the experimenter directs the attention of the S to the relative sizes. This might reasonably be assumed to be important in the intermediate-size problem, because the intermediate-size relation is difficult to see—on both empirical and theoretical grounds. Empirically, it is known that the age at which the intermediate-size relation is recognized by a majority of children is later (i.e., older) than for the two-stimulus relation (see Reese, 1968). Theoretically, the intermediate-size relation should be harder to perceive because it requires two two-stimulus comparisons (and for other reasons—see Reese, 1968, pp. 238, 239). Other evidence suggests that perception of the relation will hasten discrimination learning (Reese, 1968).

Assume that the attentional response is conditioned to the verbalizations provided to the experimental groups, as illustrated in Fig. 7. Comparing this model with the attention models in Figs. 1 and 2 shows that the difference is that the stimulus analyzer is switched in by the verbal response in the Fig. 7 model instead of being switched in by S_c. Mediation is involved in the Fig. 7 model, but it is the attentional response that is mediated and that results in the production of the cues to which the terminal response becomes conditioned.

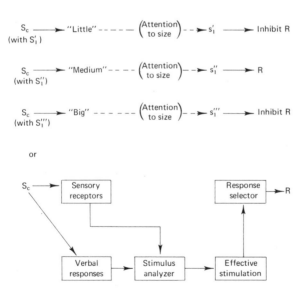

Fig. 7. Attention model for Reese (1966) study. Note that the attentional response is mediated.

Under these assumptions, attention theory would predict the faster learning of the original discrimination by the experimental Ss. If these Ss emit the size names during the test, they should also transpose more than the control Ss, who might never have seen the relation and might have learned the discrimination on the basis of absolute cues alone. If so, then the greater saliency of the relational cues in the experimental groups would also produce more transposition on the one-step test: Since the transposition by the control Ss on this test is predicted even if these Ss fail to respond to the relation, even more transposition is predicted in Ss who see the relation. On the three-step test, responding to absolute cues should produce less transposition, as it apparently did in the control group. On the assumption that the experimental groups responded only to relational cues during training, there should be no reduction in transposition at three steps, but on the assumption that they responded to both the relational and the absolute cues, the reduction in their transposition at three steps is predicted (see Reese, 1968). Note that the assumption that Ss responded to absolute cues requires a modification of the models shown in Fig. 7, which show only mediation of attentional responses. The modification in the upper part would be to add a solid arrow connecting each symbol representing an absolute size (e.g., S_1') to the terminal response (for S_1', "Inhibit R"). The modification in the lower part would be to add a solid arrow between the "sensory receptors" box and the "response selector" box.

If the size names were not emitted by the experimental Ss during the test, then these Ss should no longer respond to relational cues, and should, therefore, behave like control Ss. Alternatively, if the size names were emitted during the one-step test and not during the three-step test, then the experimental Ss should have exhibited a transposition curve like the dotted line in Fig. 6. Since neither of these results was obtained, this attentional model (Fig. 7) requires the assumption that the Ss emitted the words during the test (and that the words mediated the attentional response), as well as the assumption of single-stage learning of responses to absolute cues.

The final attentional model assumes that attention to relational cues is conditioned to S_c, as shown in Figs. 1 and 2. Note that it is not necessary to assume that the S spontaneously emits the size names during the test, since the attentional response is not mediated by size names. This model, as the ones already considered, explains the superior performance during training of the experimental groups, relative to the control group. In the transposition tests, S_c is not the same as in training because of the changes in the absolute sizes of the elements and the magnitude of the change in S_c is greater at three steps than at one step. Since the test S_c arouses attention as a result of generalization, the attentional response should be weaker—especially at three steps—than during training. There should, in other words, be less attention to relational cues with increasing "distance," and therefore less transposition with increasing distance, as was obtained. Note that it is not necessary to assume that the S responds to absolute cues at all (as required in the Fig. 7 model as modified in the discussion).

One might wonder whether the set model will work here. It seems to me that if attention is ruled out of the set model, it does not work, but in the absence of a precise theory of set this is only an impression. I suppose one might argue that the experimenter's verbalizations increase motivation (for example), perhaps by demonstrating to the S the experimenter's interest. Presumably, the increased motivation could facilitate performance in original learning and in the tests, but this is really inconsistent with any precise theory of motivation. To permit the prediction of improved performance with increasing motivation, it must be assumed that the correct response is dominant. In this experimental situation, this is clearly false during training, and therefore increasing motivation should interfere with performance. Furthermore, motivation theory could not explain the details of the transposition data. It is true that the correct response is dominant at the end of training, and therefore that high-drive (i.e., experimental) Ss should be superior to low-drive (control) Ss. However, it would be reasonable to index the response hierarchy by observation of the performance of the presumed low-drive Ss, and then to predict that whatever response is dominant for them will be exhibited even more strongly by the high-drive Ss. This expectation was not confirmed because the experimental Ss tended to transpose, while the control Ss tended to give absolute responses. (The decreasing trend in transposition responses in the control group might be more accurately described as an increasing trend in absolute responses.) This particular set interpretation does not work.

Other possibilities include the acquired distinctiveness of cues (as described by Reese, 1962), acquisition of the discrimination set, stimulus familiarization, and warm-up. The acquired distinctiveness of cues resulting from the addition of the size names would facilitate learning in the experimental groups, but even if the experimental Ss emitted the names during the test, there would be no basis for predicting more transposition, since the basis of transposition is not a discriminative process but a transfer process. For the same reason, discrimination set cannot work. In addition, there is no good reason to assume differential discrimination set in the experimental and control groups since the control Ss eventually learned the original discrimination and therefore presumably acquired a discrimination set.

Since the control Ss required more trials to learn the original discrimination, they should have become more familiar with the stimuli than the experimental Ss did. It could be that the greater stimulus familiarization in the control Ss resulted in a higher probability that these subjects would notice the change in the stimuli from the training phase to the testing phase. It is known that noticing the change reduces transposition (Reese, 1968). However, this account assumes that transposition was reduced in the control group and was "normal" in the experimental groups, but in fact comparison with other studies suggests that it was the control group that was "normal" (see Reese, 1968).

The groups may have differed in warm-up, since they received different numbers of training trials. However, there should have been more warm-up in the control group than in the experimental groups, and since warm-up should produce facilitation, the control group should have been superior to the experimental groups. Thus, the warm-up difference does not explain the results.

Related to the warm-up difference, the fact that the control group required more trials to learn the original discrimination also implies that they made more errors. The errors, which are failures as far as the S is concerned, might produce frustration or some other drive that arouses competing responses. However, there is no reason to expect greater competition at three steps than at one step, hence no reason to expect a distance effect. Furthermore, this account is like the stimulus familiarization account in that it predicts reduction of transposition in the control group rather than facilitation in the experimental groups, and, as already noted, the data suggest that the latter occurred.

It appears, then, that the attention models illustrated in Figs. 1, 2, and 7 provide the best fits to the data from both phases. Since the attention models in Figs. 1 and 2 are more parsimonious, in that they do not require the assumption of single-stage learning (as the Fig. 7 model does), they might be preferred, and in that case there is no evidence from the study to support an inference that mediation occurred, not even mediation of an attentional response.

This example shows that what might have appeared to be a straightforward study of verbal mediation turned out on close analysis of the procedure, controls, data from all phases, data from other studies, and alternative models and theories to provide little if any justification for an inference that mediation occurred. The inferences that are acceptable are the ones that survive such an analysis; and in order for a single inference to be convincing, it must be the *only* one that survives the analysis.

References

Beck, L. W. Constructions and inferred entities. *Philosophy of Science,* 1950, 17, 74-86.
Bugelski, B. R. Images as mediators in one-trial, paired-associate learning: II. Self-timing in successive lists. *Journal of Experimental Psychology,* 1968, 77, 328-334.
Bugelski, B. R. Words and things and images. Presidential address presented at the meeting of the Eastern Psychological Association, Atlantic City, April 1970.
Eimas, P. D. Attentional processes. Chapter 9 (with some material from other contributors). In H. W. Reese & L. P. Lipsitt (Eds.), *Experimental child psychology.* New York: Academic Press, 1970. Pp. 279-310.
Flavell, J. H., Beach, D. R., & Chinsky, J. M. Spontaneous verbal rehearsal in a memory task as a function of age. *Child Development,* 1966, 37, 283-299.

Goss, A. E. Early behaviorism and verbal mediating responses. *American Psychologist,* 1961, **16,** 285-298. (a)

Goss, A. E. Verbal mediating responses and concept formation. *Psychological Review,* 1961, **68,** 248-274. (b)

Hull, C. L. *Principles of behavior.* New York: Appleton, 1943.

Jeffrey, W. E. The effects of verbal and nonverbal responses in mediating an instrumental act. *Journal of Experimental Psychology,* 1953, **45,** 327-333.

Jeffrey, W. E. Variables in early discrimination learning: I. Motor responses in the training of a left-right discrimination. *Child Development,* 1958, **29,** 270-275.

Jeffrey, W. E. Transfer. Chapter 7 (with parts contributed by H. W. Reese & D. S. Palermo). In H. W. Reese & L. P. Lipsitt (Eds.), *Experimental child psychology.* New York: Academic Press, 1970. Pp. 223-262.

Kendler, H. H., & Kendler, T. S. Reversal-shift behavior: Some basic issues. *Psychological Bulletin,* 1969, **72,** 229-232.

Lachman, R. The model in theory construction. *Psychological Review,* 1960, **67,** 113-129.

Longstreth, L. E. Motivation. Chapter 10 (with one part contributed by P. D. Eimas). In H. W. Reese & L. P. Lipsitt (Eds.), *Experimental child psychology.* New York: Academic Press, 1970. Pp. 311-362.

Norcross, K. J., & Spiker, C. C. The effects of type of stimulus pretraining on discrimination performance in preschool children. *Child Development,* 1957, **28,** 79-84.

O'Connor, N., & Hermelin, B. Discrimination and reversal learning in imbeciles. *Journal of Abnormal and Social Psychology,* 1959, **59,** 409-413.

Paivio, A., & Yuille, J. C. Mediation instructions and word attributes in paired-associate learning. *Psychonomic Science,* 1967, **8,** 65-66.

Paivio, A., Yuille, J. C., & Smythe, P. C. Stimulus and response abstractness, imagery, and meaningfulness, and reported mediators in paired-associate learning. *Canadian Journal of Psychology,* 1966, **20,** 362-377.

Palermo, D. S. Imagery in children's learning: Discussion. In H. W. Reese (Chm.), Imagery in children's learning: A symposium. *Psychological Bulletin,* 1970, **73,** 415-421.

Pepper, S. C. *World hypotheses: A study in evidence.* Berkeley, Calif.: University of California Press, 1942.

Reese, H. W. Verbal mediation as a function of age level. *Psychological Bulletin,* 1962, **59,** 502-509.

Reese, H. W. Imagery in paired-associate learning in children. *Journal of Experimental Child Psychology,* 1965, **2,** 290-296.

Reese, H. W. Verbal effects in the intermediate-size transposition problem. *Journal of Experimental Child Psychology,* 1966, **3,** 123-130.

Reese, H. W. *The perception of stimulus relations: Discrimination learning and transposition.* New York: Academic Press, 1968.

Reese, H. W. Implications of mnemonics research for cognitive theory. Paper presented at the Southeastern Conference on Research in Child Development, Athens, Georgia, April 1970. (a)

Reese, H. W. Set. Chapter 8 in H. W. Reese & L. P. Lipsitt (Eds.), *Experimental child psychology.* New York: Academic Press, 1970. Pp. 263-278. (b)

Reese, H. W., & Overton, W. F. Models of development and theories of development. In L. R. Goulet & P. B. Baltes (Eds.), *Life-span developmental psychology: Theory and research.* New York: Academic Press, 1970. Pp. 115-145.

Sokolov, E. N. Neuronal models and the orienting reflex. In M. A. B. Brazier (Ed.), *The central nervous system and behavior: Transactions of the third conference.* New York: Josiah Macy, Jr., Foundation, 1960. Pp. 187-276.

Spence, K. W. The postulates and methods of 'behaviorism.' *Psychological Review,* 1948, **55,** 67-78.

Spiker, C. C. Associative transfer in verbal paired-associate learning. *Child Development,* 1960, **31,** 73-87.

Spiker, C. C., & Norcross, K. J. Effects of previously acquired stimulus names on discrimination performance. *Child Development,* 1962, **33,** 859-864.

Zeaman, D., & House, B. J. The role of attention in retardate discrimination learning. In N. R. Ellis (Ed.), *Handbook of mental deficiency.* New York: McGraw-Hill, 1963. Pp. 159-223.

The Maintenance of Behavior by Self-Generated Stimuli and Reinforcement[1]

Frederick H. Kanfer

University of Cincinnati
Cincinnati, Ohio

Introduction

A behavioral approach to human psychology would be best served by a model that can clearly describe all of the variables necessary for prediction of behavior in terms of publicly observable activities. In the early days of behaviorism, Watson and others attempted to formulate such a psychology. More recent developments in psychological theory, and especially in application of psychological techniques to the modification of behavior disorders, have sharply highlighted the necessity for a behavioristic model to account for the critical role of self-regulatory mechanisms in modifying the input–output relationships inherent in the old S–R model. Other psychological theories have proposed complex models for information processing, self systems, and similar constructs

[1] This paper was prepared in conjunction with research supported in part by Research Grant MH 17902-02 from the National Institute of Mental Health, U.S. Public Health Service.

to account for the fact that supplementary sources of stimulation, based on the person's prior history of experiences, must be considered in order to sharpen prediction, especially in the case of the individual. The essence of most personality theories has been the concern with individual differences. They have been attributed either to cumulative learning experiences or to parameters in the physical and biological make-up of the individual or their interactions. In addition, enduring structures or traits have been postulated which characterize the person's differential sensitivity to environmental inputs and especially his differential reactions to himself.

I want to address myself only to those features of self-regulatory behavior that may help to explain the processes by which a person maintains his own behavior in the absence of any immediate environmental support or feedback, to some of the conditions which describe a person's reaction to himself and to the manner in which he can modify his own action. It is evident that these phenomena cover only a small portion of the domain of private experiences. From a pragmatic point of view, the mark of a socialized person is his ability to maintain behavior, originally shaped by the sociocultural environment, when this environment is temporarily not an effective controlling influence. Consequently, the genesis of self-directed and self-reinforced behaviors and their failure to develop in consonance with social expectations, has been of central interest to personality theorists.

In this paper, I shall attempt to review a tentative conceptualization, integrating recent research and some speculations about the processes of self-reinforcement, self-monitoring, and self-control. The particular questions which require explorations in this approach are

1. How can a person supplement the momentary, external controlling variables by self-produced consequences? This question will lead us to review the concept of self-reinforcement (sr) and its supporting research findings.

2. What relevant data are available to conceptualize the individual's response to his own behavior? This question raises the problem of accounting for feedback effects of a person's actions. Special attention is given here to self-observation, the deliberate attending to one's actions and their effects, as a means of providing cues for further behavior.

3. What experiments and theorizing can aid in understanding self-control? In its broadest sense, this question addresses itself to the exploration of means by which individuals can initiate behavior change by altering the conditions for optimal reinforcement of a new behavior sequence.

Our attempt at conceptualization is one that seeks to integrate experimental findings and to provide a guideline toward future research and toward practical application in clinical facilitation of behavior change. Its utility is measured by contributions to new behavior modification methods as much as by its value in providing a framework for expanding laboratory-animal based learning principles to encompass complex human behaviors.

A Tentative Working Model of Self-Regulation

In a previous paper (Kanfer, 1967), we have suggested that the conditions for reinforcing one's own behavior may first require attending to one's behavior or self-monitoring in order to establish whether the conditions of reinforcement are fulfilled. It was further suggested that this self-monitoring system may go into effect only under those conditions in which the normal chains of behavior are not run off smoothly or when other external or internal events provide cues for which no highly trained response is available.

At the present time, it is suggested that the process of self-regulation can be better understood by consideration of a number of component processes which closely articulate in any smooth execution of human actions. Figure 1 illustrates the hypothetical interrelationship between these processes.

It is assumed that the sequence starts with the input following the execution of a response. Two such sources of input have generally been discussed by psychologists: (1) environmental consequences and (2) internal response-produced cues. The former refer to the varied consequences (environmental changes) contingent on the person's responses as he is affected by them. The latter refer to the proprioceptive, verbal-symbolic, or autonomic consequences triggered by R_A. R_A can represent any act that is not strongly linked to a succeeding response. It is this group of response-produced stimulus functions that has been viewed by protagonists of the mediational hypothesis as the starting point of a covert event sequence. Our figure suggests that, in addition, either as part of the background stimulation or triggered off by R_A, a set of other variables comes into play, including prior experiences with similar situations, effects of instructions, standards or performance criteria, past success or failure on R_A, and prior reinforcement schedules for R_A. When R_A is a well-established link in a behavior chain, and/or when feedback conditions are represented by parameters of variables with near zero controlling strength, R_B occurs as the next link in the chain, illustrating a simple element in a chain in which R_A serves merely to set the occasion (as a discriminative stimulus S^D) for R_B. However, when a decision about R_A adequacy is required (for example, in the acquisition of new chains, in situations requiring decisions about R_A as an adequate response to meet a prescribed standard, in interrupted behavior chains, or when consequences of R_A lead to conflicting cues for R_B), the sequence leads to the next step, often described as self-evaluation. Our model suggests that this step can be seen as a conditional discrimination in which the content of the previous step (the inputs from R_A plus current situation and inputs from prior

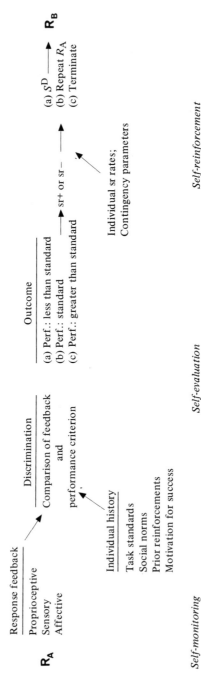

Fig. 1. A working model of self-regulation.

42

experiences) serve as the stimuli determining the self-evaluative response. The outcome of this discrimination is the S's judgment that his performance of R_A exceeds, equals, or falls below the comparison criteria. Within a certain range of motivational conditions, set by the person's history, the task and the demand characteristics of the situation, the 'judgment' serves as a S^D for positive or negative self-reinforcement (sr+ or sr−). Under some conditions, behavior will continue with repetition of R_A until performance is improved. Under other conditions R_B is made if the criteria for R_A are met, or an alternate response is made if the discrimination outcome is a 'failure' experience and the S's habitual response to evidence of failure can be carried out. Thus, the self-reinforcing operations are suggested to rest on the outcome of a discrimination in which the person evaluates the adequacy of his actions.

The various stages of the working model can be related to the research areas that are reviewed here. Self-monitoring or self-observation reflects the early stage in which recording of the conditions for R_A, response execution, and the consequences of R_A on the person or his environment may be required. Training in observing these events should increase accuracy of the information on which the subsequent discrimination is based. Recent work by Bem (1965, 1967) has further highlighted the role of self-perception. The person's recall of his own past performance may serve as a basis for prediction of his own behavior or the behavior of others. The *self-report*, apart from its strong dependence on the audience, can be correlated with (or identical to) the self-monitoring stage or with the *self-evaluation* stage. Distinctions by some authors of verbal self-reports as 'cognitive' or 'phenomenological' appear to correspond to the different points in the working model that serve as cues for verbalization. *Self-evaluation* research, indeed some operations designed to test the self-concept, can be anchored to the discrimination outcome. The observed terminal behavior can be manipulated by varying the information of the items to be discriminated. For example, past performance, social norms, performance criteria (goals) on the one hand, and controlled feedback to the S about his performance of R_A on the other hand, should and do affect self-evaluative responses. In addition, these self-evaluative responses can be directly modified by reinforcement of the verbal response (Kanfer and Duerfeldt, 1967a).

The Role of Response Feedback

Our working model suggests that, at the psychological level, some verbal, perceptual or physiological feedback for activation of the self regulation sequence is needed as a trigger. Numerous psychological theories in the areas of learning, perception, and motivation accommodate the concept of the feedback loop, i.e., the continued adjustment of a person's behavior as a function of his preceding behavior. One group of theories suggests that feedback is continuous and that sensory, affective, and proprioceptive inputs serve either as direct controlling stimuli for subsequent behavior or as concurrent events which have *intrinsic* reinforcing properties for the preceding response. In this approach, the motivational components of behavior are often traced to the correlates of the response itself, its affective or value parameters. The findings in animal work that revealed maintenance of some behaviors without support by some external consequence, e.g., novelty seeking, effort expending or fellow-animal watching behaviors, were especially persuasive for the intrinsic motivation concept. At a more complex level, some self-regulatory behaviors have been ascribed to affective conditioning of intrinsic response correlates to cognitive features of a situation by a process called internalization (Aronfreed, 1968). Thus, the concept of sr is reserved for conditions in which the inherent value (affective) of the task acquires direct control over the behavior and, if the value is positive, maintains the rate of occurrence of the behavior in the presence of the cues evoking the response plus affective value. It is apparent from our figure that we do not include such a possible sequence under *self*-regulation because it lacks the special properties of self initiated action which, in turn influences the probability of occurrence of a subsequent response sequence (see Kanfer, 1967, Kanfer and Phillips, 1970, for a full definition). In addition, the affective conditioning hypothesis is empirically difficult to test and some data (e.g., Solomon & Turner, 1962) suggest that proprioceptive feedback is not indispensable for learning.

A second group of theories, much more relevant to our topic, uses a feedback loop model, patterned after the servo theory of engineering, that describes the self-correcting control systems of such devices as thermostats or automatic aircraft pilots. In these models, a discontinuity or threshold concept is used and a reference system is required for activation of any operations that would intervene between R_A and R_B of our figure. In our working model as well, only a deviation from a standard range, an error, should activate the self-regulation system. There is only little experimental evidence of which I know, to support the discontinuity concept. Mandler (1964) has proposed the hypothesis that interruption of organized response sequences produces a state of arousal. Mandler and Watson (1966) and, in a recent dissertation at the University of Cincinnati, Sher (1970) have provided support for this hypothesis. However, the concept is not infrequently encountered in personality theories. The alerting function of ego-alien behavior, of responses inconsistent with one's self-perception, or of dissonant attitudes are widely noted and alleged to be sources of tension, maladjustment or conflict in most psychodynamic personality theories. In fact, both verbal confrontation in interview therapy and videotape feedback have been used widely for the purpose of providing objective feedback, in the hope that it would activate self-corrective behaviors. The hypothetical model includes a comparison mechanism that matches the evaluation (or feedback) of the present response with the established criterion.

The state of no-discriminable-difference between evaluation of one's performance and the standard serves as a signal for cessation of further correction and the progression to the next stage, the administration of sr or execution of R_B. The execution of the response which matches the criterion may be the reinforcing event itself. In fact this assumption is implicit in some response feedback theories that consider intrinsic motivation to be directed toward goal achievement or confirmation of a previously established hypothesis (Hunt, 1965). In his social comparison theory, Festinger (1954) has suggested a human drive to evaluate one's own behavior. The person is portrayed as an active organism, assessing, matching, and correcting his behavior.

The final link in a model of comparison mechanism involves the support of the behavior by self-generated reinforcement. In Festinger's theory, the reduction of the drive toward self-evaluation could represent the terminal event with reinforcing properties for the preceding response. A more direct concern with the motivational aspects of self-evaluation is found in Hill (1968). In a review of the reinforcing properties of positive and negative evaluations, Hill suggested that evaluative information may come to acquire secondary positive and negative reinforcing values because of its status as discriminative stimuli with regard to primary reinforcers. This interpretation stems from the assumption that evaluative statements by adults, and eventually by the child himself, are highly correlated in a person's developmental history with the availability of positive and negative reinforcers.

Affective correlates of achievement alone may also serve as differentially reinforcing events maintaining performance that is at or beyond criterion requirements. A theoretical approach which endows the self evaluative process per se with reinforcing properties is best characterized as one in which an *intrinsic* self-reinforcing mechanism is posited. As we have noted, Aronfreed (1968) has differentiated intrinsic self-reinforcement in internalization from the current usage of the terms by endowing performance correlates *directly* with value or reinforcing properties, without the introduction of an evaluation stage on which sr administration is contingent. Thus, response feedback is directly linked to motivational effects.

It is possible to conceptualize yet another focus of self-reinforcement. If no intrinsic reinforcing properties are proposed for a self-evaluative event, it can be suggested that the evaluative discrimination provides an outcome on which further self-reinforcing operations are contingent. The degree to which these two stages can be separated differs in experimental operations and as a function of the task and the explicitness with which external reinforcing operations had previously been applied to the behavior.

The recent literature on verbal learning has yielded several illustrations of the phenomena of human self-adjustment with which we are concerned. For example, the facilitative effects of knowledge of results on learning and performance has been widely described. Knowledge of results in our working model can be viewed as the outcome of a comparison between the performance criterion and the *S*'s present performance, either provided by the experimenter or by the *S* himself. A similar view is expressed by Locke, Cartledge, and Koeppel (1968). They have suggested that the motivational effects of knowledge of results (KR) are modified by the learner's standards of evaluation, the goals which he sets himself for performing the task. Thus, the simple concept of KR as a reinforcing event is expanded by these writers to include some type of prior goal or reference level against which performance is compared. The formulation fits the working model proposed here. Research findings in the verbal learning literature have led Adams (1968), Eimas and Zeaman (1963), and others to propose similar mechanisms that endow KR with motivational properties. If one accepts the assumption that man is inherently motivated by goal achievement and that behavioral sequences are influenced by prior standards which act as discriminative stimuli in stopping the error correcting sequence or initiating renewed effort toward meeting the criterion, the remaining task is to fill in this broad sketch by providing data to describe the specific variables which influence standard-setting and the actions based on the outcome of the self-evaluation. A more puzzling theoretical problem lies in accounting for the process of storing past experiences, and for the mechanisms by which the organism compares present and past performances (or matches standards) and continues or ceases corrective behavior as a result of this comparison.

Bandura (1969a) suggests that "any reinforcement ensuing from confirmation of the correctness of one's response ... is probably mediated by self-reinforcement [p. 238]." This agrees with the present formulation in suggesting that self-reinforcing operations can be considered as *separate* elements in the behavioral sequence, contingent upon, but not identical with, the self-evaluative behavior. A distinction is required between feedback effects as response-produced cues in simple chains of behavior and the use of feedback to select among alternate subsequent responses. It is only the latter use of feedback that is of interest in self-regulation. Whereas the former effects merely set the occasion for occurrence of R_B, differentiated feedback effects serve to guide the organism in selecting specific alternatives. The introduction of a discrimination stage has been suggested on the basis of animal research by Logan and Wagner (1965) and Mowrer (1960). In the human, the availability of a verbal repertoire for self-evaluation provides the potential for refining the discrimination—the self-evaluation—on which further behavior is based. The separate modifiability of sr and self-evaluations (Kanfer & Duerfeldt, 1967a) supports the hypothesis that each response class can be influenced by different operations in humans and that their interdependence may vary as a function of the standards provided for appropriate sr, commensurate with a given outcome of the evaluation.

Self-Reinforcement

Cautela (1969) has suggested the term *covert* reinforcement to describe a clinical procedure in which a patient is required to present himself with imagined reinforcing stimuli in order to modify the response probability of a preceding behavior. Cautela (1967, 1969) has used this procedure in covert sensitization as an alternative to aversion therapy and has reported clinical successes. Covert reinforcement deals with behavior which is presumed to follow either the E's or the S's instructions to present himself with imagined descriptions of some event. In our own experimental work and in that of other investigators on sr, the procedure has emphasized a paradigm in which the reinforcing stimulus is an observable event, often the physical appropriation of a material reinforcement. In a strict sense then, the procedure involves the S's administration of external reinforcements in the absence of any immediate control over such administration by anyone except the S. Self-reinforcement of operant behaviors represents a special type of self-initiated behaviors. Skinner (1953) has defined one property of sr+ by stating that it "presupposes that the individual has it in his power to obtain reinforcement but does not do so until a particular response has been emitted [pp. 237-238]." Whereas this definition emphasizes the contingency of sr on particular discriminative stimuli it does not provide a full definition of the class of behaviors to be discussed here. Self-administered reinforcing stimuli can be of the positive (sr+) or of the aversive (sr−) type. The administration is usually contingent on the conditional discrimination described in Fig. 1. It may follow negative performance, or a disturbing thought, or any other behavior that the person evaluates against some previously established reference level. The self-reinforcing event may be verbal, such as the statement "I was right," or "This was a stupid thing to do." It can be the execution of a complex motoric act such as buying a dress following weight loss in a reducing program, or rewarding oneself with a vacation after prolonged successful work. The essence of the definition of sr lies in the fact that the sequence is initiated by the person and is contingent on some self-prescribed criterion for his activities.

As we have noted, the term "self-reinforcement" has often been used by theorists to talk about hypothetical processes. The empirical support for an sr concept has come from research that has addressed itself to several different features of sr. A number of studies have demonstrated that the experimental operations characterized as sr are subject to manipulation by variables that are also known to affect other instrumental responses (e.g., Kanfer & Marston, 1963a, b; Kanfer & Duerfeldt, 1968a; Bandura & Kupers, 1964; Marston, 1965; Liebert & Ora, 1968). Other studies have described the motivational effects of self-reinforcing operations on the behavior that they follow (e.g., Bandura &

Perloff, 1967; Kanfer & Duerfeldt, 1967b). Finally, a series of studies has addressed itself to the problem of relating sr operations to the self-evaluation process on which they are asserted to be dependent.

In our efforts to develop an empirical basis for understanding the sr concept, we began with a series of studies in which *S* was presented with a relatively ambiguous task: for example, the partial learning of a verbal discrimination task, or the discrimination of near threshold perceptual stimuli. The general paradigm has included an initial phase during which *S* is exposed to the learning task. In the first phase, *E* generally administers reinforcement, either contingent upon a correct response or noncontingently according to a predetermined schedule. In the second phase, *S* is requested to take over *E*'s task of administering reinforcement by activating the reinforcement dispenser to obtain a light, a token, or a piece of candy. The *S* is asked to reward or criticize himself, depending on his judgment that his response on a given item is correct or adequate. In this procedure, self-reinforcing operations are directly related to *S*'s judgment of the adequacy (or accuracy) of his response. Results of these studies have previously been summarized (Kanfer, 1967). One early and consistent finding in several experiments has shown that in an ambiguous situation, *S*s who receive no further external feedback tend to match the rate of previously administered external reinforcement by self-reinforcement. The closeness of the match is affected by the nature of the sr and by the rate of prior external reinforcement. For example, a low rate of positive, external reinforcement is matched by a proportionately higher rate of sr+ than a high rate of prior positive external reinforcement. When criticism or negative external reinforcement is given, *S*s tend to match these rates by producing fewer sr— responses. The interaction between rate of external reinforcement and sr rate for sr— and sr+ is reversed. A higher rate of prior negative reinforcement is followed by a larger decrement sr— than a low rate of prior negative reinforcement. One critical item affecting *S*'s decision to reward himself or to punish himself is the *E* mediated norm of reinforcement for the experimental performance.

A basal level of administration of self-rewards and self-criticisms appears to be associated with individual differences. For example, *S*s differ in their general rate of sr across experiments of different content (Kanfer, Duerfeldt, & LePage, 1969).

Our working model suggests that information required for judging one's behavior may come from previous experiences, such as a pretraining phase in an experiment, or from immediate feedback during execution of the response. In a recent study (Dorsey, Kanfer, & Duerfeldt, 1971), we examined the effects of combining varying socially mediated prior reinforcement with changes in feedback during *S*'s performance. A matching-to-sample task was used which permitted variation of the level of difficulty by modifying exposure time of the stimuli. The effects of direct sensory feedback then would be expected to modify the effects of prior socially mediated sr. In a factorial design, *S*s were given either 30, 50, or 70% noncontingent, positive external reinforcement while the task difficulty remained constant. All *S*s received the same number of trials in Phase I. During Phase II, *S*s were asked to reward their own performance if they believed that they had been accurate. Each of the three training groups was split so that one-third of the *S*s obtained a more difficult perceptual task, one-third a less difficult task and for the remaining *S*s the task remained the same as in Phase I. Task difficulty was varied by changing time of exposure for the perceptual stimuli from 0.06 seconds either to 0.10 or to 0.03 seconds. The results indicated that the two variables operated in an additive fashion. Higher sr rates followed higher prior external reinforcement and lower sr rates were obtained when the task became more difficult. Therefore, a high level of prior external reinforcement tended to make *S*'s criteria for self-rewards more liberal, while increased difficulty tended to make such criteria more conservative. For *S*s who had obtained a high rate of external reinforcement, the frequency of undeserved srs was higher, while increases in task difficulty lowered the rates of both correct and incorrect srs. The judgments about one's own performance and the contingent sr appeared to depend on both the prior cues presented to *S* and those inherent in the execution of the task.

A series of studies established the effectiveness of various parameters on the rate of sr responses. Such variables as magnitude of the obtainable reward, instructions about stringency or leniency of criteria for sr, and level of competence for the task are among variables which were shown to have effects in altering sr rates. Once sr rates were established in one situation, some generalization was also obtained for sr rates on similar tasks.

One interesting finding concerns the relative independence of two separate aspects of sr, self-reward and self-criticism. Two studies (Kanfer & Duerfeldt, 1968a; Kanfer, Duerfeldt, & LePage, 1969) showed that modification of self-rewarding behavior does not necessarily affect *S*'s rate of self-criticism for the same or a similar task. Furthermore, differences in sr+ rates that could be attributed to individual differences and were noted at the outset of the experimental procedure, did not correlate with similar differential rates of sr−. These data suggest that in a description of the self concept as a set of attitudes, self-rewarding and self-criticizing tendencies should not be presumed to be simply inversely related. It is important to differentiate among all persons who tend to show a high rate of self rewards, those who show a high rate of self-criticisms, r, and those who show a low rate. While the former may represent individuals who are continuously attentive to the quality of their behavior output, the latter would represent individuals who are relatively unrealistic in their self satisfactions. Since sr+ would be expected to maintain current behaviors while sr− (as an aversive event) would tend to change behavior, one would expect much greater variations in individuals with high sr− rates.

Our working model proposes that a person's self prescribed standards are compared to his judgment about his performance and that habitual sr patterns further determine the type and magnitude of self-rewards given for achieving some success in approximating the standard. Excessively high standards or an enduring pattern of high self-criticism rates should yield a tendency toward habitually low self-evaluation. If response feedback is ambiguous, low self appraisal of performance would add further to negative outcomes of the self evaluation. Katz (1967) and Heckhausen (1969) have recently attempted to relate the development of achievement motivation to the child's development of self reinforcing behaviors. Studies of the joint effects of standard-setting and sr patterns promise to contribute, through future research, an increased understanding of school achievement and its correlates with parental and socioeconomic factors.

In our own research we have explored the relationship between achievement level, as judged by teachers, and sr. We found that the rate at which children will give themselves undeserved self-rewards is highly correlated with their class standing, as judged by teacher's ratings in their grade school classes. However, with increasing age, from first to sixth grade, the number of undeserved self-rewards on a simple task tends to decrease, although the difference between high-achieving and low-achieving Ss is maintained (Kanfer, 1966; Kanfer & Duerfeldt, 1968b). Children rated as standing below average in class achievement gave themselves significantly more undeserved sr+ than above average children. On a visual discrimination task, the number of undeserved (incorrect) sr+ was also higher for the children rated low in class standing. It is not clear from these data whether the results are attributable to more lenient criteria for sr+ administration or lower performance criteria. The results do indicate the relationship between achievement and self-reinforcing behavior. The motivational properties of self-reinforcing operations have been demonstrated in several laboratory studies (Marston & Kanfer, 1963; Bandura & Perloff, 1967). In addition, the practical advantage of sr over external reinforcement has been demonstrated in school children in a recent report by Lovitt and Curtiss (1969). The authors found that higher academic response rates were achieved when their 12-year-old S managed his own contingency system as opposed to one that was managed by his teacher. Johnson and Martin (1970) compared the effects of self-monitoring and externally monitored reinforcement systems in second grade school children. Reinforcement was managed by a token system, either controlled by the teacher or by the child himself. Self-reinforcement was shown to maintain discrimination behavior at the same rate and accuracy level as external reinforcement. Johnson and Martin required their children to make the statement "I was right" prior to activation of a reward-dispensing apparatus. They considered the verbal positive self-evaluation as a conditioned reinforcer, supported by token reinforcement and thereby acquiring motivational reinforcing properties.

It is interesting to note that sr standards learned by observation of a model in turn can modify *S*'s tendency to reward the behavior of others in similar tasks. These findings were obtained both with children (Bandura & Kupers, 1964) and by Marston (1965) in college students. The implications of these findings for educational systems are fairly obvious. The data suggest that a teacher's disposition toward evaluating her own performance and her propensity for sr+ and sr— administration may serve not only as a model to her children, a phenomenon amply demonstrated by Bandura and his co-workers, but also in the teacher's judgment of the performance of her pupils.

In addition to modification by direct reinforcement, by prior external reinforcement and by other variables already mentioned, sr behavior can also be transmitted by observation of sr behavior in others. The many studies exploring parameters that facilitate such transmission of sr behaviors have been summarized by Bandura (1969a) and require no further description here.

The weight of the accumulated research on sr clearly indicates not only the feasibility of study of this portion of self-regulatory behaviors, but suggests also the importance of the relationship between various stages in our working model. Availability of immediate feedback, prior experiences in setting standards for a given task, prior established patterns of rates of sr+ and sr— all tend to affect a person's judgment of his own performance, his satisfaction with it, and his further action based on the outcome of his self evaluation. Recent adoption of the laboratory precedures for treatment of clinical problems (e.g., Rehm & Marston, 1968; Goodlet & Goodlet, 1969) indicate the practical potentialities of the products of sr research and theorizing.

Self-Monitoring and Self-Control

As we turn back to our working model, we note that other stages of the self-regulatory process have also come under recent experimental investigation. For practical reasons one area of concern has been the area described as self-control. The mechanisms responsible for the nonexecution of a response in the presence of available reinforcers or the tolerance of aversive stimulation even when an escape response is available have been related most frequently to the anticipation of punishment or anxiety. For example, Aronfreed (1968) has suggested that anticipatory anxiety, resulting from past punishment experiences, is associated with environmental cues for execution of a previously punished response and the self-controlling behavior reduces such anxiety by inhibition of the temptation or by engagement in other behaviors. Our approach to self-control research and its application in the clinical area has rested more heavily on Skinner's definition of the process. Essentially, we consider the term self-control most appropriate for defining situations in which the behavior is initially under control of two sets of conflicting reinforcing contingencies. Usually, the behavioral act has immediate positive consequences, but long range aversive consequences. For example, smoking, overeating, and a wide range of antisocial behaviors are difficult to eliminate, because these behaviors are frequently accompanied by immediate favorable consequences. In the tolerance of aversive stimulation such as heroic acts of suffering, the positive consequences may occur later in time but may be of larger magnitude than the immediate aversive consequences. In each situation, the particular response to be controlled must be viewed as the terminal link in a chain of behaviors leading to the undesirable behavior. Skinner (1953) defines self-control as a process in which "an organism may make the punished response less probable by altering the variables of which it is a function. Any behavior which succeeds in doing this will automatically be reinforced [p. 230]." Execution of self-control thus requires the manipulation of a *controlling* response in such a way that the contingent *controlled* response becomes either less probable or impossible.

Figure 2 describes the schema for the two situations, *"resistance to temptation"* and *"heroism."* The upper part of the figure indicates the theoretical position that execution of the tempting response is inhibited because of anticipatory anxiety and control is maintained by the aversion relief experienced through anxiety reduction. The lower part suggests a broader conceptualization. Once the decision toward self-control is made (a matter which itself requires investigation, but will not be covered in detail here), the temptation sequence can be interrupted by a variety of devices. All of them share the outcome of lowering the probability of the tempting response. Figure 3 presents some of the methods available for inhibiting the tempting response. It

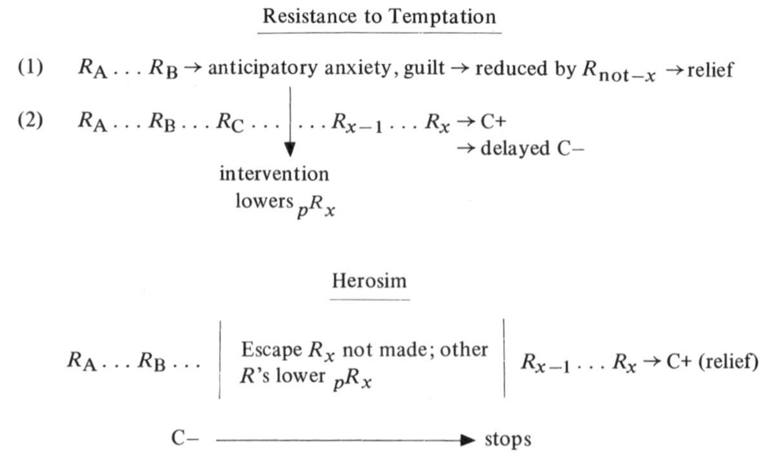

<u>Resistance to Temptation</u>

(1) $R_A \ldots R_B \rightarrow$ anticipatory anxiety, guilt $\rightarrow$ reduced by $R_{not-x} \rightarrow$ relief

(2) $R_A \ldots R_B \ldots R_C \ldots \Big| \ldots R_{x-1} \ldots R_x \rightarrow C+$
                                            $\rightarrow$ delayed C−

              intervention
              lowers $_pR_x$

<u>Herosim</u>

$R_A \ldots R_B \ldots$ $\Big|$ Escape R_x not made; other R's lower $_pR_x$ $\Big|$ $R_{x-1} \ldots R_x \rightarrow$ C+ (relief)

        C− $\longrightarrow$ stops

Fig. 2. Self-control I.

will be noted that in all cases the definition of self-control requires that it be the person himself who initiates interruption of the tempting response chain. Control of undesirable behavior by external agents may utilize the same methods. For example, removal of the positive consequences of some behaviors such as the addition of unsavory substances to food by a cook, or physical restraint of a drug-addicted person are possible means of stopping the sequence. However, since they are initiated by external agents, they would not qualify as cases of self-control. Nevertheless, in practical situations, a person can initiate his own behavior change by requesting others to manipulate either stimulus control or response consequences in such a way that the probability of the critical response changes. Therefore, the person arranges his own controlling program by turning over control to others. Many examples of such controlling devices are encountered in everyday life. Alcoholics may turn their money over to their companion when going out for an evening in order to reduce the probability of buying drinks. A wife may solicit her husband's or friend's help in preparing food in order to reduce her temptation to snack. Alarm clocks and timers serve to facilitate self-control for most of us. In situations in which others are invited to arrange the controls, the main practical problem lies in the hazard of building up counter controlling behaviors. For example, we tease our friend to let us have a drink, a cigarette, or a candy bar; we avoid our colleagues whom we asked to remind us of our pledge to cut down on lunches. Such behavior then puts the controller in a bind by pitting threats of changes in our interpersonal behaviors against the controller's execution of the agreed restrictive measures.

Self-control usually deals with situations in which the tempting response has prepotency and past experiences have built up reinforcing events favorable to execution of the undesired behavior. As a result, self-control initially is difficult to maintain and may require supplementary environmental supports. Once a rearrangement of response probabilities and consequences is achieved, the tempting behavior eventually decreases in frequency. Successful self-control thus changes the behavioral sequence so that "temptation" no longer presents a problem under most circumstances. However, when the earlier controlling variables of the tempting response are reestablished or the consequences are changed again, the problematic behavior can reappear.

Means for Achieving Self-Control

Figure 3 lists five ways in which self-control can be accomplished. Most clinical practices for establishing self-control represent combinations of these means. Intervention begins early in the behavioral chain, with R_A as the link selected for intervention. By establishing a competing response with highly

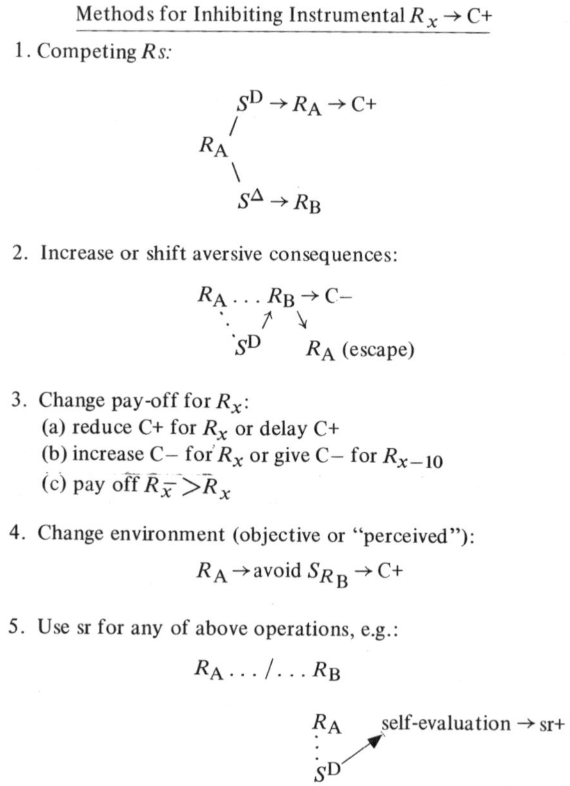

Methods for Inhibiting Instrumental $R_x \to$ C+

1. Competing Rs:

$$S^D \to R_A \to \text{C+}$$
$$R_A$$
$$S^\Delta \to R_B$$

2. Increase or shift aversive consequences:

$$R_A \ldots R_B \to \text{C}-$$
$$S^D \qquad R_A \text{ (escape)}$$

3. Change pay-off for R_x:
   (a) reduce C+ for R_x or delay C+
   (b) increase C– for R_x or give C– for R_{x-10}
   (c) pay off $\bar{R}_{\bar{x}} > \bar{R}_x$

4. Change environment (objective or "perceived"):

$$R_A \to \text{avoid } S_{R_B} \to \text{C+}$$

5. Use sr for any of above operations, e.g.:

$$R_A \ldots / \ldots R_B$$

$$R_A \qquad \text{self-evaluation} \to \text{sr+}$$
$$S^D$$

Fig. 3. Self-control II.

rewarding consequences, (C+) the chain may be interrupted after the R_A link takes on discriminative functions for the newly introduced behavior and its consequence.

A second method consists of bringing the aversive consequences (C–) of the tempting response into play prior to the completion of the behavior chain. Training and reinforcement for an escape response should help in disrupting the previous chain.

A third method consists of changing the consequences for the tempting response (R_x). This can be done by reduction of the positive consequences, or introducing a delay. For example, a person can arrange an eating sequence so that he delays food intake after an initial disposition to seek food, or by selecting less tasty items. Increasing aversive consequences for the tempting behavior or applying aversive consequences to prior links in the chain (R_{x-10})

should also alter the probability of the controlled response (R_x). Finally, alternate and more desirable responses $(R_{\bar{x}})$ are connected to reinforcing events of equal or greater magnitude than the original response, but by means of alternate response chains. This method is similar to the one used for establishing competing responses.

Another method for altering the probability of the tempting response lies in changing the environment. In this approach, the person is taught to avoid or escape environments in which the probability of the controlled response is high. For example, the alcoholic avoids taverns, invitations to cocktail parties, and similar situations. It is clear that this method is effective in theory, but difficult to execute in practice. The social environment often offers support for the tempting behavior under many conditions. It may also require a person's presence in a tempting environment for attainment of other desirable consequences. Thus, optimum achievement of available social and material reinforcers may make it difficult to avoid environments in which temptation occurs.

We have noted that the initial period in any self-controlling program is the most difficult. Since supervision or external control is often difficult and undesirable, training in utilization of any of the previous methods by positive self-reinforcement is used to strengthen self-controlling techniques.

A brief summary of current clinical methods may help to illustrate our conceptual framework. Detailed descriptions of these methods are available in several recent reviews (Bandura, 1969b; Cautela, 1969; Kanfer & Phillips, 1970). Narrowing stimulus control or establishing competing responses is illustrated in modification of study habits (Fox, 1962), in the control of obesity (Ferster, Nurnberger, & Levitt, 1962). Use of self-instructions (e.g., O'Leary, 1968) and the use of self-monitoring to establish a competing response (Kanfer & Phillips, 1970) as well as the proverbial use of cold showers or athletic activities to compete with sexual arousal are examples of means for facilitating control. Skinner (1953) notes the effectiveness of interposing a delay before execution of the final response. Others have reported connecting old discriminative stimuli to new responses such as chewing peppermint candy or other eating responses incompatible with smoking behavior.

Homme (1965) and Cautela (1969) and Davison (1969) advocate the use of self-generated imaginal or verbal responses to serve either as competing responses or to bring aversive consequences into play early in the behavioral chain. Utilization of self-reinforcement together with training of competing responses is involved in Bandura's technique of modeling (1969b) and Rehm and Marston's (1968) technique of training sr for alternate behaviors. Changes in consequences have been suggested for such techniques as self-delivered shock, self-punishment by paying a large fine after execution of the tempting response, and similar behaviors. Contract management (Sulzer, 1962; Pratt & Tooley, 1964) changes response consequences and provides for alternate behaviors as competing responses to enhance self-control.

Self-Monitoring

Recent attention has been devoted to closer examination of the role of self-monitoring in behavior control. In our conceptual schema (Fig. 1), it is seen that any means by which response feedback is clarified or classified would contribute toward making it easier for the person to assess the discrepancy between performance standards and his achievement. This simplification of the self-evaluating task should permit more realistic execution of self-reinforcing operations. It should also facilitate planning toward effective alteration of the undesirable behavior. Self-control should, therefore, be easier to achieve if the person can specify the desired terminal behavior and can obtain clear feedback during his attempt to change.

Recent studies and clinical reports have supported this expectation. Self-monitoring alone has been reported to be sufficient to bring about changes in patient behaviors. In fact, although originally used only as a method of data collection, attention has recently been drawn to the fact that such self-reports may be reactive measures, modifying the very behavior which they are intended to describe. A review of this area (Kanfer, 1970) suggests that the utility of self-observation in therapy may depend on the patient's commitment to change, the incompatability between the observing response and the symptomatic behavior, the magnitude of reinforcement for observation and for change, the inherent reinforcing consequences of the observed behavior, the timing for self-observation in reference to the symptomatic behavior, and similar variables. Apart from the interesting methodological problems and the relevance to the broader issue of the utility of self-reports, deliberate self-observation has practical utility because it can provide response feedback to a degree of clarity not often encountered in daily behaviors. Numerous earlier studies on self-confrontation, be it by the therapist's verbal statements or by photographs, or by television playback, share the implicit assumption that such feedback can bring about self-directed change. From our working model, it would be reasoned that such information input may be most useful when a person can also be helped to use it for comparison against performance standards and for attaching differential consequences to various outcomes to this comparison.

Self-monitoring is clearly one method by which private events can be further explored. Therefore, its methodology, the philosophical and experimental requirements for its proper use and knowledge of the conditions which affect the self-report are of critical interest to theoreticians and practitioner alike.

In the present paper, I have attempted to present a working model for the dual purpose of raising research issues in the investigation of self-regulatory processes and for integrating experimental findings and reports from the clinical literature into a pragmatic as well as theoretically sound framework. I have touched only upon a few of the research areas which have relevance to a better understanding of self-regulatory processes. For example, most of my work has dealt with the role of operant behaviors. Recent reports have indicated that respondents (which may play a significant role in the response feedback loop) can be brought under operant control. Areas of research that deal more specifically with investigating the effects of self-prescribed standards and behavior have also been barely mentioned. Nevertheless, I believe that the research direction discussed in this paper has supported the faith of researchers in the applicability of a model basically derived from a behavioristic learning analysis to private events. Ultimately, an understanding of processes which are now loosely called "self" should permit not only refinement in our theorizing about the nature of human functioning but also in our effectiveness as experts in the practical matter of changing human behavior.

References

Adams, J. A. Response feedback and learning. *Psychological Bulletin,* 1968, **70**, 486-504.

Aronfreed, J. *Conduct and conscience: The socialization of internalized control over behavior.* New York: Academic Press, 1968.

Bandura, A. *Principles of behavior modification.* New York: Holt, 1969. (*a*).

Bandura, A. Vicarious and self-reinforcement processes. Unpublished Ms. Stanford University, 1969. (*b*).

Bandura, A., & Kupers, C. J. Transmission of patterns of self-reinforcement through modeling. *Journal of Abnormal and Social Psychology,* 1964, **69**, 1-9.

Bandura, A., & Perloff, B. Relative efficacy of self-monitored and externally imposed reinforcement systems. *Journal of Personality and Social Psychology,* 1967, **7**, 111-116.

Bem, D. J. An experimental analysis of self-persuasion. *Journal of Experimental Social Psychology,* 1965, **1**, 199-218.

Bem, D. J. Self-perception: An alternative interpretation of cognitive dissonance phenomena. *Psychological Review,* 1967, **74**, 183-200.

Cautela, J. R. Behavior therapy and self control: Techniques and implications. In C. M. Franks (Ed.), *Behavior therapy: Appraisal and status.* New York: McGraw-Hill, 1969.

Cautela, J. R. Covert sensitization. *Psychological Record,* 1967, **20**, 459-468.

Davison, G. C. Self-control through "imaginal aversive contingency" and "one-downsmanship." In J. D. Krumboltz & C. E. Thoresen (Eds.), *Behavioral counseling: Cases and techniques.* New York: Holt, 1969.

Dorsey, T. E., Kanfer, F. H., & Duerfeldt, P. H. Task difficulty & noncontingent reinforcement schedules as factors in self-reinforcement. *Journal of General Psychology,* 1971. In press.

Eimas, P. D., & Zeaman, D. Response speed changes in an Estes' paired-associate "miniature" experiment. *Journal of Verbal Learning and Verbal Behavior,* 1963, **1,** 384-388.

Ferster, C. B., Nurnberger, J. I., & Levitt, E. B. The control of eating. *Journal of Mathetics,* 1962, **1,** 87-109.

Festinger, L. A. A theory of social comparison processes. *Human Relations,* 1954, **7,** 117-140.

Fox, L. Effecting the use of efficient study habits. *Journal of Mathetics,* 1962, **1,** 75-86.

Goodlet, G. R., & Goodlet, M. M. Efficiency of self-monitored and externally imposed schedules of reinforcement in controlling disruptive behavior. Unpublished manuscript, University of Guelph, 1969.

Heckhausen, H. Die Interaktion der Sozialisations-variablen in der Genese des Leistungsmotive. In H. Thomae (Ed.) *Socialisation. Handbuch der Psychologie,* 7, Bd. Göttingen: Hogrefe, 1969.

Hill, W. F. Sources of evaluative reinforcement. *Psychological Bulletin,* 1968, **69,** 132-146.

Homme, L. E. Perspectives in psychology—XXIV: Control of coverants, the operants of the mind. *Psychological Records,* 1965, **15,** 501-511.

Hunt, J. McV. Intrinsic motivation and its role in psychological development. In D. Levine (Ed.) *Nebraska Symposium on Motivation,* Lincoln, Nebraska: Univ. of Nebraska Press, 1965.

Johnson, S. M., & Martin, S. Self-evaluation as conditioned reinforcement. Mimeo. Report, Univ. of Oregon, Eugene, 1970.

Kanfer, F. H. Influence of age and incentive conditions on children's self-rewards. *Psychological Reports,* 1966, **19,** 263-274.

Kanfer, F. H. Self-Regulation: Research, Issues, & Speculations. Presented at the Ninth Annual Institute for Research in Clinical Psychology, "Behavior Modification in Clinical Psychology," at the University of Kansas, April 3–5, 1967.

Kanfer, F. H. Self-monitoring: Methodological limitations and clinical applications. *Journal of Consulting and Clinical Psychology,* 1970, **35,** 148-152.

Kanfer, F. H., & Duerfeldt, P. H. Effects of pretraining on self-evaluation and self-reinforcement. *Journal of Personality and Social Psychology,* 1967, **7,** 164-168 (*a*).

Kanfer, F. H., & Duerfeldt, P. H. Motivational properties of self-reinforcement. *Perceptual and Motor Skills,* 1967, **25,** 237-246 (*b*).

Kanfer, F. H., & Duerfeldt, P. H. Comparison of self-reward and self-criticism as a function of types of prior external reinforcement. *Journal of Personality and Social Psychology,* 1968, 8, 261-268 (*a*).

Kanfer, F. H., & Duerfeldt, P. H. Age, class standing, and commitment as determinants of cheating in children. *Child Development,* 1968, **39,** 545-557 (*b*).

Kanfer, F. H., Duerfeldt, P. H., & LePage, A. L. Stability of patterns of self-reinforcement. *Psychological Reports,* 1969, **24,** 663-670.

Kanfer, F. H., & Marston, A. R. Determinants of self-reinforcement in human learning. *Journal of Experimental Psychology,* 1963, **66,** 245-254 (*a*).

Kanfer, F. H., & Marston, A. R. Conditioning of self-reinforcing responses: An analogue to self-confidence training. *Psychological Reports,* 1963, **13,** 63-70 (*b*).

Kanfer, F. H., & Phillips, J. S. *Learning Foundations of Behavior Therapy.* New York: Wiley, 1970.

Katz, I. The socialization of academic motivation in minority group children. In D. Levine (Ed.), *Nebraska Symposium on Motivation.* Lincoln, Nebraska: University of Nebraska Press, 1967.

Liebert, R. M., & Ora, J. P. Children's adoption of self-reward patterns: Incentive level and method of transmission. *Child Development,* 1968, **39,** 537-544.

Locke, E. A., Cartledge, N., & Koeppel, J. Motivational effects of knowledge of results: A goal-setting phenomenon? *Psychological Bulletin,* 1968, **70,** 474-485.

Logan, F. A. & Wagner, A. R. *Reward and punishment.* Boston: Allyn & Bacon, 1965.

Lovitt, T. C. & Curtiss, K. A. Academic response rate as a function of teacher and self-imposed contingencies. *Journal of Applied Behavior Analysis,* 1969, **2,** 49-53.

Mandler, G. The interruption of behavior. In D. Levine (Ed.), *Nebraska Symposium on Motivation.* Lincoln, Nebraska: University of Nebraska Press, 1964.

Mandler, G. & Watson, D. L. Anxiety and the interruption of behavior. In C. D. Spielberger (Ed.), *Anxiety and behavior.* New York: Academic Press, 1966.

Marston, A. R. Initiation, self-reinforcement, and reinforcement of another person. *Journal of Personality and Social Psychology,* 1965, **2,** 255-261.

Marston, A. R. & Kanfer, F. H. Human reinforcement: Experimenter and subject controlled. *Journal of Experimental Psychology,* 1963, **66,** 91-94.

Mowrer, O. H. *Learning theory and behavior.* New York: Wiley, 1960.

O'Leary, K. D. The effects of self-instruction on immoral behavior. *Journal of Experimental Child Psychology,* 1968, **6,** 297-301.

Pratt, S., & Tooley, J. Contract psychology and the actualizing transactional field. Special Edition # 1 (Theoretical Aspects in Research), *International Journal of Social Psychiatry,* 1964, 51-69.

Rehm, L. P., & Marston, A. R. Reduction of social anxiety through modification of self-reinforcement: An instigation therapy technique. *Journal of Consulting Psychology,* 1968, **32,** 565-574.

Sher, M. Pupillary dilation during recall and following interruption of recall. Unpublished Ph.D. dissertation, University of Cincinnati, 1970.

Skinner, B. F. *Science and human behavior.* New York: Macmillan, 1953.

Solomon, R. L., & Turner, L. H. Discriminative classical conditioning in dogs paralyzed by curare can later control discriminative avoidance responses in the normal state. *Psychological Review,* 1962, **69,** 202-219.

Sulzer, E. S. Reinforcement and therapeutic contract. *Journal of Consulting Psychology,* 1962, **9,** 271-276.

Construing Hypnosis as Modifiable Behavior

Lewis B. Sachs

West Virginia University
Morgantown, West Virginia

Confusion begins with the definition of hypnosis. Some investigators have primarily emphasized the antecedent conditions, others have focused solely on the response consequences, and the remaining have stressed a variety of intervening states or traits. The resulting lack of clarity, combined with the tendency of many investigators to refer to hypnosis as an explanation rather than as a class of behavior, has been responsible for diverting research into issues that are essentially definitional in nature.

For instance, in an effort to substitute task-motivation for hypnosis as an explanation, Barber and his co-workers (Barber, 1961, 1962a, b, c, d, 1966; Barber & Calverley, 1962; Barber & Deeley, 1961; Barber & Hahn, 1962) have repeatedly demonstrated that brief task-motivating or exhortation instructions are as effective as traditional hypnotic inductions. However, Ludwig and Lyle (1964) have pointed out that hypnosis need not be regarded as a sleeplike state, and induction procedures need not be limited to passive inductions, but can include alert inductions similar to Barber's exhortation procedure. Similarly, by repetitiously contrasting hypnotic induction with noninduction procedures many other investigators have attempted to demonstrate the superiority and hence the necessity of specific hypnotic states or trances. While both approaches have provided information on the behavior of hypnotic theorists or researchers, the extensive research efforts assessing the effectiveness of presumed nonhypnotic antecedents and the absence or presence of presumed essential intervening states have provided very little information regarding the particular behaviors under investigation.

In contrast to the frequent assumption of many psychologists that private responses are somehow unlawful or their investigation unscientific, both the subjective or private and the objective responses were included in the current presentation of hypnotic behaviors. The intention of construing hypnotic behavior as modifiable was to focus attention directly on the hypnotic behaviors themselves. The successful modification of these behaviors would not only support the construction of hypnotic behavior as modifiable but more importantly would increase the utility of such behaviors. Furthermore, the successful modification or increase of both the objective and subjective hypnotic behaviors would be of importance, as previously, only limited numbers of Ss were capable of performing hypnotic behavior.

The first purpose of this chapter is to provide an historical perspective on the assumption of hypnosis as a stable characteristic of the individual, as variously cast in terms of neurophysiological mechanisms, physiological states, and personality traits. Second, this chapter will review the literature regarding the modification of hypnotic behavior, an area of particular relevance to that of private events, as the analysis and alteration of private events provided a successful means of increasing hypnotic behaviors. Finally, this chapter will briefly discuss some uses of hypnotic behaviors.

Historical Perspective

Early historical conceptualizations viewed hypnosis as dependent upon a particular underlying mechanism and consequently as a characteristic of only certain individuals. For instance, Charcot (1882), Binet and Fere (1888), and Janet (1920) presented hypnosis as a pathological condition based on a neurological predisposition to hysteria. Janet also believed in a dissociation process similar to the positions of Prince (1909), Sidis (1910), and Burnett (1925) who viewed hypnosis as a state of dissociation based on unconscious memories. The work of Pavlov (1934) and Kubie and Margolin (1944) linked hypnosis to a modified form of sleep based on cerebral inhibition. Various other investigators ranging in time from Hart's (1882) work to Eysenck's (1947) more recent position, have viewed hypnosis in terms of specific neurophysiological processes. Each of these conceptualizations of hypnosis have implied the stability of hypnosis and the necessity of some form of physiological intervention for the modification of an individual's hypnotizability.

Many of the more recent theoretical formulations regarding the nature of hypnosis have shifted from physiological to psychological orientations. The current psychological formulations also represent a continuation of the historical notion of hypnosis as dependent upon some underlying stable characteristic of the individual. For instance, the trance theory of Shor (1959) was based on the assumption of at least one permanent attribute of mental functioning being a necessary condition for hypnosis. The psychoanalytic theory of Gill and Brenman (1959) interpreted hypnosis as a function of ego processes and transference. The developmental-interactive theory of Hilgard and Hilgard (1962) postulated hypnosis as a function of specific experiences early in childhood. For the psychological orientations, the modification of the assumed stable hypnotic abilities would necessitate changes in the basic personality makeup of the individual.

The extensive research in the area of assessment of hypnotic abilities has also implied that hypnosis was an extremely stable individual characteristic. The work of Schmidkunz (1944), Lowenfeld (1901), and Bramwell (1903) categorized 10% of the population as able to attain a deep level of hypnosis. Further confirmation for the consistency of the distribution of hypnotic abilities has been obtained from the recent normative data reviewed by Hilgard (1965), indicating 13% of the population as capable of deep hypnosis. In a review of hypnotic susceptibility scales, Hilgard (1965) concludes that under standard conditions, hypnotic susceptibility is a dependable trait, with retest correlations ranging between 80 and 90. This stability was assumed to be a function of an underlying true hypnotic ability score with slight error from either individual resistance or compliance. Unfortunately, the replicability of the hypnotic assessment results has often been viewed as constituting evidence for hypnosis as an entity, incapable of significant modification.

Stability has also been implied from areas of research attempting to investigate the underlying mechanisms of hypnosis. For instance, Barber (1965a) has reviewed the studies concerned with the physiological correlates of the hypnotic trance, Barber (1965b) has reviewed the physiological effects of hypnosis, Barber (1964) and Hilgard (1965) have reviewed the numerous studies that have investigated the psychological correlates of hypnosis, and Hilgard (1965) and Evans (1966) have reviewed the factor-analytic research on hypnosis. The studies represented in these reviews of hypnotic research have shared the assumption of constancy or stability in their search for the basic underlying states, traits, or factors of hypnosis. The number of studies included in these extensive reviews indicates the strength of the assumptions regarding the nature of hypnosis, as researchers only fixated in their continued search for significant correlates of hypnosis. However, such investigations have not been able to find any invariant physiological or psychological correlates, nor any definite set of factors associated with hypnotizability.

Modification of Hypnotic Abilities

The traditional constructs regarding hypnosis have directed many studies in search of the presumed stable and basic entities underlying hypnotic phenomena and have thereby served to delay systematic efforts to modify these behaviors. Fortunately, the neglect of such an important area has not been total, since many individual hypnotists have reported incidences of clinical success in increasing hypnotizability. For instance, as early as 1846 Esdaile claimed that lengthy induction procedures allowed most of his patients to become deeply hypnotized. By postulating a universal capacity for individuals to attain a hypnotic state, Bernheim (1884) initiated a controversial challenge to Charcot's position of hypnosis as an underlying constitutional predisposition. Vogt (1896) claimed that the alternation of hypnotizing and awakening his Ss allowed many to reach a deep level of hypnosis. Erickson (1957) reported a resistant S that required 300 hours of labor before a trance could be successfully induced. Blum (1966) reported that both a medium and a low hypnotizable S were able to score in the high hypnotizable range after a dozen hours of training.

In a very important study, Pascal and Salzberg (1959) were the first to have demonstrated that a systematic training procedure led to significant increases in hypnotic performance. Most of their Ss were able to complete the specific hypnotic tasks that were presented in an ascending order of difficulty. Training effectiveness was evaluated by comparison of the percentage of subjects passing particular tasks with the earlier normative data reported by Bernheim (1947). The authors concluded that the significant increases in hypnotizability were attributable to the successive specific steps involved in their systematic training procedure. However, interpretation of the obtained increases was difficult as many variables other than successive specific steps confounded the comparison with the earlier findings of Bernheim. Moreover, the rapidity of training (20–45 min) suggests that motivational components contributed more to the increased hypnotic behavior than the manipulation of learning parameters.

Giles (1962), utilizing the same training procedure as employed by Pascal and Salzberg, was able to replicate their finding of an increased percentage of Ss capable of successful hypnotic behavior. This study also indicated the necessity of experience on the part of the hypnotist, as only 23.5% of the first 17 Ss were able to attain a deep trance in contrast to 55.2% for the last 29 Ss to participate in the training procedure. In evaluation of the results, Giles noted that the comparisons across studies were weakened by the subjective judgment involved in the assessment of the depth of hypnosis and by the varied samples selected for investigation.

Wiseman and Reyher (1962) indicated that one of the biggest obstacles to the further development of hypnosis as an applied technique and research tool has been the difficulty in deepening hypnotic trance. In an attempt to alleviate this problem, they developed a training procedure utilizing dreams for deepening hypnosis. Training effectiveness was based on a comparison of amnesia scores for *S*s who had undergone the dream deepening procedure to *S*s not subjected to the deepening procedure. The results indicated a significant increase in the training *S*s' amnesia ratings. Although training led to an increase in the percentage of *S*s capable of attaining total amnesia, the method did not lead to a significant increase in the percentage of *S*s able to experience some amnesia. The authors suggested that this technique may not be useful for implementing major changes, but serve more as a facilitator when resistances are relatively weak. The authors concluded that the results supported the hypothesis that the dream deepening method facilitates the production of total amnesia and, inferentially, a deepening of the hypnotic trance.

Shor, Orne, and O'Connell (1962) reported that most *S*s soon reach a plateau of hypnotic performance beyond which no appreciable improvement occurred regardless of the hypnotist, methods employed, or amount of subsequent training. The authors assumed that the stability of hypnosis, particularly in the deep region of the hypnotizability continuum, was a function of the *S*s' possession of exceptionally high cognitive-ability components. However, Shor, Orne, and O'Connell (1966) performed a study based on the assumption that hypnotic training sessions would increase a *S*'s hypnotizability. Therefore, instead of defining hypnosis as a single score on a limited test, they defined hypnotizability as the maximum hypnotic depth achieved in as many intensive hypnotic training sessions as the *E* needed in order to feel confident that a stable plateau in the *S*'s hypnotic performance had been reached. This definition of hypnotizability depended upon the hypnotist's judgment of the *S*'s inability to improve with further training.

Training consisted of a variety of unspecified techniques, which the authors believed would maximize hypnotic performance. The *S*'s stable plateau of hypnotic performance was rated in four categories (less than light, light, medium, and deep), on the basis of objective hypnotic behavior and the *S*'s own report. The correlation between posttraining hypnotic susceptibility as measured on the Stanford Hypnotic Susceptibility Scale (SHSS), Form B, and depth of hypnotizability rating was significantly higher than the correlation between pretraining hypnotic susceptibility as measured on the SHSS, Form A, and depth of the hypnotizability rating, and was offered as evidence for the utility of the assessment of plateau hypnotizability. However, interpretation of this obtained correlational increase was not possible, since the authors did not report the pre- and posttraining scores, thus precluding direct analysis of the effectiveness of training sessions on the modification of hypnotizability, although the results indicated that none of the Ss who had not had prior hypnotic experiences were able to attain a deep hypnotizability rating.

Shor and Cobb (1968) characterized research on the modification of hypnotizability as one of the most basic questions regarding the nature of hypnosis. To test the universality of hypnotizability the authors attempted to increase each individual's plateau performance. Plateau performance was now more operationally defined as no improvement on two consecutive testings on Form C on the SHSS, where each test was intervened by at least two intensive clinical training sessions. The E was allowed freedom to choose from any available hypnotic procedures for training Ss. Although the authors did not analyze their results, the pre- and posttraining scores were reported. Analysis of the obtained mean change score of 1.5 between the initial test and plateau performance revealed an insignificant difference ($t = 1.87$, $df = 7$, $p < .10$; one tailed). In fact, only three of the eight Ss showed any improvement after a variety of traditional hypnotic training methods. This finding seriously questions the utility of the concept of plateau performance. However, the authors' subsequent efforts to increase the Ss' plateau performances were successful, as five of eight Ss improved after employment of new methods of hypnotic training. The new training techniques consisted of the following: a sensory-isolation type situation with controlled hypnotic input for periods of time ranging from 15 to 41 hr, self-hypnosis sessions particularly before retiring at night, placebos under the guise of a mild psychedelic drug, and a brain-wave synchronizer utilizing a flashing light. The mean posttraining change score (3.1) was found to be a significant improvement over plateau performance ($t = 2.6$, $df = 7$, $p < .025$; one tailed). Although the posttraining scores represented a statistically significant increase, the fact that three of the eight Ss did not show any improvement after individual training over two summers indicates some limitations for this training procedure.

In contrast, Hilgard, Weitzenhoffer, Landis, and Moore (1961) noted a high degree of consistency for Ss across varied hypnotic tests and across different hypnotists when routine hypnotic inductions were used. Hilgard and Hilgard (1962) presented hypnotic susceptibility as a stable personality characteristic based on the following evidence: first, the high test–retest reliability with the same hypnotist; second, the high test–retest reliability with different hypnotists; third, the high correlations over tests differing in method of induction and test content.

In a subsequent study As, Hilgard, and Weitzenhoffer (1963) explored the changes in hypnotizability in moderately susceptible Ss after repeated individualized training sessions, on the assumption that individual training might be superior to routine inductions. The 4–10 hr of training ranged from a variety of induction techniques to actual psychotherapy with the subject. The resulting posttraining mean increase of 3.9 was statistically significant, although the authors claimed not to have been able to modify hypnotizability dramatically. They concluded that hypnosis was a fairly stable trait, as there were only very slight gains with no appreciable correlation between intial scores and gains after practice, or between the number of sessions and the amount of gain.

In an extension of the As *et al.* study, Cooper, Banford, Schubot, and Tart (1967) provided individual training sessions ranging from 7 to 16 sessions of 1–2 hr duration. The use of the Stanford Profile Scale of hypnotic susceptibility conʑisting of difficult tasks made it possible to avoid confounding results by imposing an upper limit on hypnotic improvement. The obtained mean increase of 2.9 after modification sessions was barely significant, and the authors pointed out that although one *S* changed as much as eight points, hypnotic susceptibility was unusually stable. At this study was a replication of the previous study of As *et al.,* it was possible for the authors to combine the results of both studies to evaluate the relationship between the *S*'s original susceptibility and subsequent modification. A rank order correlation of .59 was obtained between initial responses and gain scores. Examination of the mean change scores from the *S*'s initial susceptibility indicated a significant mean gain of 7.1 for the *S*s on the higher half of the susceptibility continuum and a mean gain of only 1.9 for the *S*s on the lower half of the continuum. The authors concluded that initially good subjects are the most likely to profit from training sessions.

Sachs and Anderson (1967) devised a new training method for the modification of hypnotic susceptibility in an attempt to facilitate both the clinical and research uses of hypnosis. Similar to the work of Pascal and Salzberg (1959), the training method was based on the assumption of hypnosis as learned behavior. A maximum number of six 50-min training sessions was inserted between pre- and posttraining tests on Forms A and C of the SHSS, with training limited to those items that an individual failed or barely passed on Form A of the SHSS. Training consisted of the synthesis of several techniques that allowed variation in individual learning rates. Despite the individualization of training, the method can be described for all *S*s in terms of four major components discussed as follows.

1. The goal of training was to provide each *S* with a clear conception of the sensory experiences associated with performance on each hypnotic task and to indicate that it would become possible as a result of training, to experience these sensations involuntarily when given the appropriate cues. This was accomplished by the utilization of actual physical stimuli, by the hypnotist's description of both the nature of the desired level of sensory experience and the process

whereby this level was attained, and by involving the *S* in his own progress. For example, to acquaint the *S* with the sensations of heaviness, heavy objects were piled on the hand to demonstrate the heaviness; later training on this item, or training on a more abstract item such as amnesia, relied more on the hypnotist's descriptions of the desired sensations. These descriptions stressed subjective or private sensations as reported by the *S*s and past experiences with components in common with the item being trained, e.g., both lethargy and exhaustion share certain components with the experience of heaviness. Repetitious exposure to these actual and imagined sensations enabled each *S* to experience items with increased clarity and vividness. Throughout the training, the *S* was instructed to focus his entire attention upon the sensations being rehearsed and to report which experiences proved to be most helpful.

2. Self-paced successive approximations were used to maximize progress for any given item. For example, *S*'s 1-sec delay in lifting his hand after being told it was extremely heavy would constitute a successful start. Following repetitions at this level, subsequent approximations to the final criterion were reached by instructing the *S*s to increase in just-noticeable-difference (JND) steps. In order to increase the latency or time required to lift the "heavy" hand, the *S* was directed to supply just enough additional imaginary weights to enable him to experience a noticeable improvement in the degree and clarity of his subsequent sensation of "heavy" hand. This procedure minimized the possibility of failure and allowed training to proceed at an optimal rate.

3. A further component of the training procedure was the use of a double-bind situation. Each *S* was requested to give a motor signal when he felt the intensity of the appropriate sensation had increased by a JND. The *S* was then challenged on the item and his objective performance measured. For example, after a subjective report of increased heaviness, the *S* was challenged to move his arm and the duration of immobilization was measured. Thus, each *S* found himself in the position of being compelled to validate his subjective experience of increased sensation with increased objective performance. Resolution of this conflict is also an analog of the cognitive dissonance paradigm. In addition, this procedure influenced the *S* to become more actively involved in the training procedure.

4. Verbal reinforcement was provided for appropriate increases in subjective or private experiences throughout the training procedure. The training hypnotist provided reinforcement in terms of verbal approval; however, verbal reinforcement was progressively decreased with further training sessions. The *S*'s self-reinforcement provided another important source of reinforcement. The primary source of self-reinforcement derived from the *S*'s own gratification upon success (e.g., *S*'s spontaneous excitement after not being able to list the "heavy" arm). It was suspected that self-reinforcement increased progressively as a function of further training, since the intensity of the reported private experiences greatly increased.

The effectiveness of the training sessions was clearly indicated by the dramatic improvement (mean increase of 6.0) on posttraining Form A performance. The significantly increased (mean increase of 4.0) performance on Form C indicated the degree of generalization of this training to related and to new hypnotic tasks. Similar posttraining changes were also obtained for each of the *S*'s subjective change scores, as measured by their subjective ratings on each of the hypnotic tasks.

A more extensive investigation designed by Kenney and Sachs (in preparation) was able to avoid many of the previous methodological difficulties in the evaluation of modification techniques. For this investigation both pre- and posttraining experimenters tested *S*s without knowledge of their participation in a modification study, thereby eliminating the potential bias from *E*'s expectation of improvement which had confounded previous studies. Prior assessment of subjective reports on changes of cognitive and perceptual tasks had not controlled for the demand characteristics of the experimental situation, which Bowers (1967) had recently shown to produce significant differences in subjective reports about hypnosis. Bowers's technique was utilized in the present study to maximize the conditions which would allow for more accurate assessment of the subjective ratings. The use of a control group was a further advantage in that it allowed comparison of just the effect of pre- and posttesting experiences without the intervention of training sessions. The inclusion of a 1-month follow-up provided an opportunity to evaluate the stability of potential improvements in hypnotizability.

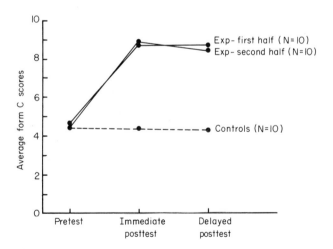

Fig. 1. Comparison of average scores for experimental and control subjects for pretest, immediate posttest, and delayed posttest.

Selected *S*s scoring between one and four (low group) and five and eight (medium group) on Forms A and C of the SHSS were subjected to the training procedure developed by Sachs and Anderson. Because there were twice as many experimental *S*s as controls, two analyses were conducted—one comparing the first ten experimental subjects (five low and five medium) with the controls, the other comparing the second half (also five low and five medium) with the controls. While this was not actually a replication, because the same control group was used twice, it did serve as a partial replication. In both cases the results indicated statistically significant improvement for the experimental compared to control *S*s. Low-group *S*s showed a mean increase of 4.0, medium-group *S*s showed a mean increase of 4.6, and the control *S*s showed no change in mean scores as shown in Fig. 1. The pre- and posttest of the Stanford Profile Scales of Hypnotizability were analyzed to test for generalization effects after the completion of the training on Form C items. The results indicated a nonsignificant mean increase of 3.2 points for the low group and a significant mean increase of 7.8 points for the medium group. The results of the 1-month follow-up for both the Form C and the profile scales indicated the stability of the obtained training gains.

In a recent study by Sachs (unpublished, 1969), seven experimental subjects received the same training technique used by Sachs and Anderson, with training progress again based on the *S*s' subjective feedback. That is, changes in objective performance were based on the shaping of subjective or private responses. However, in contrast to prior studies, all training sessions were conducted without a prior hypnotic induction. In fact, *S*s were specifically instructed not to allow themselves to become hypnotized. The results indicated that training without hypnotic inductions still led to statistically significant improvements on both objective scores and subjective ratings. The obtained mean increase on the training scale, Form A of the SHSS, was 3.6 and the mean increase for the generalization test, Form C of the SHSS, was 2.6. No significant pretest–posttest differences were obtained for the seven control *S*s receiving an equal amount of training time consisting of repetitious rehearsal on the training scale tasks. The lack of improvement for the control group receiving mere repetition was in close agreement to results previously reported by Barber and Calverly (1966), who gave *S*s a standardized hypnotic induction and a standardized battery of test suggestions over eight individual sessions, and noted a slight decrement in hypnotic susceptibility with repeated practice.

In a further attempt to validate the results of training, Sachs (in press) applied the Sachs and Anderson technique to the modification of hypnotic analgesia. The results of shaping hypnotic analgesia indicated not only a significant reduction of subjective reports of experienced pain but also a significant decrease in blood-pressure scores during analgesia. The blood pressure and subjective reports of pain were measured during the presentation of continuous pain source which allowed comparison under both a hypnotic analgesic and a hypnotic relaxed condition. The reduced blood pressure scores and the results of an anonymous questionnaire regarding the validity of the subjective reports constituted evidence against interpretation of the training results as mere response to the demand characteristics of the experimental situation or simply subject compliance.

The use of modeling procedures represents another approach to the modification of hypnotizability. Salter (1941) utilized a hypnotized model with reported success in his efforts to demonstrate appropriate hypnotic behaviors. In a study directed at the demand characteristics of hypnosis, Orne (1959) indicated that many *S* who had observed the occurrence of a particular hypnotic behavior during a demonstration of hypnosis spontaneously exhibited that behavior during hypnosis. Zimbardo (informal communication, 1969) reported 18 of 19 high school *S*s with no previous experience in hypnosis achieved a somnambulistic state with 9-12 hr of training. Subjects were given intensive training in concentration, focusing their attention, and in avoiding distraction. Zimbardo also felt that it was important to dispel the *S*'s fears about hypnosis, by using such techniques as correcting misconceptions through counter information and letting *S*s observe a model *S* being hypnotized. However, evaluation of just modeling effectiveness was confounded by the use of the other techniques. Modeling effectiveness was demonstrated in a subsequent study by Marshall and Diamond (1969) using modeling procedures and obtaining a significant average mean change score of 2.47. Other investigators have also begun to research the parameters of the hypnotic modeling procedure. In particular, Diamond (informal communication, 1970) has examined the effect of both behavioral and verbal modeling cues, DeVoge (informal communication, 1970) has examined the effects of nonreinforcement and positive reinforcement over both high and low status models, and Havens (informal communication, 1970) has extended his examination to the effects of negative reinforcement on hypnotic modeling. If the group modeling procedures can match the extent and durability of changes possible as a function of individual training procedures, the practical advantages would make it the procedure of choice.

The Utility of Hypnotic Behaviors

The purpose of this last section is to discuss briefly two general uses of hypnotic behaviors. First, it provides the means for increasing or decreasing the number and intensity of selected stimulus conditions. For instance, in the analysis of the reinforcing consequences of cigarette smoking, the author has found it possible to alter the taste of tobacco, the sight of exhaled smoke, and various tactile sensations and assess their relative contribution to subsequent smoking rates. In general, the establishment of greater stimulus control would be of advantage to the analysis and modification of any particular behavior. Second, the possible hypnotic manipulation or reversal of conditions serves as a very useful control procedure. For instance, comparison of a *S*'s smoking rate on days with sight of exhaled smoke to days without sight of exhaled smoke. The use of hypnosis would allow intrasubject comparison across varied therapeutic treatments rather than necessitating evaluation in relation to arbitrarily chosen placebo-control conditions. In fact, Lindsley (1969) has shown that some presumed placebo conditions were not completely devoid of specific treatment effects, as mere daily charting of specific behavior was sufficient to produce change.

A specific, but very important further use of hypnosis is for the reduction of pain. The ineffectiveness of morphine, the most widely used pain killer, increases the importance of the control of pain as a further application of hypnosis. Beecher and his associates (1959) found that roughly one-third of patients suffering postoperative pain gained as much relief from a placebo as morphine; for another third, morphine was more effective than placebo, while for the final third neither morphine (in safe doses) nor placebo were effective.

By considering pain as a multidimensional response, Hilgard and his associates (1967) have avoided the confusion regarding the selection of the appropriate measure of pain. For instance, the private or subjective pain responses have not usually been considered as valid measures, although overt measures, as heart rate and blood pressure changes which were initially validated against private responses, are considered valid measures. In 1966, Hilgard initiated a very important program of systematically investigating pain under laboratory conditions. Hilgard and his associates (in preparation) have assessed the effects of hypnotic analgesia, hypnotic relaxation, relaxation, aspirin, placebo, demand characteristics, and a wide range of pain intensities on both the overt and covert pain responses. On the basis of these studies, Hilgard (1969) has been able to conclude that the subject's verbal pain-state report was more capable of discriminating fine differences in stimulus conditions, more reliable upon repetition, and more lawfully related to changed stimulus conditions than any physiological measure of pain. Most important, the results of these studies also clearly demonstrated the utility of hypnotic procedures for the reduction of pain. Further confirmation of the effectiveness of hypnosis for pain reduction has been reported by McGlashan, Evans, and Orne (1969), and Sachs (in press).

In conclusion, hypnotic behaviors such as hallucinations, analgesias, amnesia, and other behaviors included on standard scales of hypnotizability, are clearly capable of significant modification. The successful modification of these behaviors has been based on the same modification or learning principles that have been used to change other behaviors.

References

As, A., Hilgard, E. R., & Weitzenhoffer, A. M. An attempt at experimental modification of hypnotizability through repeated individualized hypnotic experience. *Scandinavian Journal of Psychology*, 1963, 4, 81-89.

Barber, T. X. Experimental evidence for a theory of hypnotic behavior: II. Experimental controls in hypnotic age-regression. *International Journal of Clinical and Experimental Hypnosis*, 1961, 9, 181-193.

Barber, T. X., & Deeley, D. C. Experimental evidence for a theory of hypnotic behavior: I. Hypnotic color-blindness without hypnosis. *International Journal of Clinical and Experimental Hypnosis*, 1961, 9, 79-86.

Barber, T. X. Experimental controls and the phenomena of "hypnosis": A critique of hypnotic research methodology. *Journal of Nervous and Mental Disease*, 1962, 134, 493-505. (a)

Barber, T. X. Hypnotic age regression: A critical review. *Psychosomatic Medicine*, 1962, 24, 286-299. (b)

Barber, T. X. Toward a theory of hypnosis: Post-hypnotic behavior. *Achives of General Psychiatry*, 1962, 7, 321-342. (c)

Barber, T. X. Toward a theory of "hypnotic" behavior: The "hypnotically induced dream." *Journal of Nervous and Mental Disease*, 1962, 135, 206-221. (d)

Barber, T. X., & Calverley, D. S. "Hypnotic behavior" as a function of task motivation. *Journal of Psychology*, 1962, 54, 363-389.

Barber, T. X., & Hahn, K. W., Jr. Physiological and subjective responses to pain producing stimulation under hypnotically-suggested and waking-imagined "analgesia." *Journal of Abnormal and Social Psychology*, 1962, 65, 411-418.

Barber, T. X. Hypnotizability, suggestibility, and personality: V. A critical review of research findings. *Psychological Reports*, 1964, 14 (Monogr. Suppl. 3-V14), 299-320.

Barber, T. X. *Physiological indices of "hypnosis": A critical evaluation.* Harding, Massachusetts: Medfield Foundation, 1965 (mimeo). (a)

Barber, T. X. Physiological effects of "hypnotic suggestions": A critical review of recent research (1960-64). *Psychological Bulletin*, 1965, 63, 201-222. (b)

Barber, T. X. The effects of "hypnosis" and motivational suggestions on strength and endurance: A critical review of research studies. *British Journal of Social and Clinical Psychology*, 1966, 5, 42-50.

Barber, T. X., & Calverley, D. S. Toward a theory of hypnotic behavior: Experimental evaluation of Hull's postulate that hypnotic susceptibility is a habit phenomenon. *Journal of Personality*, 1966, 34, 416-433.

Beecher, H. K. *Measurement of subjective responses: Quantitative effects of drugs.* New York: Oxford Univ. Press, 1959.

Bernheim, H. M. *De la suggestion dans l'état hypnotique et dans l'état de veille.* Paris: Librairie scientifique et philosophique, 1884.

Bernheim, H. M. *Suggestive therapeutics* (translated and revised French edition by Christian A. Herter). New York: London Book Co., 1947.

Binet, A., & Fere, C. *Animal magnetism.* New York: Appleton, 1888.

Blum, G. S. Programming people to simulate machines. In S. S. Tomkins & S. Messick (Eds), *Computer simulation of personality,* New York: Wiley, 1966. Pp. 127-157.

Bowers, K. S. The effects of demands for honesty on reports of visual and auditory hallucinations. *International Journal of Clinical and Experimental Hypnosis*, 1967, 15, 31-36.

Bramwell, J. M. *Hypnotism.* New York: Julian Press, 1956. [Originally published 1903.]

Burnett, C. T. Splitting the mind. *Psychological Monograph,* 1925, **34,** No. 2.

Charcot, J. M. Essai d'une distinction nosographiqu.> des divers états compris sous le nom d'Hypnotisme. *Comptes Rendus de l'Académie des Sciences,* 1882, **44.**

Cooper, L. M., Banford, S. A., Schubot, E., & Tart, C. T. A further attempt to modify hypnotic susceptibility through repeated individualized experience. *International Journal of Clinical and Experimental Hypnosis,* 1967, **15,** 118-124.

Erickson, M. H. Deep hypnosis and its induction. In L. M. LeCron (Ed.), *Experimental hypnosis.* New York: Julian Press, 1957. [Originally published 1850.]

Esdaile, J. Mesmerism in India and its practical application in surgery and medicine (1846). *A history of experimental psychology* (2nd edition) Edwin G. Boring. New York: Appleton, 1957.

Evans, F. J. The structure of hypnosis: A factor analytic investigation. Unpublished doctoral dissertation, Univ. of Sydney, 1966.

Eysenck, H. J. *Dimensions of personality.* London: Kegan Paul, 1947.

Giles, E. A cross-validation study of the pascal technique of hypnotic induction. *International Journal of Clinical and Experimental Hypnosis,* 1962, **10,** 101-108.

Gill, M. M., & Brenman, M. *Hypnosis and related states.* New York: International Univ. Press, 1959.

Hart, E. Hypnotism and humbug. Nineteenth century. January, 1882. [As reported by Bramwell, M. J. *Hypnotism, its history, practice, and theory.* Philadelphia: Lippincott, 1930.]

Hilgard, E. R. Lawfulness within hypnotic phenomena. In G. H. Estabrooks (Ed.), *Hypnosis. Current problems.* New York: Harper, 1962, pp. 1-29.

Hilgard, J. R., & Hilgard, E. R. Developmental-interactive aspects of hypnosis: Some illustrative cases. *Genetic Psychology Monograph,* 1962, **66,** 143-178.

Hilgard, E. R. *Hypnotic susceptibility.* New York: Harcourt, 1965.

Hilgard, E. R., Cooper, L. M., Lenox, J., Morgan, A. H., & Voevodsky, J. The use of pain-state reports in the study of hypnotic analgesia to the pain of ice water. *Journal of Nervous and Mental Disease,* 1967, **144,** 506-513.

Hilgard, E. R. Pain as a puzzle for psychology and physiology. *American Psychologist,* 1969, **24,** 103-113.

Hilgard, E. R., Weitzenhoffer, A. M., Landes, J., & Moore, R. K. The distribution of susceptibility to hypnosis in a student population: A study using the Stanford Hypnotic Susceptibility Scale. *Psychological Monograph,* 1961, 75 (8, Whole No. 512).

Janet, P. *Major symptoms of hysteria.* New York: Macmillan, 1920.

Kubie, L. S., & Margolin, S. The process of hypnotism and the nature of the hypnotic state. *American Journal of Psychiatry,* 1944, **100,** 611-622.

Lindsley, O. R. Should we decelerate urges or actions?: Thou shalt not covet. Paper presented at the meeting of the American Psychological Association, Washington, D.C., August, 1969.

Loewenfeld, L. *Der Hypnotismus.* Wiesbaden: Bergman, 1901.

Ludwig, A. M., & Lyle, W. H., Jr. Tension induction and the hyperalert trance. *Journal of Abnormal and Social Psychology,* 1964, **69,** 70-76.

McGlashan, T. H., Evans, F. J., & Orne, M. T. The nature of hypnotic analgesia and placebo response to experimental pain. *Psychosomatic Medicine,* 1969, **31,** 227-246.

Marshall, G. D., & Diamond, M. J. *Increasing hypnotic susceptibility through modeling.* Stanford Univ.: Department of Psychology, 1969 (mimeo).

Orne, M. T. The nature of hypnosis: Artifact and essence. *Journal of Abnormal and Social Psychology,* 1959, **58,** 277-299.

Pascal, G. R., & Salzberg, M. C. A systematic approach to inducing hypnotic behavior. *International Journal of Clinical and Experimental Hypnosis,* 1959, 7, 161-167.

Pavlov, I. P. *Conditioned reflexes.* New York: Oxford Univ. Press, 1934.

Prince, M. Experiment to determine co-conscious (subconscious) ideation. *Journal of Abnormal and Social Psychology,* 1909, **3**, 37.

Sachs, L. B., & Anderson, W. L. Modification of hypnotic susceptibility. *International Journal of Clinical and Experimental Hypnosis,* 1967, **15**, 172-180.

Sachs, L. B. Modification of hypnotic behavior without hypnotic inductions. Unpublished study, West Virginia Univ., 1969.

Sachs, L. B. Comparison of hypnotic analgesia and hypnotic relaxation during stimulation by a continuous pain source. *Journal of Abnormal Psychology,* 1970, **76**, 206-210.

Salter, A. Three techniques of autohypnosis. *Journal of General Psychology,* 1941, **24**, 423-438.

Schmidkunz, H. Zur Statistik des Hypnotismus. *Wiener medizinische Wochenschrift,* 1944, **23**, 1022-1024.

Shor, R. E. Hypnosis and the concept of the generalized reality-orientation. *American Journal of Psychotherapy,* 1959, **13**, 582-602.

Shor, R. E., Orne, M. T., & O'Connell, D. N. Validation and cross-validation of a scale of self-reported personal experiences which predicts hypnotizability. *Journal of Psychology,* 1962, **53**, 55-75.

Shor, R. E., Orne, M. T., & O'Connell, D. N. Psychological correlates of plateau hypnotizability in a special volunteer sample. *Journal of Personality and Social Psychology,* 1966, **122**, 721-726.

Shor, R. E., & Cobb, J. C. An exploratory study of hypnotic training using the concept of plateau responsiveness as a referent. *American Journal of Clinical Hypnosis,* 1968, **10**, 178-197.

Sidis, B. *The psychology of suggestion.* New York: Appleton, 1910.

Vogt, O. Zur Kenntnis des Wesens und der psychologishen Bedeutung des Hypnotismus. *Zeitschrift für Hypnotismus,* 1894-1895, **3**, 277; 1896, **4**, 32, 122, 229.

Wiseman, R. J., & Reyher, J. A procedure utilizing dreams for deepening the hypnotic trance. *American Journal of Clinical Hypnosis,* 1962, **5**, 105-110.

A Second Look at
Systematic Desensitization

Alfred Jacobs

West Virginia University
Morgantown, West Virginia

and

Milton Wolpin

University of Southern California
Los Angeles, California

Over a decade has elapsed since the publication of *Psychotherapy by Reciprocal Inhibition* (Wolpe, 1958). Wolpe's clear specification of the theoretical basis of the systematic desensitization method of treatment and of the operations which it employed held an immediate appeal for research-minded clinical psychologists. Lazovik and Lang (1960) supplied an important contribution to the technology of research on systematic desensitization by adapting Wolpe's methods to the study of relatively common fears and avoidant behaviors. Lazovik and Lang thereby created a large pool of potential *S*s and provided standardized techniques for the study of fear in the psychological laboratory. The consequence was the generation of a large number of studies by psychologists attempting to evaluate the importance of specific components and variables to the effectiveness of systematic desensitization techniques of treatment.

Some may argue that the variables involved in the treatment of phobias, as proposed by Wolpe, are different in degree and kind from the variables involved in the treatment of common fears in otherwise normal *S*s. Empirical evidence rather than polemics should eventually settle this issue. However, the study of fears in normal *S*s has its own social legitimacy in any case, since common fears in normals by far outnumber the phobia frequency in the general population and are not less deserving of treatment.

The material to follow reviews the research that we, our students, and others have contributed which bears on the role of experienced fear and relaxation in *S*s as they have cognitively rehearsed approaches to fear-provoking stimuli. The research relates to the necessity for the rehearsals to proceed in a manner graduated with reference to the amount of fear evoked. We shall also refer to some material on imagery, and to some recent studies that have attempted to evaluate the importance of expectations of success of treatment by *S*s in desensitization treatments.

In general, we have followed what Lang (1969), in his excellent review, has referred to as the dismantling strategy in our endeavor to evaluate the variables responsible for the efficacy of the desensitization techniques.

Fear and Avoidance in Desensitization

In this section we address ourselves to two topics: first, the necessity of preventing fear responses from occurring during desensitization as in the counter-conditioning paradigm; and second, to relationships between fear and avoidance generally. A more formal analysis of the first issue is related to the fact that psychologists identify two processes, extinction and counter conditioning, which purport to cause fear responses to dissipate. Counter conditioning or response substitution demands that the fear response occur as infrequently or as weakly as possible during treatment for success. Extinction demands that the fear response be elicited as strongly as possible in order for it to dissipate itself. The counter-conditioning paradigm in systematic desensitization, as presented by Wolpe, required the substitution of a response. For example, the relaxation response, was substituted for the original anxiety response to the symbolic representation of the fearful object in order to ensure that the anxiety response, which motivates avoidance behavior, will not occur on consequent presentations of the fearful stimulus. The basis for extinction types of treatment such as the implosive method of Stampfl (Stampfl & Levis, 1967) is that repeated exposures to feared objects or perhaps to symbolic representations thereof, that the organism is prevented from avoiding in the absence of the aversive reinforcement, may lead to fewer and weaker fear and/or avoidance responses. The theories concerned with extinction and counter conditioning are excellently reviewed in Bandura's book, *Principles of Behavior Modification* (1969).

It is, of course, possible that both maximizing or minimizing fear responses is more effective than if moderate amounts of fear are elicited to the fearful event or some symbolic representation of it. In the material to follow, we shall review the evidence on this issue and present some of the material that we have gathered suggesting that it is unnecessary to prevent fear from occurring during symbolic rehearsals of responses to feared objects in order to facilitate approach responses. Furthermore, our evidence suggests that even increasing the fear experienced during rehearsals does not impair the effectiveness of treatment.

In the second part of this section, we shall review some of the material gathered by others and ourselves on the relationships between verbal reports of fear of objects and avoidance behavior, and between verbal reports of fear of academic test situations and test performance. The evidence suggests to us that the verbal and other behavioral so-called measures of "fear" have very little relationship to each other, and, therefore, that it is implausible to expect that the prevention of a fear response accounts primarily for the success of systematic desensitization.

The problem of whether it is necessary for fear to be absent during desensitization is confounded by the problem of whether it is necessary for S to be relaxed during desensitization. Primarily, we shall try to address ourselves here to the former problem. Wolpin and Raines (1966) (to be reported in more detail later), using a small number of snake phobic patients, omitted relaxation during rehearsal and presented images at, or close to the top of the hierarchy, and achieved success in inducing Ss to handle snakes after short periods of desensitization. The authors reported that significant amounts of fear were observed in Ss during this successful desensitization. Another study that had led to some suspicion about the necessity for the absence of anxiety during desensitization is that of Cautela (1966). Cautela employed a modification of Wolpe's procedures in which he asked patients to report the disappearance rather than the onset of anxiety during visualization. As a consequence, Ss were exposed to periods of anxiety lasting up to 15 sec at a time before reinstatement of relaxation was undertaken. However, improvement occurred in approximately the same general proportions reported by Wolpe.

Rachman (1966) compared a flooding condition designed to intensify fear reactions during visualization with the reciprocal inhibition group from a 1965 study (Rachman, 1965). The flooding conditions differed from the standard reciprocal inhibition procedures in that both relaxation and hierarchies were omitted and descriptions were deliberately made as terrifying as possible. Rachman presents statistically unanalyzed curves which suggest that three Ss in his reciprocal inhibition condition improved whereas the flooding group did not. However, the results can hardly be considered conclusive in view of the failure to control for experimenter and sampling biases as well as the small size of his groups.

It might be appropriate at this point to refer again to Stampfl's implosive therapy (Stampfl & Levis, 1967) in which high levels of anxiety are aroused in patients until signs of spontaneous fear reduction occur. A number of laboratory studies based on objective measures of behavioral change to feared small animals (Kirchner & Hogan, 1966; Hogan & Kirchner, 1967) or snakes (Hogan & Kirchner, 1968) suggest that the increasing of anxiety during treatment is superior to control conditions.

In view of the controversial role of anxiety in desensitization, it seemed worthwhile to us to direct some dissertations towards the study of the effect on avoidance of anxiety reported by Ss during the desensitization process. The first (Myerhoff, 1968) used a technique derived from a study by Wolpin (1966) which had strongly supported the conclusion that induction of muscular tension in human Ss increased the anxiety experience while visualizing scenes. Wolpin read scenes to be imagined by 36 nonphobic volunteer Ss when they were instructed to relax, in normal states, and instructed to tense muscles, counter balancing the order of presentations. Subjects rated the scenes as significantly more frightening when they were imagined during a state of tension than of relaxation or during tension than under natural conditions. Scenes used by Wolpin in this study were not derived from the fears of his Ss.

Myerhoff designed a study to determine whether Ss instructed to imagine scenes derived from their own reported fears would report more subjective fear when in the state of muscular tension than when in their "natural state" instructed. Myerhoff (1967) selected 11 Ss from a group of psychiatric aides in a state hospital who had indicated much or very much fear of snakes and spiders on a modified fear survey schedule. Scenes describing increasing proximity to snakes were read verbatim to Ss in the context of no instructions regarding body states or instructions to maintain a state of muscular tension. The tension condition Ss were instructed to tense up specific muscle groups which were highly visible to the experimenter during trials, following Wolpin's (1966) proceedings of having Ss clench their fists, lift their toes and heels in the air, beatle their brows, clench their teeth and squeeze eyes shut. Subjects were required to rate the amount of fear experienced immediately following each presentation, and fear was significantly greater under conditions of muscular tension than under natural conditions.

Myerhoff then recruited 75 students enrolled in introductory psychology classes who had reported fear on the fear survey schedule of rats, mice, snakes, or spiders. Two experimental groups were formed; both performed ten rehearsals in imagination per session for three sessions of standardized scenes that were presented to the Ss for visualization by E. A tension group performed the rehearsal of their scenes while maintaining a state of muscular tension and a natural group without maintaining muscular tension, but without relaxation. The groups did not differ in terms of subjective fear scores or avoidance scores before treatment. A control group was administered the same pre- and posttests as the two experimental groups. The procedure was as follows:

(1) Subjects approached a snake as closely as they were able.
(2) Subjects went to a second room and made a fear rating.
(3) Subjects again approached the snake and made a fear rating (Test B).
(4) After desensitization, Ss approached the snake to the same point they had in Test B and made a rating (Test X).
(5) Subjects approached the snake as closely as they could and rated fear (Test Y).

The study was presented to all Ss as a study of fears rather than as a study of treatments.

The tension group reported significantly more fear during desensitization than the natural group. Figure 1 shows that mean subjective fear ratings for the

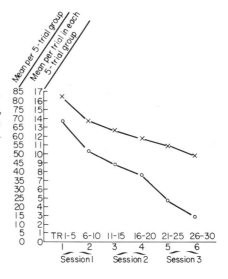

Fig. 1. Mean subjective fear ratings for six groups of five trials each group, separately for the Natural (O) and for the Tension (x) groups. [Reproduced by permission from Myerhoff (1968).]

natural group and the tension group decreased significantly in fear associated with visualization over the course of desensitization. However, the hypothesis that Ss in the tension group would become sensitized (show increases in subjective fear as treatment progresses) was not supported by an increase in subjective fear scores to the series of presentations. Both the natural and tension groups show significant decreases in fear after desensitization, but the decrease in fear is significantly greater for the tension group at the point of closest approach to the feared object before desensitization. Figures 2 and 3 present the means of subjective fear and avoidance scores at all the pre- and postcriterion tests for fear and avoidance. It can be observed that the mean subjective fear scores for the tension group tend to be lower after treatment than those for the natural or control groups. The mean fear score at Test X is almost significantly lower (between the 5 and 10% level) for the tension than the natural group. The avoidance scores for both the tension and the natural groups also decreased significantly from the precriterion Test B to the final Test Y, although the

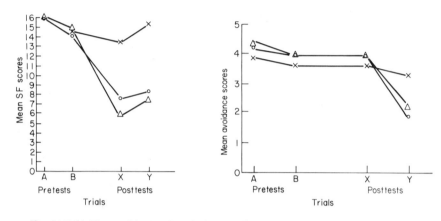

Fig. 2. (left) Mean subjective fear (SF) scores for each trial, by group [($\triangle$): Tension; (O): Natural; (x): Control]. All groups automatically equated at SF = 16, Trial A. [Reproduced by permission from Myerhoff (1968).]

Fig. 3. (right) Mean avoidance scores for each trial by group. All groups [($\triangle$): Tension; (O): Natural; (x): Control] taken to AS B = AS X for SF−X score. [Reproduced by permission from Myerhoff (1968).]

control group did not. There are no significant differences between the tension and natural groups in the avoidance score at Test Y.

The Myerhoff study provides strong support for the proposition that the presence of anxiety during desensitization does not necessarily sensitize the S so that he is more fearful or more avoidant of phobic objects after treatment as had been suggested by Wolpe (1958). The significantly greater decrease in subjective fear in the muscular tension group raised the issue of whether a suggestion effect of having worked harder during desensitization or having done something additional could account for the difference. Therefore, a second study was designed to follow this issue.

The second study (Jacobs, Edelman, & Wolpin, 1969; Edelman, 1968) used 54 snake phobic Ss assigned to three equal groups on the basis of scores on the Byrne Repression–Sensitization Scale. The Byrne R–S Scale was included to explore the relationship of response styles in fearful situations to treatment effectiveness. Three treatment conditions were used. Subjects in the low anxiety condition remained in a state of muscular relaxation during visualizations of approaching a fearful object. Subjects in the intermediate anxiety condition performed a routine motor task (finger tapping) and the *S*s in the high anxiety condition maintained a state of muscular tension during visualization as induced in Myerhoff's study. All three groups were engaged in some order of activity to provide for the possible distracting or suggestion effects of engaging in muscular activity during treatment.

The amount of subjective fear reported at the point of closest approach to the feared stimulus was determined for all *S*s and the point of closest approach recorded before and after treatment. Subjects visually rehearsed items in a standard ten-scene fear hierarchy during two sessions and reported subjective fear estimates elicited during each visualization on a ten-point scale of subjective fear. Subjects were recruited in the same manner as in the Myerhoff study except they were promised $5 to be paid at the completion of the study.

The study assumed that the three experimental conditions would be associated with different levels of fear during treatment. The second assumption was that the level of fear experienced from visualizations of fear evoking scenes would decrease with repetitious visualizations. Separate analyses of variance were conducted on fear ratings of Scenes 2, 4, 6, 8, and 10 and supported both assumptions for each of the five analyses. Moreover, each analysis suggests that the decrease in subjective fear scores over repetitions was independent of the type of treatments.

An incidental finding was that a significant interaction occurred between repetitions and defense in the analysis of variance for Scenes 2 and 4. The fear rating of sensitizers, which lies between those of repressors and intermediates, dropped lower than those of either repressors and intermediates by the fifth repetition of the scene. The same trend is observed in Scene 6, but disappears in Scenes 8 and 10. Therefore, the reduction in intensity of mild or moderate verbal responses of fear seems to occur more rapidly during cognitive rehearsals for sensitizers than for other *S*s.

The analysis of variance for avoidance scores after treatment yielded an *F* ratio of less than 1, suggesting that any differences in avoidance of the feared stimulus resulting from the type of treatment or levels of fear reported during rehearsal, were not reliable. This is in spite of the fact that all treatment groups showed substantial though not statistically significant improvement. The *F* ratio of 42.9, degrees of freedom 1,1 is associated with a probability of less than .10. The necessity of considering a therapist variable as random in the plan of statistical analysis and the consequent reduction in degrees of freedom from 36 to 1 make the achievement of statistical significance exceedingly difficult in this comparison.

The analysis of variance for subjective fear scores also failed to yield any significant differential effects due to treatments. The *F* ratio falls short of statistical significance, and thus fails to validate the hypothesis that treatments would lead to differential decreases in fear reported to the fearful stimulus on the basis of differential anxiety level during desensitization. Here again, however, there are strong indications of an overall treatment effect although the F ratio of 141.3, df 1,1 reaches only the 10% level of significance because of the loss of degrees of freedom. Two effects not directly relevant to the major hypotheses were significant. The F ratio, significant at the .05 level, suggested that Ss who

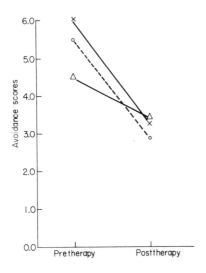

Fig. 4. Pre- and posttherapy avoidance scores for repressors ($\triangle$), sensitizers (x), and intermediates (O). [Reproduced by permission from Edelman (1968).]

scored in the middle range of the R–S Scale obtained overall avoidance scores which were higher than those of sensitizers or repressors. Second, Fig. 4 shows the slope for intermediate defense Ss and sensitizers to be steeper than that of repressors indicating significantly less improvement for repressors than for the other two groups.

It was clear at this point that instructing Ss to imagine doing what they feared could be depended on to lead to improvement even if Ss were allowed to remain anxious while imagining. However, a more severe test was designed.

Wolpin worked with Evans (1968) in a study in which 19 snake-phobic female Ss visualized scenes of approaching and picking up a snake while verbalizing what they were imagining. Evans administered a painful electric shock to the wrist of the S's preferred hand as she verbalized that she was picking up the snake. There were 10 shock-visualizations per session and a total of four sessions. Both the no-treatment control and the experimental group decreased in subjective fear on posttest with no significant difference between groups. The approach behavior of the experimental group increased more than that of the control group, the difference being significant at the .05 level.

An electric shock is usually experienced as aversive and typically has the effect of reducing the probability of the response upon which it is contingent. Results of Evans raise questions regarding the nature of mediating processes when aversive conditioning is used in therapeutic procedures. For example, is it simple straight automatic aversive conditioning that gets a transvestite to stop dressing as a woman?

The three studies by Myerhoff, Jacobs, Edelman, and Wolpin, and Evans present strong evidence for the fact that the level of anxiety during desensitization within the ranges of anxiety manipulated in the present studies bears relatively little, if any, relationship to subsequent fear and avoidance of feared objects. The Edelman study suggests, however, that the Ss, typical methods for dealing with fear and avoidance may be relevant.

Donner and Guerney (1969), who had Ss press a button when they were anxious during visualization of test situations, report that a significant positive relationship existed between increases in grade point averages and number of button presses during visualization. Subjects who were in the top half of the button-pressing distribution of scores (most anxious and least relaxed during cognitive rehearsals) showed a significantly greater grade point change than those in the lower half. The results are again contrary to the notion that anxiety present during visualization is detrimental to treatment, and suggest that it may, indeed, facilitate treatment.

The second general issue to which this section is addressed is that of the relationships between fear and avoidance scores. The low correlations in the Edelman study between subjective fear ratings during desensitization and avoidance scores raised the issue of the extent of the relationships between verbal reports of fear and measures of avoidance behavior. We examined the correlations between subjective fear scores and avoidance scores and found, for example, that the correlation between subjective fear scores before treatment and avoidance scores at that point was .01. However, the correlation between fear after treatment and approach to the phobic object was significant at the .01 level, $r = .52$. Higher correlations are found between changes in subjective fear scores and changes in avoidance scores, although not impressively higher. However, the size of such correlations would seem to be partially at least a consequence of the restrictive range of values in the scales used to measure subjective fear and avoidance.

In examining the sensitizer population of the Edelman study particularly, it seemed clear that fear and avoidance behaviors were largely independent of one another. That is to say, avoidance behavior does not necessarily seem to be a consequence of fear among sensitizers. Such a conclusion is in accordance with the clinical descriptions of sensitizers as individuals who confront rather than avoid the source of anxiety. The repressors, on the other hand, are distinguished somewhat from other Ss by virtue of positive and significant correlations;

$r = .72$ between posttherapy fear and posttherapy avoidance behavior measures. High positive correlations were also observed between subjective fear reported during treatment and posttherapy avoidance behavior and fear in the repressors. The repressors are the only group to support Wolpe's speculation that high fear during visualization may detract from the effectiveness of treatment. We may speculate that in repressors fear and avoidance behavior are more intimately related, that is, repressors characteristically react to fear by avoiding fearful stimuli as Byrne (1964) has suggested. Paradoxically, however, the repressors in the Edelman experiment not only reported more fear of the phobic object before treatment than the other two groups, but also approached closest to it of any of the other groups before treatment.

An additional source of pertinent data here is Dixon (1966). Dixon compared the effects of 18 sessions of group desensitization designed to reduce examination fears, plus two training sessions in relaxation, to 20 sessions of group counseling. She found significant improvements in both groups after treatment in fear survey schedule scores and in a performance on a symbol-substitution perceptual-motor task. She also observed increments in grade point average after treatment of about the same magnitude in both groups, significant in the case of the counseling group and not quite as significant in the case of the systematic desensitization group. However, she found no significant superiority for either treatment over the other on any measure. No significant changes were observed on a test anxiety questionnaire.

Corroboration of Dixon's results has occurred recently in a study by Crighton and Jehu (1969) who found no differences in effectiveness of systematic desensitization and psychotherapy in treatment of examination anxiety.

Dixon found practically no significant relationships between her measures of fear, nor between her measures of fear and performance before treatment. However, in the systematic desensitization group, after desensitization, the correlation of the test anxiety questionnaire with grade point average and with performance on the perceptual motor task, increased to almost significant levels (although the correlations in the .40 area do not account for an impressive part of the variance), but not so in the counseling group. The results are similar to those observed in the Edelman study where subjective fear scores were not related to snake avoidance before systematic desensitization-like treatment, but significantly so afterwards.

Such results lead us to suggest that systematic desensitization may function in a different way than ordinarily proposed. Systematic desensitization training may improve the ability of the Ss to discriminate subjective states of fear, improving the reliability of their ratings so that the underlying relationship between fear and avoidance may manifest itself. It may suggest to Ss that their performance should be lowered if they are aware of a high level of anxiety or that they should report more fear if they are aware of a poor performance.

Desensitization training may merely convince Ss that fear and avoidance are highly associated whereas in fact they are not.

Dixon found no significant relationships in any of the groups between decreases in test anxiety scores and changes in performance tests. No significant relationships between initial measures of anxiety and changes in performance were observed in the systematic desensitization group. Those Ss in the counseling group who had the highest Mood Adjective Checklist scores (MAACL) before treatment (the highest situational anxiety) increased most in grade point. For the combined groups, the higher the test anxiety scores before treatment, the greater the improvement in the symbol performance task; the higher the MAACL before treatment, the greater the increase in grade point. The relationship between high initial anxiety and increases in academic performance bears some similarity to results in the Donner and Guerney study (1969) and the Lieberman study (1969) to be reported.

Lang (1968) also emphasizes the fact that different measures of fear behavior, even though taken in the same session from the same S, did not yield reponses of the same relative strength. Lang points out that correlations among avoidance, self-ratings of fear, observer ratings, and Ss' ratings of general fear level are not impressively highly correlated. Lang asserts that the failure of autonomic activity to relate in any direct way to verbal or overt motor measures of emotion or change in psychotherapy has already been abundantly documented. He also concludes that there are gross individual differences in the response of Ss to desensitization. He has observed that some show primary gains in overt behavior, and others change little in approach but report less fear or appear more relaxed.

As a consequence, Lang is led to the strategy that one should apply specific techniques to the specific behaviors or systems that one wishes to change. In the treatment of verbal or cognitive behavior, Lang suggests that the S may be instructed to reinforce himself for his successes, or can be encouraged to place cognitions in opposition to distressing thoughts or actions. In the treatment of overt motor behavior, a program of reinforcement of overt motor responses, or role-playing may be useful techniques. Lang suggests that the autonomic responses may be themselves directly amenable to training. He describes briefly his own work demonstrating the ability of human Ss to stabilize or reduce cardiac rate when they are provided with appropriate feedback and instructions. We may add that the rapidly expanding bio-feedback literature (Jacobs & Felton, 1969), for example, provides support for Lang's contention that many previously presumed involuntary responses are trainable.

An additional source of evidence related to verbal and behavioral measures of fear is a recent article by Fazio (1969). Fazio's study is of particular interest because he obtained normative data on avoidance responses of an unselected group of college students to a large insect. He did this rather than sampling in a very restrictive range of Ss who verbalize high avoidance and fear as in the results reported by Lang and Edelman. In the latter studies one might anticipate low correlations between verbalizations of fear and approach behavior due to restrictions of range in either or both dimensions. However, the highest correlations found by Fazio between questionnaire fear items or item composites and rated overt test behavior was less than .50 and, therefore, accounted at best for only 25% of the behavioral variance. Fazio suggests that the magnitude of the correlation may be increased if the stimuli in the verbal situation were more similar to those in the overt response situation. For example, if Ss were asked how afraid they would be if they were asked to handle the insect, or in the case of the snake phobias, if they were asked to pick up a harmless snake for 30 sec rather than to rate their fear of the phobic object on a scale of 0–5.

A final study which should be included in this section is that of Lieberman (1969) since hers was an attempt to study desensitization techniques and their effectiveness with regard to so-called normal fears. That is, rather than selecting Ss complaining of excessive test anxiety, Lieberman desensitized a portion of an introductory psychology class. The Ss were randomly assigned to a desensitization group, placebo group, or control group. Twenty-six Ss were in each group. Subjects were given a test anxiety questionnaire before a course examination was scheduled and four presentations of an approach–avoidance verbal scale constructed by the author to measure avoidance and approach tendencies toward the examination in the time interval between the scheduling of the course exam and its occurrence. For the desensitization group between the first and second administration of the approach–avoidance verbal scale, a tape recording was presented consisting of muscle relaxation instructions followed by six short scenes related to taking an exam which were visualized according to the instructions on the tape. Two sessions of group desensitization were performed. A placebo group had a tape recording consisting of muscle relaxation training followed by a short discussion on the history of modern education the same number of times.

Figure 5 shows the response strength to the avoidance statements with successively closer trials to the course exam. Significant increases in the amount of avoidance among trials occurred, but not of approach or neutral statements.

It was predicted that the tendency to avoid would increase at a lower rate with the desensitization group than in the placebo or the control groups because it was expected that the desensitization would effectively lower the drive upon which the avoidance tendency is based. The trend of differences among the three group-means is not statistically significant. In fact, the decrease in avoidance tendency reports in the placebo group after treatment is slightly greater than that of the desensitization group.

It was also predicted that the Ss in the desensitization group would perform more adequately on the course examination compared to the previous one. A statistical comparison of the relative performance of the three groups confirmed the expectations. Although no significant decreases in fear were observed in the desensitization group, significant increases in grade point occurred. So-called normal or rational fear, i.e., fear supported by social consensus, may be different from phobic, or other types of so-called fear-motivated behavior.

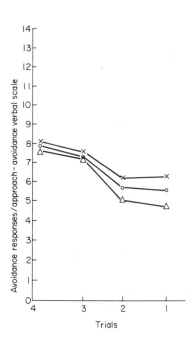

Fig. 5. Response strength to avoidance statements with successively closer trials to the course exam, in the desensitization group (O), the placebo group (x), and the control group (△). [Reproduced by permission from Lieberman (1969).]

In any case, it may be wise to question the assertion of students, who volunteer as *S*s in studies designed to reduce test anxiety, that it is primarily the consequences of their feelings of fear that impair performance on examinations in the absence of strong evidence that such is indeed the case. Conversely, one may question in such experiments whether it is the reduction in fear about tests which leads to improvement in grades or test performance. It is equally plausible that test scores and grade-point averages are more likely to change in volunteers who commit themselves to a type of "new year's resolution" by selecting to undergo various treatments and are strongly enough motivated to complete them. The evidence reviewed here that it may be the high anxiety *S* who improves the most suggests to us that it may be the student who is "most worried about grades" whom we are identifying. Increases in fear about *not* studying and/or changes in study habits may accompany such a commitment to a treatment procedure. A weekly treatment session may also serve as a "string around the finger" reminder to study. We have little if any evidence on such matters.

We would like to expand this criticism to include some other conclusions about the studies on desensitization. For example, for the most part, such studies have paid little attention to the role of the approach responses which Ss are practicing during visualizations. It may be worthwhile to compare the effectiveness of visualizing approaching phobic objects as contrasted with just visualizing the phobic object. We should add that it is clear that the importance of such approach response practice is recognized by practitioners of assertion training (Lazarus, 1968). However, the practice of approach habits on a cognitive level, and any affective attitude change such as from dangerous to harmless, may be relevant to the success of treatment.

Wolpin, Frankel, Zinsmeyer, and Paris (1970) are in the process of completing a study which involves three conditions for the treatment of snake phobic Ss. They are concerned with answering two different types of questions: (a) a theoretical one, i.e., is it necessary to practice approach behavior (in the imagination) in order to have an increase in approach behavior (as well as a decrease in subjective fear)?; and (b) does a given variation of an implosion procedure work?

With regard to the theoretical question, in the procedures of both Wolpe and Stampfl, one imagines approach behavior. What would happen if instead, one practiced: (a) either not getting as close, in imagination as one did in a pretest or; (b) (in imagination) not getting as close and then engaging in explicit escape behavior? It may be sufficient to simply be exposed to the anxiety-arousing stimulus in such a way that anxiety is aroused (allowing for extinction to occur) while not approaching the feared stimulus. In this way, we would separate out the effects of practicing approach behavior from the effects of an extinction process.

In the Wolpin *et al.* study, each Ss is asked, prior to visualizing each approach to the snake, to imagine an anxiety-arousing situation, specific to him and based on material derived from an interview and responses to a fear survey both obtained before treatment. Therefore, we ensure that anxiety occurs during all visualizations. The scenes vary from trial to trial. Immediately after the scene is developed, S is instructed to visualize approaching the snake. In condition A, he visualizes proceeding to a point 3 ft further away than he had been in the pretest, staying there for 15 sec, and then terminating the scene. In condition B, S also begins by visualizing an anxiety-provoking scene, and imagines himself proceeding, once again, to a point 3 ft further away than he had been in the pretest. However, after remaining at that point for 15 sec, S then visualizes turning around and leaving the room.

We are still collecting data. However, the approach scores show that thus far, six of eight Ss in condition A have shown improvement and ten of 12 in condition *B*. In comparison, seven out of 15 no-treatment controls have shown increased approach behavior.

In the third treatment condition, developed by Frankel, *S*s are asked to imagine themselves in a fearful situation, an encounter with a feared snake for *S*s in the study being reported. They are asked to describe their fantasy and stay with it, continually reporting what they experience. The *S* is not allowed to discontinue his fantasy until he reports a successful conclusion to this encounter. Rather than *E* developing the fantasy, as in Stampfl's procedure, it is composed by *S* and thus the imagery comes from *S*. Only three of nine *S*s have shown improvements in approach score so far. The low rate of success is puzzling as Frankel has been quite successful with it clinically, with, among other conditions, fear of earthquakes, sexuality, and enclosed places (Frankel, 1970).

There has been relatively little attention to other plausible explanations that may contribute to, if not account for, the success of the desensitization technique. One may refer to such variables as the demand characteristics of situations, or the necessity to reduce dissonance. After *S* has spent a considerable investment in time in an elaborate and somewhat uncomfortable or fearful procedure, for which he initially volunteered and in which he has sometimes been led by instructions to expect a symptom reduction, and where he has been encouraged by experiencing less fear about his visualizations of a feared object, how could he not move closer to or touch the snake? The role of expectations, beliefs, and attitudes would appear to be very relevant in such processes as the above description of desensitization.

The Edelman (1968) study for example, suggests that typical habits or styles for dealing with fear and avoidance, for example, confronting versus avoiding, may account for part of the variance of treatment effects. In a more general sense, we have words like 'courage' which we apply to nonavoidance responses made by people in situations where the social concensus might be that intense levels of fear are elicited and most people would be expected to avoid. Therefore, one might suspect that a model based solely on fear and avoidance is a unimotive-habit analysis of behavior whereas a multimotive-habit description of avoidance and approach responses may be a more fruitful approach.

Specifically, the studies (Myerhoff, 1968; Edelman, 1969; Evans, 1968) reported, strongly suggest that fear induced during desensitization does not make *S*s more fearful or avoidant of feared objects, and, in fact, such *S*s actually become less fearful and approach more closely after visualization. Furthermore, there is the suggestion that the level of fear reported during visualization, assuming that it decreases as visualizations progress, is irrelevant to fear and avoidance of the phobic object.

Finally, our data and the data of others show little, if any, relationship between reports of fear and avoidance behavior toward feared objects or events before desensitization. We have speculated about the meaning of the evidence which exists for the significant relationships after desensitization. The low relationships between verbal reports of fear, motor behavior, and physiological measures may represent poor measuring devices. These might include, for example, the discrepancies between the verbal scales which ask for one overall statement about fear of snakes and the motor scale which requires perhaps independent responses such as touching and picking up. On the other hand, such minimum relationships may represent the fact that the global concept of fear is not a very useful one. Mischel (1968) has raised the issue of whether personality descriptions are useful since prediction of behavior seems to be so situation or stimulus specific. Similarly, broad concepts like fear-motivated avoidance may not be practical. One may not only have to identify the stimulus setting, but also designate which fear or avoidance response we are concerned with as well. In any case, the relationships between the verbal reports of fear and avoidance behaviors are so low that we are very skeptical that desensitization directly decreases avoidance by reducing fear, since the variance that the two behaviors share in common is so meagre.

Hierarchies and Relaxation

It is quite commonly suggested that it is important not to proceed too rapidly through a hierarchy because one may create excess anxiety and thus sensitize rather than desensitize the patient. Wolpe, for example, suggests completing two or three steps per session (Wolpe, 1958).

Concerned with this question, Wolpin and Pearsall (1965) worked with a snake-phobic in-patient woman, diagnosed as neurotic. During the first seven sessions, the therapist became well acquainted with the patient, trained her in muscle relaxation, and developed a 20-step hierarchy. Desensitization with the patient instructed to relax began in the next session. After proceeding through ten steps of the hierarchy, the therapist discerned that something was remiss. Inquiry revealed that a supposedly relaxing background scene was not, in fact, relaxing. The therapist changed the scene, started from the first step again, and by the time the session was over (it lasted 75 min), the patient was able to proceed through the entire hierarchy. The patient proceeded to the office shortly thereafter and with some manifest enthusiasm picked up and fondled what had previously been a very feared snake. Behavior on follow-up, 23 days later, was almost identical.

Wolpin and Raines (1966) then explored the need for either relaxation or a hierarchy. Two *S*s each were assigned to: (a) exposure to all hierarchy items, in ascending order of fear evoking aspects with no instructions regarding muscles; (b) to the same level of hierarchy with muscles tensed; and (c) exposure to only the "top of the hierarchy" items (in long scenes, often several minutes in length and sometimes 10 min or more) with no relaxation. The snake phobic *S*s showed marked improvement, all of them picking up the snake after treatment and five of six doing so again on follow-up approximately a month later. Criticisms of this brief pilot study might include: (a) therapist and tester were the same person; (b) there was modeling during the pre- and posttests; and (c) the procedures were anything but well controlled, with something on the order of a therapy session preceding each visualization period. The results nonetheless did raise the distinct possibility that neither relaxation nor the hierarchy are crucial.

In the Myerhoff (1967) study referred to earlier, *E* instructed each *S* to visualize a very curtailed hierarchy consisting of a seven-item scene with repetitions of each scene per session. The rapidity with which the top of the hierarchy was reached is illustrated by items one and two in the scene that follows: 1. Picture yourself going over to the cage with the top open. You can clearly see the spider (snake, rat) moving around inside the cage. Do you see that clearly? 2. You reach inside the cage, put both hands around the spider, hold him, lift him out. He does not bite. Subjects showed a significant increase in approach behavior with no difference between a group given no relaxation instructions and one instructed to tense muscles during visualizations, although an extended hierarchy was not employed in either case.

Jaffe (1968), in a study on expectations to be reported in more detail later, repeated Myerhoff's operations, using the same curtailed hierarchy and no muscle relaxation instructions and found decreases in fear and avoidance for his *S*s. Krapfl and Nawas (1970) have also contributed a relevant study, showing that taped random presentation of hierarchy items and a taped order, beginning with the strongest fear evoking items and proceeding to the least, were not significantly less efficacious than socially presented or taped presentations using the classical graduated hierarchy.

It seems clear that the presentation of hierarchy of graduated or fear stimuli is not necessary to the success of desensitization.

Relaxation

In a formal study, Lang and Lazovik (1963) were able to demonstrate improvement in snake-phobic *S*s assigned to standard desensitization procedures, while training in hypnosis and relaxation failed to modify the phobic behavior.

Lang, Lazovik, and Reynolds (1965), in a study to be discussed in more detail later, included an additional group to check for placebo effects. Subjects in this group, after training in relaxation and hierarchy construction, were given the rationale that a better understanding of oneself and learning to relax deeply would help overcome fears, again with snake-phobic Ss. Once again the standard desensitization groups came out best showing significantly greater fear reduction than controls. Lang *et al.* conclude that hypnosis training in muscle relaxation, hierarchy building, and their continued use in a therapeutic context do not in themselves produce change in fear behavior. However, there are a number of criticisms which we will make later which leave this conclusion open to question.

Rachman (1965) investigated the necessity of utilizing relaxation when using a hierarchy, and in addition the value of relaxation alone. Spider phobics, three per group, were assigned to the following conditions: exposure to hierarchically arranged stimuli plus relaxation; exposure to hierarchically arranged stimuli without relaxation; relaxation alone and no treatment controls. Only those Ss in the condition with exposure to stimuli plus relaxation showed marked reductions in fear, as measured by self report and an avoidance test. The small number of Ss, as well as indications that the therapist served as a tester, indicate the need for caution regarding these results.

Lomont and Edwards (1967) pursue the question of the necessity of reciprocally inhibiting anxiety through the use of muscular relaxation, as compared to straight extinction procedures, in modifying the anxiety and avoidance reactions of snake-phobic Ss. The Lomont and Edwards study included a reciprocal inhibition group which relaxed immediately following each visualization and a muscular tension group which tensed after each presentation. Evidence that we have reported suggests that muscular tension during visualization is associated with verbal reports of increased fear. The Lomont and Edwards procedure is in contrast to the usual reciprocal inhibition procedure in which relaxation is initiated prior to and maintained throughout visualization. Both groups in the Lomont and Edwards study were instructed to remain tensed during actual visualization. As they report "the mean change for each of the two treatment groups on each of the five variables was tested by a *t* test and none was found to be significant." However, this notwithstanding, with "insignificant treatment effects," they conclude that "the evidence of this experiment that relaxation is important in systematic desensitization ... favors a learning concept, such as reciprocal inhibition, as the explanation of desensitization."

Davison (1968) investigated the necessity of developing responses incompatible with anxiety when engaging in desensitization procedures using muscle relaxation as the incompatible response. He developed four conditions: (a) relaxation paired with graded aversive stimuli; (b) relaxation paired with irrelevant stimuli; (c) exposure to graded aversive stimuli without relaxation; and (d) no treatment. The greatest improvement in approach behavior at posttest, was for the group where relaxation was paired with graded aversive stimuli, which contained the only Ss achieving significant reductions in avoidance behavior. The other two treatment groups did not differ significantly from each other or from the no-treatment controls.

However, indications show there was only one therapist, raising the possibility of biasing effects. In addition, there is no demonstrated evidence that the pseudodesensitization group 'believed' in their treatment, i.e., visualizing things from childhood. Especially this becomes a consideration when it is specified that some of the items (to be visualized) were neutral in content; it is more likely that the prevalent notion is that you have to recall trauma to feel better or improve, etc. If so, this would mitigate against Ss belief in the procedure. In addition, when Ss in the pseudodesensitization condition signaled anxiety, they were told to maintain the image as it is "important for the experimental design." This procedure would hardly be likely to develop faith in the procedure or to increase expectations of benefits. Subjects were not interviewed to assess the credibility of the pseudotherapy condition. It would be intriguing, in the light of the rapidly growing body of literature on the effects of placebo and especially expectancy that we will report later, to discover a credible pseudotherapy which is able to generate no improvement, as Davison reports.

A study by Cooke (1968) investigating the need for relaxation as an anxiety inhibitor, appears to lack the controls necessary for drawing any conclusions. The number of scene presentations per condition are not specified. Cooke assumed that "it is not necessary to use change scores from pretest to posttest," presumably pretest means and variances would be equal. Cooke reports, "When S reported anxiety, or T observed anxiety, relaxation instructions were given for a period of at least one minute." He does not report whether visualization was discontinued at this time.

Folkins, Lawson, Opton, Jr., and Lazarus (1968), in a very interesting study, compared four groups: an analog of therapeutic desensitization; relaxation; cognitive rehearsal; and no-training control. The stress or anxiety producing situation was a film of an industrial accident. Results suggest that repeated exposure, without relaxation, to an anxiety-arousing stimulus, is more effective than with relaxation, quite different from what would be predicted from a reciprocal inhibition model.

There are, nonetheless, aspects of the study that lead to some concerns. They obtained positive results on only one of three self-report measures and only two of four measures of autonomic reactivity, failing to get the expected differences in heart rate and in one of three measures of skin conductance, the failure being during the most stressful part of the film. Thus, it would appear that replication is in order; nonetheless their results are intriguing.

The studies that we have reported do not provide support for the proposition that graded presentations of stimuli or relaxation are necessary to the success of desensitization, nor even provide an impressive facilitative function.

Imagery

So far as is known, as yet, very little has been reported of studies regarding the role of imagery in fear-reducing procedures. We have some unanalyzed data at present from the Edelman study (1968). Maybe it is a bit difficult for good, solid behaviorists to admit to the existence of such a variable.

Miller (1950) reports that emotional (GSR) responses to thoughts are similar to the responses made to verbal statements representing the thought, utilizing aversive stimulation. Barber and Hahan (1964) report findings consistent with Miller's. Subjects were exposed directly to a stressful experience, i.e., painful, cold, and also imagined it. Responses to the imagined experience, as measured by self reports and various indications of autonomic activity, were similar to those produced by the actual stressful experience. Grossberg and Wilson (1968), found that neutral images generate less autonomic arousal than do fearful ones, as one might expect, but also discovered that reading descriptions to Ss of fear-provoking situations did not lead to as much arousal as did instructions to imagine these same scenes as they were being described by Weitzman's (1967) interviews with patients, regarding the nature of the imagery occurring during desensitization sessions, revealed the occurrence of flows of visual imagery. Visualization of the initiating scene is soon transformed, and, at the time of termination of imagining by the therapist, the images of the patient are quite removed in their content from the initiating stimulus.

Weinberg and Zaslove (1963) interviewed three Ss undergoing systematic desensitization; their Ss all reported "diluting" fearful images from time to time by changing the context to a more secure setting. All Ss reported variations in the clarity and intensity of images.

There is clearly a great deal to explore with regard to the role of imagery in desensitization. How does one ensure that S visualizes what E requests? How are images enhanced for those who are currently capable of producing nothing but weak ones? What is the relationship between images and imageless thoughts? Are they identical with regard to their utility in the approaches being considered? How long do suggested images persist and is duration related to improvement?

One role that might be played by imagery, in desensitization procedures, is suggested by data from a study by Wolpin (1966) which began with an attempt to study the vividness of imagery under relaxed and tensed conditions. Wolpin found that Ss who were relaxed reported visualizing such scenes as an ocean with soft, gentle, low waves, whereas Ss whose muscles were tensed reported larger waves and a more stormy body of water.

In the Wolpin study, normal Ss were asked to imagine eight different scenes, with muscle states varying from usual to relaxed, to tensed, all Ss appearing in all conditions and order-effects were controlled.

A scale was developed to measure responses of Ss using such characteristics of images spontaneously reported by a number of pilot Ss, as activity, vividness, friendliness, frighteningness, etc.

There are only two reliable differences between the relaxed and usual conditions, i.e., on the "relaxed" and "rapid" items. By contrast, under relaxed, as compared to tensed conditions, scenes are reported as more relaxed, less frightening, safer, less weird, sounds are softer, people are friendlier and the entire situation in general appears more attractive.

If these results could be replicated, they would suggest that Wolpe's procedures, in addition to changing the response Ss make to an anxiety evoking stimulus, may also change the perception of the Ss. If one is asked to imagine a frightening situation while deeply relaxed, one may imagine it in a way that he does not ordinarily perceive in his "usual" state, given that he is highly anxious in that situation. It may be that aspect of the state of relaxation or tension, existing essentially on a cognitive level, that is crucial and that muscle activity is irrelevant. This has already been suggested by Davison (1968) and Folkins *et al.* (1968).

Donaldson (1969) compared implosive therapy with snake-phobic Ss to positive imagery therapy, an adaptation of Leuner's initiated symbol projection (1966). In this latter procedure, Ss imagine approach behavior (no hierarchy, no relaxation) while E tries to keep anxiety to a minimum. This is done by having the S: (a) Confront the creature and stare it down; (b) feed it until it is very full; and (c) become friendly with it. In addition, Ss in imagination make use of anything from physical barriers to help from others necessary to retain the feeling of complete safety.

Both experimental groups showed significant increases in approach behavior with no significant difference between them, and no improvement for a nontreated control group.

Finally, an abstract of a dissertation by Perloff recently received (Perloff, 1970), compared four groups: Desensitization group in which aversive stimuli were paired with muscular relaxation; in a second group the aversive items were paired with positive imagery alone; in a third group neutral imagery was paired with aversive items; and a notreatment control group. Perloff reports that the desensitization utilizing positive and neutral imagery did not differ from each other, but both produced significantly greater increases in approach behavior and more positive attitudes towards snakes than either desensitization with relaxation or the control condition. Perloff reports that the gains for the imagery groups were more general than for the desensitization groups.

Expectancy

We believe the evidence suggests that neither relaxation, a graduated hierarchy, nor the absence of anxiety during cognitive rehearsals are essential to the therapeutic effect of the systematic desensitization process. A number of other authors have begun to doubt that the counter-conditioning process is the basic ingredient responsible for the success of the systematic desensitization techniques. The survey of the literature to follow has convinced us that there is reasonable basis for the belief that the cognitions of *S*s have a powerful influence on the effectiveness of systematic desensitization.

The work of Rosenthal (1964), Goldstein (1962), and others, showing that the expectancies of therapists, experimenters, and patients are important agents in the changing of behavior, have stimulated a number of experimenters to study systematically the role of expectancy in systematic desensitization technique. A number of strategies suggest themselves as approaches to the problem some of which have already been explored. One could manipulate the expectations of success by instructions which state that systematic desensitization is a proven, effective treatment method or a promising experimental approach, or as a means of study to find out if it has any effectiveness or that it probably does not work. Credibility of such instructions or sets may be increased by real or bogus feedback of progress, which may also increase the credibility of earlier and later statements made directly or implied by the therapist or the experimenter, that treatment will be effective or that the *S*s will be better able to perform the target or problem behavior.

A number of studies have pursued this first strategy. In the first of these, Leitenberg, Agras, Barlow, and Oliveau (1969), told female *S*s that desensitization was a therapy that had been found effective in treating such fears as those of snakes and *S*s were given verbal praise for successful completion of hierarchy items. A second condition was disguised as an experiment on physiological responses to feared objects. Subjects were informed that physiological responses would be recorded while they visualized fearful objects. The *S*s were instructed that they would be taught to relax during sessions in order that extraneous factors might not affect the recording of physiological responses. The third group was a no-treatment waiting control group.

Avoidance scores at the end of treatment revealed that the systematic desensitization group with therapeutic instructions and positive reinforcement decreased significantly more in avoidance scores than either of the control groups. The group which received neither therapeutic instructions nor selective reinforcement did not differ significantly in avoidance after treatment from that of the waiting control. However, there was a significant within-group increase in approach to the snake from pre- to posttest in the disguised desensitization group, whereas none was noted in the control group. The increase in approach behavior for the graduated hierarchy-relaxation-therapeutic instructions-positive reinforcement group was more than twice as great as that for just the hierarchy relaxation with bogus instructions.

The authors conclude that therapeutic instructions and selective positive reinforcement can enhance beneficial effect of the systematic desensitization therapy. However, since each of the experimental groups was exposed to the snake on two occasions during treatment, it is possible that the decrease in the avoidance scores of the desensitization group not given therapeutic instructions may be attributable to exposure to the phobic object rather than to systematic desensitization per se. Exposure to the phobic object in itself may decrease fear and avoidance. Such results were found by Myerhoff (1968) where significant numbers of Ss decreased subjective fear scores on the second of two precriterion tests and a systematic decrease in avoidance scores was also noted in the absence of any therapeutic interventions during the first session. A second shortcoming of the Leitenberg study is the absence of any data on the credibility of the bogus instructions that only physiological responses were being studied.

A second study by the same authors (Oliveau, Agras, Leitenberg, Moore, & Wright, 1969) was similar in method to the first study. In addition, half of each group was reinforced for progress through the hierarchy so that four subgroups were produced. An analysis of changes in avoidance scores showed that the therapeutic instructions were significantly more effective than the study of physiological responses to pain instructions. However, significant decreases in snake avoidance scores occurred for all groups. The mean change in avoidance scores for the group with therapeutic instructions and positive reinforcement was again more than twice as great as that for the group given the study of physiological responses instructions and no reinforcement. The authors conclude that the significant changes occurring in this last group referred to support the hypothesis that the procedure of systematic desensitization alone produced a therapeutic effect. Here too, as in the previous study, four exposures to the feared object, that is, the snake *in vivo,* plus a failure to assess credibility of the therapeutic nontherapeutic instructions, weaken this conclusion. Both studies show that therapeutic instructions play a very powerful role in the success of the desensitization technique.

Oliveau (1969) managed to get 78% of the Ss of the previous study to follow-up sessions 10 months later. The mean avoidance scores on this follow-up session were very similar to those that had occurred on the posttest. An interview revealed that those Ss who did not believe the experiment was designed to alleviate their fears showed significantly poorer approach scores. However, the author pointed out that behavioral improvement occurred even for the Ss who stated that the procedure should not have changed their fear. Most of the Ss in the follow-ups said their feelings about snakes had been changed by the experiment, and approximately half of the S attributed the change in their behavior either entirely or in part to their experience with the snake itself rather than to the desensitization process. The author points out that the reliability of verbal reports about attitudes, 10 months after the conduct of the experiment, is somewhat open to question. It would be very worthwhile to assess the credibility of the therapeutic and nontherapeutic instructions sets and their relationship to changes in avoidance scores immediately after the conclusion of such a study.

A second strategy involves the comparison of systematic desensitization to other elaborate and credible complex sets of operations which are introduced as treatment techniques, but have no other particular purpose but the manipulation of the Ss' credibility and belief systems regarding the success of treatment. The strategy has been pursued by Marcia, Rubin, and Efran (1969) who have attempted to demonstrate that such complex pseudotherapies achieve successes similar to those of systematic desensitization. In the most recent and better designed study, the authors instructed Ss in a pseudotherapy condition called a T-scope group, that treatment would be based on well-established psychological principles such as the irrational and unconscious natures of phobias and the suppressibility of responses by mild aversive stimulation. Subjects were told that phobic stimuli would be presented subliminally to evoke phobic responses which would then be shocked.

One hundred pseudopresentations of the stimuli and 16 random shocks were administered to Ss over a period of eight sessions. A galvanic skin response (GSR) technician showed the Ss a printout of improvement in physiological responses after each session. Low expectancy-of-success groups were told that a crucial element was lacking and that, therefore, improvement would not be expected. Similar instructions in order to create high and low success expectancy groups for systematic desensitization were reported by the authors to be unsuccessful because the Ss forgot or ignored the information and the Es were unable to reinforce the expectancy because they were kept blind. This suggests that the Es in the T-scope therapy were not blind or had cues such as the printout presentation, and that the differences between high and low expectancy T-scope groups may be contaminated by E's bias. Marcia *et al.* also report that initial avoidance tests were dissimilar, necessitating dropping of Ss in data analysis, and resulting in marked differences in numbers of male and female Ss in different groups. Other evidence exists (Fazio, 1969) which suggests that male and female Ss are differential in fear reporting as well as perhaps in their response to the demand characteristics of situations. Therefore, Marcia *et al.* have introduced another source of potential bias in their results. High- and low-level expectancy desensitization groups were combined, for reasons that are not clear, although the authors explain that the comparisons were not biased because the low expectancy desensitization group improved slightly more than the high; a finding difficult to explain in terms of expectancy theory.

The results revealed that improvement scores did not differentiate between the desensitization and the high expectancy T-scope group, but that each group improved significantly more than the low expectancy T-scope group or the waiting controls. There was some slight superiority of improvement for the desensitization group over all the others. It is of interest that although a posttreatment interview was held, the authors did not report whether they questioned Ss to ascertain the effectiveness of their attempt to create high or low expectancies of success.

Jaffe (1968), in a recent study addressed to the expectation issue, using the same procedure as did Myerhoff, worked with Ss' fear of snakes. Subjects received no instructions regarding their muscles, i.e. no relaxation, no tension. One group of Ss was informed that it would undergo a satisfactory treatment for fear of snakes. A second group of Ss was given the same treatment, and was informed that it were in a "dummy" (notreatment) control and would be offered treatment at the end of the experiment.

A third group (placebo condition) was shown high speed tachistiscopic projections of travel scenes and simple arithmetic problems (paralleling the work of Marcia, Rubin, and Efran (1969). Subjects were told that they were seeing "subliminal" fear stimuli and that the purpose of working the arithmetic problems was to "reciprocally inhibit" the fear responses brought about by the fear stimuli which operated unconsciously. A fourth group served as a no-treatment control.

The treatment group with positive expectations achieved the most improvement, both behaviorally and for self reports and improved significantly more than the "dummy" group on all measures, while improving significantly more than the placebo group on the approach test and one of the subjective fear measures. The placebo group equaled the "dummy" treatment group on all measures and exceeded it on one subjective report scale. The notreatment control showed a significant decrease in avoidance behavior (least of all groups) but no change on the subjective ratings. Jaffee's results again support the importance of expectations of success from treatment.

The point of departure for Valins and Ray (1967) is that during the process of systematic desensitization Ss are instructed to instruct themselves to relax while in the presence of stimuli that are ordinarily frightening. If Ss are convinced that they are able to relax, they may also believe that the feared stimulus no longer has the same effect on them. Therefore, the cognitive change may lead to behavioral change. The authors report two experiments where Ss were given bogus reports that their heart rate was not changed to the presentation of the snake or the snake slide, but that heart rate accelerated when slides showing the word SHOCK occurred, at which time a mild electric shock was actually delivered to them. The control Ss were told that they were listening to extraneous sounds which they were to ignore since the E was interested in their vasomotor and finger temperature reactions to the slides and shocks.

No difference was obtained between experimentals and controls in approaching a live snake at the end of the experiment except when those Ss from both groups who had reported they had touched a snake sometime before were eliminated from the sample. The criterion for effectiveness of treatment was whether *S*s would touch a snake without money being offered or for one, two, or three dollars (pressure applied). Analysis of the pressure applied suggests that the experimental *S*s require less pressure to touch the snake than do the controls. The advantage of the pressure applied evaluation over the more traditional approach measures used to estimate the effectiveness of treatment is not clear. The lack of initial avoidance scores, particularly with regard to the use of an incentive for touching snakes, is a major shortcoming of the study since nine out of 11 control *S*s touched the snake. No evidence is available regarding how many *S*s would have touched the snake for one, two, or three dollars before any treatment at all. The improvement in the second study is also possibly attributable to the exposure of both groups of *S*s to the live snake during the second session of trials rather than to any manipulation of cognitions.

A third, general strategy is ordinarily dealt with in terms of controlling for placebo effect. This strategy involves comparisons between the effects of systematic desensitization and other sets of operations which are presumed to have no therapeutic or beneficial effects generally, or relative to the specific criterion towards which the desensitization is pointed. These control groups are included primarily to control for the effects of the belief of *S*s that they will improve after undergoing some procedure. However, some so-called placebo conditions, for example, teaching *S*s how to relax, may indeed produce beneficial effects.

Three other generally well-designed and frequently cited studies that have employed some sort of control for placebo effects or expectations of treatment being successful as part of more general investigations of systematic desensitization report that systematic desensitization is much more effective than placebo controls. We have some reservations about their methodology and conclusions. The first of these, Paul (1966, 1967) studied individuals' reported stress about public speaking. Subjects received systematic individual desensitization, or insight oriented psychotherapy, or an attention-placebo treatment or were in an untreated control group. In the tension placebo, *S*s were administered a placebo with strong suggestions that the drug that they had received effectively reduced the occurrence of anxiety in stressful situations and following the administration of the drug, *S*s performed a supposedly stressful task which in fact produced feelings of drowsiness.

Primarily, we are interested in comparing the desensitization group, the attention placebo group, and the control group in Paul's studies. Clearly, the improvement scores favor the desensitization group. However, the scores in this group are systematically and quite a bit higher in general than in the attention placebo group before treatment. As a matter of fact, the actual performance of the placebo group is superior, although probably not significantly so, on three out of the four specific anxiety scales, and practically equal on the fourth to those of the desensitization group after a 2-year follow-up. Similarly, two of the three personality test scores presented favor the placebo control group over the desensitization group. In situations like this where the scores for the one experimental subgroup are systematically higher than others to begin with, one may very well suspect that random assignments to groups may have resulted in a subgroup which, because of momentary and temporary considerations, produced higher scores during pretest than the other groups in the experiment. In such a case, difference in scores may not adequately represent different effects of treatments. Since Hovland and Pritzser (1957) suggest a positive relationship between initial extremity and accomplished change, it is important to ensure that the changes are not attributable to the room for change to occur. We are somewhat skeptical whether even analysis of covariance adequately deals with such problems, since its assumptions are not easily met.

A second study by Davison (1965) found a complete reciprocal inhibition procedure to produce significant decrements in snake fear while control conditions were ineffective. The controls consisted of: (1) relaxation "pseudo-conditioning," in which muscular relaxation was paired with imaginal stimuli irrelevant to snakes; (2) systematic desensitization without relaxation; (3) no-treatment control which received only pre- and posttreatment criterion tests. Since the number of hierarchy items completed had been previously demon-strated to relate to improvement and because *S*s who were relaxed during visualization might be expected to proceed more rapidly up the hierarchy test, Davison yoked the number of visualizations in the control groups to those in the desensitization group. As a consequence, *S*s in the experimental group have the advantage of receiving repetitions geared specifically to their individual requirements, that is, to their success experiences, or their decrease in anxiety experiences or their beliefs about achieving progress, whereas *S*s in control groups do not. Davison's findings of superiority in reciprocal inhibition over systematic desensitization without relaxation may be partially attributable to these factors.

A third study by Lang *et al.* (1965) referred to earlier, used a treatment called pseudotherapy in which an effort was made to involve the *S* in a treatment procedure that was therapeutically neutral except for the therapist–client relationship. During the first 15 min of the therapy hour, the *S* was asked to imagine a series of scenes which he had previously described as pleasant or relaxing.

The last 30 min was keyed to the hierarchy items and provided starting points for discussion of nonanxiety provoking aspects of the *S*'s life. The pseudo therapist did attempt to prevent phobic responses (discussions of the phobic material) from being made in the context of the therapy hour. Pseudotherapy *S*s were instructed that previous research suggested that people with fears like theirs had higher levels of autonomic tonus than others and that "some psychologists held" that if this generally high tonus level could be reduced, the way would be paved for a general reduction of fears. It is not clear from Lang's article whether or not some doubt about this success of treatment was also injected in instructions for the desensitization Ss, that is for example, "some psychologists hold." Criterion avoidance and fear scores for the pseudotherapy group are generally significantly poorer than those in the desensitization group, as found by Lang *et al.* (1965).

Although the authors conclude that changes in fear behavior have not been produced in the pseudotherapy group, no evidence is provided that a statistical test of the increment in approach responses was performed. The increment in approach for the desensitization group was .27, of the pseudotherapy group .14, and of the no-treatment controls $-.19$. On the basis of nonsignificant t tests between the control and pseudotherapy group, the authors combine their results into one group to compare with the desensitization group so that the entire analysis is open to question.

Lang used the hypnotic susceptibility scale and found that it was highly related to initial avoidance scores of Ss, but not related to change scores and somewhat related to fear thermometer change scores in the control group. It is unfortunate that correlations between hypnotic susceptibility and posttest scores in fear and avoidance were not also presented for the systematic desensitization group.

Other strategies that might be tried could involve the manipulation of the expectancy of success or failure of the therapist, or the selection of therapists with different expectancies of success or failure, the selection of Ss with differential expectations of success in treatment and perhaps even varying the credibility of different sets of instructions.

An interesting study of this type by Cohen (1969), which was concerned with reduction of test anxiety, actually asked Ss for their expectations about anxiety reduction before, during, and after treatment. The expectancy of anxiety reduction after the third session was almost twice as large as pretreatment expectancy for anxiety reduction in five groups of Ss tested. It is also suggested by the data that the mean expectation of anxiety reduction by Ss who dropped out after only half of the desensitization course was completed, was lower than that of four of five other experimental groups.

We must conclude, after reviewing these studies on the effects of expectation and belief in systematic desensitization and systematic desensitization-like studies that there is strong evidence to support the notion that people can be persuaded and influenced and convinced to perform feared acts. Very little study has directed itself predominantly to such questions as what is the suggestion value of different kinds of systematic desensitization instructions, what expectations are formed by various components of the technique itself, and how are these related to fear and avoidance.

The most direct studies, those of Oliveau (1969) and Leitenberg *et al.*

(1969) show a very clear superiority as a treatment device for desensitization when it is presented as such and when Ss are encouraged for progress as compared with cases where Ss are led to believe that it is an experiment in physiology. The changes for the former condition are more than twice as great as the latter, and would be even more impressive if a ratio approach scale were used instead of a linear one.

With regard to the question of whether desensitization is any more than an elaborate technique for increasing Ss expectations of success with feared objects, the evidence is not clear at this point. Experimenters who study desensitization have tended to approach reasonably intelligent college students who serve as Ss as some kind of black boxes, rather than as hypothesis-forming, suspicious, very complex systems, who are very unlikely to believe exactly what they are told by instructions. Adequate verbal reports are rarely obtained from Ss in experiments regarding their hypotheses and expectations about the nature of the experiment.

We are forced to conclude that the study of how one changes cognitive variables, attitudes, belief systems, and what relationship such changes have to overt behavior is important for evaluating the systematic desensitization procedure.

References

Bandura, A. *Principles of behavior modification.* New York: Holt, 1969.

Barber, T. X., & Hahan, K. W., Jr. Experimental studies in "hypnotic" behavior: Physiological and subjective effects of imagined pain. *Journal of Nervous and Mental Disease,* 1964, **139**, 416-425.

Byrne, D. Child rearing antecedents of repression-sensitization. *Child Development,* 1964, **35**, 1033-1039.

Cautela, J. R. Behavior therapy approach to pervasive anxiety. *Behavior Research and Therapy,* 1966, **4**, 17-24.

Cohen, R. The effects of group interaction and progressive hierarchy presentation on desensitization of test anxiety. *Behavior Research and Therapy,* 1969, **7**, 15-26.

Cooke, G. Evaluation of the efficacy of the components of reciprocal inhibition psychotherapy. *Journal of Abnormal Psychology,* 1968, **73**, 464-467.

Crighton, J., & Jehu, D. Treatment of examination anxiety by systematic desensitization or psychotherapy in groups. *Behavior Research and Therapy,* 1969, **7**, 245-248.

Davison, G. The influence of systematic desensitization relaxation, and graded exposure to imaginal, aversive stimuli on the modification of phobic behavior. Unpublished Doctoral dissertation, Stanford Univ., 1965.

Davison, G. C. Systematic desensitization as a counter conditioning process. *Journal of Abnormal Psychology,* 1968, **73**, 91-99.

Dixon, F. Systematic desensitization of test anxiety. Unpublished doctoral dissertation, Univ. of Southern California, 1966.

Donaldson, D. W. Positive imagery technique and impulsive therapy. Unpublished doctoral dissertation, Fuller Theological Seminary, 1969.

Donner, L., & Guerney, B. Automated group desensitization for test anxiety. *Behavior Research and Therapy*, 1969, **7**, 1-13.

Evans, W. O. The effectiveness of visual imagery on phobic behavior when accompanied by electric shock. Unpublished doctoral dissertation, Fuller Theological Seminary, 1968.

Edelman, M. Anxiety level and the repression-sensitization dimension in desensitization therapies. Unpublished dissertation, Univ. of California, 1968.

Fazio, A. F. Verbal behavioral assessment of a specific fear. *Journal of Consulting and Clinical Psychology*, 1969, **33**, 705-709.

Folkins, C. H., Lawson, K. D., Opton, E. M., Jr., & Lazarus, R. S. Desensitization and the experimental reduction of threat. *Journal of Abnormal Psychology*, 1968, **73**, 100-113.

Frankel, A. S. Treatment of a multisymptomatic phobic by a self-directed, self-reinforced imagery technique. *Journal of Abnormal Psychology*, in press, 1970.

Goldstein, A. P. *Therapist-patient expectancies in psychotherapy.* New York: Pergamon, 1962.

Grossberg, J. M., & Wilson, H. Physiological changes accompanying the visualization of fearful and neutral situations. *Journal of Personality and Social Psychology*, 1968, **10**, 124-133.

Hogan, R. A., & Kirchner, J. H. Preliminary report of the extinction of learned fears via short-term implosive therapy. *Journal of Abnormal Psychology*, 1967, **72**, 106-109.

Hogan, R. A., & Kirchner, J. H. Implosive, electric verbal, and bibliotherapy in the treatment of fears of snakes. *Behavior Research and Therapy*, 1968, **6**, 167-171.

Hovland, C., & Pritzser, H. Extent of opinion change as a function of amount of change advocated. *Journal of Abnormal and Social Behavior*, 1957, **54**, 257-261.

Jacobs, A., & Felton, G. Visual feedback of myoelectric output to facilitate muscle relaxation in normal persons and patients with neck injuries. *Archives of Physical Medicine and Rehabilitation*, 1969, **50**, 34-39.

Jacobs, A., Edelman, M., & Wolpin, M. Anxiety level and desensitization. Unpublished manuscript, 1969.

Jaffe, L. W. Nonspecific treatment factors and deconditioning in fear reduction. Unpublished doctoral dissertation, Univ. of Southern California, 1968.

Kirchner, J. H., & Hogan, R. A. The therapist variable in the Implosion of phobias. Psychotherapy: *Theory Research and Practice*, 1966, **3**, 102-104.

Krapfl, J. E., & Nawas, M. M. Differential ordering of stimulus presentation in systematic desensitization. Unpublished manuscript, 1970.

Lang, P. J., & Lazovik, A. D. Experimental desensitization of a phobia. *Journal of Abnormal and Social Psychology*, 1963, **66**, 519-525.

Lang, P. J., Lazovik, A. D., & Reynolds, D. J. Desensitization, suggestibility and pseudopsychotherapy. *Journal of Abnormal Psychology*, 1965, **70**, 395-402.

Lang, P. J. Fear reduction and fear behavior problems in treating the construct. *Research in Psychotherapy, 1968*, **3**. Pp. 90-102. American Psychological Corporation, Inc.

Lang, P. J. The mechanics of desensitization and the laboratory study of human fear. In C. M. Franks (Ed.), *Behavior Therapy.* New York: McGraw-Hill, 1969.

Lazarus, A. Behavior therapy in group. In G. Gazda (Ed.), *Basic Approaches to Group Psychotherapy and Group Counselling.* Springfield, Illinois: Charles Thomas, 1968. Pp. 149-175.

Lazovik, A. D., & Lang, P. J. A laboratory demonstration of systematic desensitization psychotherapy. *Journal of Psychological Studies*, 1960, **11**, 238-247.

Leitenberg, H., Agras, W., Barlow, D., & Oliveau, D. Contribution of selected positive reinforcement and therapeutic instructions to systematic desensitization therapy. *Journal of Abnormal Psychology*, 1969, **74**, 113-118.

Leuner, H. The use of initiated symbol projection in psychotherapy. Monograph, New York: The Psychosynthesis Research Foundation, 1966.

Lieberman, S. A temporal approach–avoidance conflict in an academic test situation. Unpublished doctoral dissertation. Univ. of Southern California, 1969.

Lomont, J. F., & Edwards, J. E. The role of relaxation in systematic desensitization. *Behavior Research and Therapy*, 1967, **5**, 11-26.

Marcia, J., Rubin, B., & Efran, J. Systematic desensitization: Expectancy change or counter conditioning. *Journal of Abnormal Psychology*, 1969, **74**, 382-387.

Miller, N. E. Learnable drives and rewards. In S. Stevens (Ed.), *Handbook of Experimental Psychology*, New York: Wiley, 1950, pp. 435-472.

Mischel, W. *Personality and assessment.* New York: Wiley, 1968.

Myerhoff, H. L. Visual imagery under varying muscle states. Unpublished manuscript, Camarillo State Hospital, Camarillo, California, 1967.

Myerhoff, H. L. Tension and anxiety in deconditioning. Unpublished doctoral dissertation, Univ. of Southern California, 1968.

Oliveau, D., Agras, W., Leitenberg, H., Moore, R., & Wright, D. Systematic desensitization, therapeutically oriented instructions, and selective positive reinforcement. *Behavior Research and Therapy*, 1969, **7**, 27-34.

Oliveau, D. Systematic desensitization in an experimental setting: A follow-up study. *Behavior Research and Therapy*, 1969, **7**, 377-380.

Paul, G. Insight versus desensitization in psychotherapy: An experiment in anxiety reduction. Stanford: Stanford Univ. Press, 1966.

Paul, G. Insight versus desensitization in psychotherapy two years after termination. *Journal of Consulting Psychology*, 1967, **31**, 333-348.

Perloff, B. Influence of muscular relaxation, positive imagery, and neutral imagery on extinction of avoidance behavior through systematic desensitization. Unpublished doctoral dissertation, Stanford Univ., 1970.

Rachman, S. Studies in desensitization. I. The separate effects of relaxation and desensitization. *Behavior Research and Therapy*, 1965, **3**, 245-251.

Rachman, S. Studies in desensitization: Flooding. *Behavior Research and Therapy*, 1966, **4**, 1-6.

Rosenthal, R. Experimenter outcome orientation and the results of the psychological experiment. *Psychological Bulletin*, 1964, **61**, 405-412.

Stampfl, T. G., & Levis, D. J. Essentials of implosive therapy: A learning theory based psychodynamic behavior therapy. *Journal of Abnormal Psychology*, 1967, **72**, 496-503.

Valins, S., & Ray, A. Effect of cognitive desensitization on avoidance behavior. *Journal of Personality and Social Psychology*, 1967, **7**, 345-350.

Weinberg, N. H., & Zaslove, M. "Resistance" to systematic desensitization of phobias. *Journal of Clinical Psychology*, 1963, **19**, 179-181.

Weitzman, B. Behavior therapy and psychotherapy. *Psychological Review*, 1967, **74**, 300-317.

Wolpe, J. *Psychotherapy by reciprocal inhibition.* Stanford: Stanford Univ. Press, 1958.

Wolpin, M., & Pearsall, L. Rapid deconditioning of a fear of snakes. *Behavior Research and Therapy*, 1965, **3**, 107-111.

Wolpin, M., & Raines, J. Visual imagery, expected roles and extinction as possible factors in reducing fear and avoidance behavior. *Behavior Research and Therapy*, 1966, **4**, 25-37.

Wolpin, M. Visualization under conditions of tensed, relaxed, and neutral body states. Unpublished manuscript, Camarillo State Hospital, Camarillo, California, 1966.

Wolpin, M., Frankel, A. S., Zinsmeyer, J., & Paris, R. Factors in the reductions of anxiety and avoidance behavior, in progress.

Covert Conditioning

Joseph R. Cautela

Boston College
Boston, Massachusetts

In the early stages of the development of learning theories, most of the theorists (Pavlov, 1927; Guthrie, 1935; Hull, 1952; Skinner, 1938) assumed that the study of relatively simple organisms under highly controlled conditions would lead to the discovery of laws which would eventually provide a basis for high predictability and control of human behavior. These theorists also assumed that theoretical models preoccupied with private events (mental activity) had no place in the development of a successful scientific psychology.

As the learning models developed, however, it became increasingly clear that private events could not be ignored if the theories were to be applicable to human behavior. Therefore, each theorist attempted to account for the occurrence of private events. Pavlov stated that words acted as a second signal system and made man capable of the symbolic processes of thinking and abstraction (1955, p. 285). Guthrie referred to mediational processes in humans as "maintaining stimuli" (1935, pp. 205-206). Hull explained planning and abstract thinking in humans as an anticipatory goal response (1952, p. 350). Skinner's viewpoint on the place of private events in the study of behavior is difficult to specify. In one 1969 article he (Skinner, 1969b) maintained the position that an inference of mediational states was unnecessary; complex behavior may be accounted for by determining the correct parameters for the functional relationship between behavior and the environment. In a 1969 book, however, Skinner (1969a) referred to private (covert) events in this way:

> So far as we know, the responses are executed with the same organs as observable responses, but on a smaller scale. The stimuli they generate are weak, but nevertheless of the same kind as those generated by overt responses. It would be a mistake to refuse to consider them as data just because a second observer cannot feel or see them, at least without the help of instruments [p. 242].

In recent years, private events (images) have been employed to modify behavior. Imagery has been paired with electric shock to reduce response frequency (McGuire & Valence, 1964). Imagery is the main component of Wolpe's desensitization method (1958), Lazarus's and Abramovitz's technique of emotive imagery (1962), and Stampfl's implosive therapy (1967). Homme (1965) has attempted to manipulate overt behavior by the manipulation of covert behavior utilizing the Premack hypothesis (Premack, 1959).

Barber has shown that direct instructions to think, imagine, or visualize in specific ways can produce dramatic physiological and behavioral effects. Barber and Hahn (1962) demonstrated that verbal reports of pain and physiological responses to pain-producing stimulation can be markedly reduced by instructing *S*s to try to think about and imagine vividly a pleasant situation during the noxious stimulation. Barber, Chauncey, and Winer (1964) found that (a) instructions to imagine vividly that water (placed on the tongue) was a sour solution produced a significant elevation in *S*s' salivary response to the water, and (b) instructions to imagine vividly that a citric acid solution was tasteless produced a significant reduction in the *S*s' salivary response to acid. Barber (1969) and Hahn and Barber (1966) asked *S*s first to watch an optokinetic drum (a revolving drum with black and white vertical stripes) and then proceeded to ascertain whether instructions to imagine vividly and to visualize the optokinetic drum give rise to nystagmoid-like eye movements, which resemble those manifested by the *S*s when they were actually watching the revolving drum. A small proportion (about 10%) of unselected *S*s manifested the involuntary nystagmoid-like eye movements which were found when the *S*s were actually looking at the revolving drum. Barber (1969, pp. 66-67) instructed *S*s, immediately before they went to bed at night, to try continually during the night to think about and to dream about a specified topic. The *S*s were awakened when EEG and rapid eye movements (REM) indicated that they were dreaming and also, for control purposes, at other times during the night. Fifty percent of the dreams reported by the *S*s were concerned directly or indirectly with the specified topic. The *S*s swore in the morning that they had actually dreamed about the specified topic and that they did not report the dreams in order to comply with the experimental instructions.

The major assumption made in this paper is that stimuli presented in imagination have similar functional relationships to covert and overt behavior as do stimuli presented externally. It is further assumed that the manipulation of covert processes can influence overt responses in a predictable manner. Investigators such as Kimble (1961) and Franks (1967) agree with this assumption. Also, I believe the evidence presented in this paper will support the assumption.

It is the purpose of this paper to demonstrate how both aversive and reinforcing stimuli presented in imagination can be used to modify behavior in a manner similar to externally applied aversive and reinforcing stimuli. The procedures used to modify behavior by presenting aversive and reinforcing stimuli in imagination, termed covert sensitization and covert reinforcement (Cautela, 1967; Cautela, 1970), will be described with examples of clinical applications. Some experimental evidence will also be presented.

Advantages of the Use of Imagery in Behavior Modification

1. Patients often drop out of treatment when aversive external stimuli are employed to reduce the probability of undesirable behavior because the procedure is so disagreeable. Investigators employing covert sensitization (a technique which presents aversive stimuli in imagination) have not reported any significant dropout rate.

2. Overgeneralization may sometimes occur when strong aversive stimuli are employed to modify behavior. The effects of covert sensitization, on the other hand, are specific to the response class that is to be eliminated.

3. The use of imagery requires little if any equipment, and procedures can be applied in almost any situation.

4. The use of imagery is not limited by practical reality. In imagination, events that the patient is unable to initiate (e.g. asking for a date) or that are impractical (e.g., witnessing a plane crash) can be made to occur.

5. Imagery can easily be used as a self-control procedure. The patient can produce the necessary imagery whenever he is confronted with situations that lead to the maladaptive behavior.

The Use of Covert Conditioning in Self-Control

Covert sensitization and covert reinforcement are used in the following manner to assist patients to gain self-control:

1. Patients are told to practice the procedures at home.
2. Patients are told to use the procedures *in vivo* whenever they are "tempted" to make the maladaptive response.
3. Patients are instructed on how to employ the procedures. If at any time after they leave therapy, they observe they are again performing the maladaptive response for which they have been treated or if new maladaptive behaviors are beginning to develop, they may once again apply the procedures to themselves.

In this way, the procedures can be used as self-control techniques for the rest of the patients' lives.

Covert Sensitization

Covert sensitization is used to treat maladaptive approach behavior such as alcoholism, homosexuality, and obesity. The procedure is labeled "covert sensitization" because neither the undesirable response nor the aversive stimulus is actually presented. These stimuli are presented in imagination only. The word "sensitization" is used because the purpose of this procedure is to build up an avoidance response to the undesirable stimulus.

In addition to the usual assessment procedures (Cautela, 1968), the client is given specific questionnaires (e.g., smoking, alcohol, eating, homosexuality) designed to elicit information concerning the maladaptive approach behavior. The questionnaires are designed to obtain the frequency of the maladaptive behavior, the type of the object preferred (e.g., brand of cigarette, type of homosexual), and the conditions under which the behavior usually occurs.

In employing covert sensitization, not only is the maladaptive behavior itself treated directly by pairing the behavior with aversive stimuli, but the anxiety (drive) component is also treated by identifying those situations which tend to be antecedent to the maladaptive behavior. After those situations are identified in which the maladaptive behavior occurs, the individual is made less anxious in these situations by desensitization or covert reinforcement. Covert sensitization may also be combined with other procedures such as thought stopping (Cautela, 1969).

Description of Procedure

The patient is told that he is unable to stop drinking in excess (or eating, or whatever is the problem to be treated) because it is a strong, learned habit which now gives him a great amount of pleasure. He is told that the way to eliminate his problem is to associate the pleasurable object with an unpleasant stimulus. The patient is then asked to visualize the pleasurable object (e.g., food, liquor, homosexual). When he can do this very clearly, he is told to raise his index finger. After he signals, he is told to next visualize that he is about to take the object (commit the compulsive act). If the object is liquor, for example, he is asked to visualize himself looking at the glass with the alcoholic beverage in it. Then he is told to visualize a sequence of events—holding the glass in his hand, bringing it up to his lips, having the glass touch his lips. When he imagines this latter scene, he is told to imagine that he begins to feel sick to his stomach. In imagination, he begins to vomit. The vomit goes all over the floor, the drink, his companions and himself. He is then asked to visualize the whole scene by himself, and to raise his finger when he can picture it and actually feel nauseous when he had the intention of drinking, gradually getting sicker as he touches the glass, raises it, etc.

A feeling of relief is provided in scenes when he turns away from the pleasurable object. He is told to imagine that as he rushes outside into the fresh, clean air, or home to a clean, invigorating shower, or whenever he is tempted to drink and refuses to do it, the feeling of nausea goes away, and he no longer feels ill.

The following is an example of the specific instructions given to a client who wanted to stop smoking:

I am going to ask you to imagine as vividly as you can. I don't want you to imagine that you are seeing yourself in these situations. I want you to imagine that you're actually in these situations. Do not only try to visualize the scenes but try to feel, for example, the cigarette in your hand, or the back of the chair in which you are sitting. Try to use all your senses as though you were actually there. The scenes that I pick will be concerned with situations in which you are about to smoke. It is very important that you visualize the scenes as clearly as possible and try to actually feel yourself in the situation.

The following is a typical scene:

You are sitting at your desk in the office preparing your lectures for class. There is a pack of cigarettes to your right. While you are writing, you put down your pencil and start to reach for a cigarette. As soon as you start reaching for the cigarette, you get a nauseous feeling in your stomach. You begin to feel sick to your stomach, as if you are about to vomit. You touch the pack of cigarettes and bitter spit comes into your mouth. When you take the cigarette out of the pack some pieces of food come into your throat. Now you feel sick and have stomach cramps. As you are about to put the cigarette in your mouth, you puke all over the pack of cigarettes. The cigarette in your hand is very soggy and full of green vomit. There is a stink coming from the vomit. Snots are coming from your nose. Your hands feel all slimy and full of vomit. The whole desk is a mess. Your clothes are all full of puke. You get up from your desk and turn away from the vomit and cigarettes. You immediately begin to feel better being away from the vomit and the cigarettes. You go to the bathroom and wash up and feel great being away from the vomit and the cigarettes.

After the scene is described to the *S* he is asked how clearly he visualized the scene, and if he felt some nausea or disgust. Then he is asked to repeat the scene himself, trying to see the cigarettes as clearly as possible and trying to see and smell the vomit.

Other scenes are given in a similar manner concerning other places in which he smokes, e.g., if he takes a cigarette after coffee in the morning, a scene is described in which he is about to smoke, but gets sick and vomits all over the table and the cigarette.

Alternating with an aversive scene is an escape or self-control scene. A typical self-control scene is:

You are at your desk working and you decide to smoke, and as soon as you decide to smoke you get this funny sick feeling in the pit of your stomach. You say to yourself, "The hell with it, I'm not going to smoke!" As soon as you decide not to smoke, you feel fine and proud that you resisted temptation.

The self-controlling-response scenes make use of two procedures that have been found to increase response probability:

(1) negative reinforcement (escape conditioning) (Mowrer, 1940);
(2) self reinforcement (Kanfer & Marston, 1963).

At each therapy session, the *S* is given 10 trials of vomiting alternating with 10 scenes of escape and self reinforcement. At the end of each session, the *S* is asked to practice the 20 scenes twice a day until the next session. Also he is instructed to say "Stop!" and imagine he is vomiting on a cigarette whenever he is tempted to smoke. At the beginning of each session, he is asked how many times he practiced and how many cigarettes he has smoked.

In treating alcoholism, a typical scene is as follows:

You are walking into a bar. You decide to have a glass of beer. You are now walking toward the bar. As you are approaching the bar, you have a funny feeling in the pit of your stomach. Your stomach feels all queasy and nauseous. Some liquid comes up your throat and it is very sour. You try to swallow it back down, but as you do this, food particles start coming up your throat to your mouth. You try to keep your mouth closed and swallow it back down. You reach for the glass of beer to wash it down. As soon as your hand touches the glass, you can't hold it down any longer. You have to open your mouth and you puke. It goes all over your hand, all over the glass and the beer. You can see it floating around in the beer. Snots and mucous come out of your nose. Your shirt and pants are full of vomit. The bartender has some on his shirt. You notice people looking at you. You get sick again and you vomit more and more. You turn away from the beer and immediately you start to feel better. As you run out of the bar room, you start to feel better and better. When you get into the clean fresh air you feel wonderful. You go home and clean yourself up.

In treating homosexuality this type of scene is employed:

I want you to imagine that you are in a room with X. He is completely naked. As you approach him you notice he has sores and scabs all over his body, with some kind of fluid oozing from them. A terrible foul stench comes from his body. The odor is so strong it makes you sick. You can feel food particles coming up your throat. You can't help yourself and you vomit all over the place, all over the floor, on your hands and clothes. Now that even makes you sicker and you vomit again and again all over everything. You turn away and then you start to feel better. You try to get out of the room, but the door seems to be locked. The smell is still strong, but you try desperately to get out. You kick the door frantically until it finally opens and you run into the nice clean air. It smells wonderful. You go home and shower and you feel so clean.

In treating obesity, we have employed this scene:

I want you to imagine you've just had your main meal and you are about to eat your dessert, which is (e.g., apple pie). As you are about to reach for the fork, you get a funny feeling in the pit of your stomach. You start to feel queasy, nauseous and sick all over. As you touch the fork, you can feel food particles inching up your throat. You're just about to vomit. As you put the fork into the pie, the food comes up to your mouth. You try to keep your mouth closed because you're afraid that you'll spit the food out all over the place. You bring the piece of pie to your mouth. As you're about to open your mouth, you puke. You vomit all over your hands, the fork, over the pie. It goes all over the table, over the other peoples' food. Your eyes are watering. Snots, mucous are all over your mouth and nose. Your hands feel sticky. There is an awful smell. As you look at this mess you just can't help it, but you start to vomit again and again until just watery stuff is coming out. Everybody is looking at you with a shocked expression. You turn away from the food and immediately start to feel better. You run out of the room, and as you run out, you feel better and better. You wash and clean yourself up and it feels wonderful.

Results of Covert Sensitization

There have been a number of studies to determine the effectiveness of covert sensitization following the first publications describing the technique (Cautela, 1966; Cautela, 1967).

The use of covert sensitization in the treatment of smoking. Some studies have evaluated the effect of covert sensitization on smoking behavior. Mullen (unpublished data, 1967) employed a control group, a group-treated covert sensitization group, and a group in which Ss were treated individually with covert sensitization. At the end of six sessions (½ hr each), the control group went from a mean of 16.3 cigarettes a day to 15.4 cigarettes a day. The mean of the group treatment covert sensitization group was 5.0 a day. A 6-month follow-up showed that the control group had a mean of 17.1 cigarettes a day and the experimental groups had a mean of 10.1 a day. No member of the control group gave up smoking, but two members of the experimental groups stopped smoking completely. Mullen reports that as early as the second session, the majority of the experimental Ss commented that they no longer enjoyed the cigarettes they smoked. In view of the small number of sessions, the follow-up results are not surprising. The experiment should have employed a placebo group.

Viernstein (unpublished data, 1968) compared covert sensitization with educational-supportive and control groups in the modification of smoking behavior. Seven sessions were used and two therapists alternated weekly in administering the procedures. Subjects subjected to covert sensitization smoked significantly less ($p < .05$) at posttreatment, and on a 5-week follow-up. She also reports that the covert sensitization Ss said that when they did smoke, they did not enjoy the cigarette. Subjects would take a few puffs, then extinguish the cigarettes. It would have been interesting to see reports of a 6-month follow-up.

Wagner (1969) compared systematic desensitization alone, covert sensitization alone, relaxation alone, and a group in systematic desensitization and covert sensitization were combined. He reports that at the end of the 30- and 90-day follow-ups, only the group combining systematic desensitization—covert sensitization was smoking significantly less than the base rate. As a result of this study, Wagner and Bragg (1968) developed a self-administering programmed recording of the systematic desensitization—covert sensitization procedure.

The treatment of alcoholism. The application of covert sensitization to alcoholic problems has been demonstrated by Ashem and Donner (1968) in a study treating 23 alcoholic male patients over a 6-week period of therapy. The patients were selected according to the following criteria: 45 years of age or less, of average intelligence as measured by the Otis Intelligence Scale, free from any sign of gross psychological disturbances assessed by the MMPI, and whose family history suggested that 6-month follow-up would be obtainable after the completion of the study. The authors employed three groups: a forward classical conditioning group (CS–UCS); a backward classical conditioning group (UCS–CS) with the visual scene presented before the drinking of alcohol is mentioned [assuming that backward conditioning is not true conditioning as Cautela (1965) suggests] ; and a no-contact control group. The treatment program consisted of nine sessions which ranged from 30 to 40 min each. Both treatment groups were relaxed before the scenes were presented. In the backward-conditioning group, patients were told to imagine they were drinking alcohol as soon as they showed overt signs of discomfort. The authors state that the patients in this group quickly made forward associations between the alcohol and the nausea. As a result, they combined both treatment groups and compared them statistically with the control group. A 6-month follow-up after treatment revealed that each member of the control group was drinking, whereas 40% of the treatment group was abstaining. Included as part of the treatment procedure, the authors taught the patients to relax when they stopped thinking of alcohol.

The authors were impressed with the results since 23 patients had been drinking on the average of 18.5 years and that the treatment sessions were given over a period of only 3 weeks.

Application of covert sensitization to sexual deviations. Barlow, Leitenberg, and Agras (1969b) treated a 25-year-old, married male who reported a 13-year history of pedophilic experiences ranging from fantasies to several instances of sexual contact. Baseline procedures involving self-reports of occasions of arousal for each day, a card-sort technique, and GSR measures were then instituted for five sessions. After training in deep muscle relaxation (Jacobson, 1938), the highest six items in the patient's 45-item hierarchy were chosen for sensitization. For example, the top item in the hierarchy was, "You are alone in a room with a very sexy looking 10-year-old girl with long, blond hair."

In each session, the patient was given relaxation instructions and presented with eight scenes. In four scenes, the patient was described approaching the girl, feeling nauseous and vomiting. The description of the nauseous scene was usually expanded and lasted 30 to 60 sec. In the remaining four scenes, the patient was described approaching the girl and beginning to feel nauseous, at which point he would turn and start walking away from the scene and immediately feel relieved and relaxed. Six acquisition sessions consisting of 48 pairings were followed by eight extinction sessions consisting of 64 scene presentations. The extinction procedure consisted of presentations of only the sexually-arousing scenes. Reacquisition was introduced after the extinction procedure.

The results indicate that during acquisition trials, in which the covert sensitization scene was paired with the sexually-arousing scene, the measures of inappropriate sexual arousal in the patient dropped sharply. In extinction, the covert sensitization procedure was omitted resulting in an increase in both measures of sexual arousal. In reacquistion, the covert sensitization procedure was introduced and measures of sexual arousal dropped to zero. The patient also reported increased heterosexual behavior during this last phase.

In the same study, Barlow *et al.* (1969b) demonstrated the efficacy of covert sensitization applied to homosexual behavior. Baseline measures of sexual arousal were first obtained from the *S,* and then, as he imagined six sexually arousing scenes, covert sensitization scenes were introduced. All measures of sexual arousal decreased sharply during the phase when covert sensitization was employed. Then, the extinction phase where the sexually arousing scenes were presented without the aversive imagery, was introduced. During extinction, all measures of arousal increased. The final phase of reacquisition was then initiated and all measures dropped to zero.

These foregoing experiments indicate that covert sensitization alone is sufficient to decrease deviant behavior. Although evidence indicates that covert sensitization is effective in treating maladaptive approach behavior, one could assert that treatment outcome is due to expectancies established in the *S*s by the covert sensitization procedure itself. Indeed, Murray and Jacobsen (1969) claim that treatment outcome in all behavior modification procedures employing imagery such as desensitization (Wolpe, 1958), implosive therapy (Stampfl, 1967), and emotive imagery (Lazarus & Abramovitz, 1962) is more parsimoniously explained in terms of the expectancies of the S who is convinced of the procedure.

In order to test this assumption, Barlow, Agras, and Leitenberg (unpublished data, 1969a) recently completed two studies bearing on the possibility that outcome effects of covert sensitization can be attributed to expectancies of the S. These investigators employed an operant paradigm to test the effect of instructions on the modification of sexual arousal in two male homosexuals. (The second study was a replication of the first.) First, they established a baseline measure of arousal, utilizing these measures:

(a) The number of times each S reported he was sexually aroused by the sight of another male or had homosexual fantasies;

(b) A rating of sexually arousing scenes from 0 (no arousal) to 4 (very much arousal) taken after each session.

(c) Changes in penile volume during the time Ss were viewing color slides of male and female nudes.

While baseline data was gathered, the Ss were trained in relaxation. In the first phase of the experiment, Ss were given instructions suggesting that relaxing while viewing the first six sexually arousing scenes in their hierarchy would decrease arousal. In other words, Ss were given expectancies opposite to the expectancies of the Es. They were told that:

Sexual arousal is characterized by certain pleasurable tension which is difficult to control. This contributes to the formation of an erection. This sexual arousal to males is learned and we are going to get rid of that tension by substituting a relaxed response for the tension state and in this way eliminate sexual arousal to males.

During the next phase (covert sensitization phase), the Ss were told that:

It is now necessary to heighten the tension a bit by pairing sexually-arousing scenes with images of vomiting. During this phase, you will probably notice an increase in your homosexual urges; but do not be alarmed, this is part of the treatment.

The relaxation phase and the covert sensitization phase were then repeated. The results show that, in general, arousal increased during the relaxation phase and decreased during the covert sensitization phase, as would be expected from the results of previous experimental studies. During the last phase of the experiment, covert sensitization was applied until there was no arousal on all measures. A 6-month follow-up revealed that Ss showed no relapse. Therefore, Ss' expectancies had no significant effect on treatment outcome.

Anecdotal evidence. In the studies previously cited, experimental procedures were employed. There are also some anecdotal studies indicating the effectiveness of covert sensitization when combined with other procedures. In a paper by Cautela and Wisocki (1969b), a detailed procedure is described on the use of male and female therapists in the treatment of homosexuality. In this procedure, covert sensitization is a crucial component of treatment, though other techniques such as thought-stopping, and covert reinforcement were employed. Cautela and Wisocki present anecdotal evidence indicating that the combination of procedures is effective. Davison (1968) reports a case in which sadistic fantasy of 10 years' duration was eliminated in five sessions over a 10-week period. Davison used a counter-conditioning technique for the patient's sexual responses (from masturbating while imagining the sadistic fantasy to masturbating while focusing on a picture of a sexy nude woman), but credits the application of covert sensitization during the third through fifth sessions as instrumental in changing the content of the client's fantasies. Cautela and Baron (unpublished data, 1970) combined covert sensitization with other behavior modification procedures to eliminate serious self-injurious behavior in a 21-year-old male. Stuart (1967) reports the behavioral treatment of eight obese Ss with a procedure derived from the work of Ferster, Nurnberger, and Levitt (1962) combined with covert sensitization. He concluded that at the time of a 32-week follow-up all patients had been successfully treated with no negative secondary reactions noted.

Anant (1967) combined relaxation, breathing exercises, and covert sensitization to treat 25 alcoholics. The Ss were 24 males and one female, ranging in age from 19 to 55. The Ss were given five treatment sessions. A session in this case was not one meeting, but a series of meetings, each series representing a stage of treatment. Anant did not specify clearly the details of the treatment sessions. He reports, however that all 25 Ss were abstinent from 8 to 15 months after treatment. No relapses occurred up to the time that the paper was written. No control group was used in this study.

Covert Reinforcement

As evidence began to accumulate to indicate that covert sensitization was an effective procedure for reducing the frequency of covert and overt behaviors, I started to speculate as to the possibility of presenting a reinforcing stimulus in imagination to increase the probability of particular responses. If an aversive stimulus presented in imagination, via instructions, had properties similar to an externally applied stimulus, why would a reinforcing stimulus presented in imagination not function in a manner similar to an externally applied reinforcement? This reasoning led to the formulation of a procedure labeled "covert reinforcement" (COR) (Cautela, 1970). The term "covert reinforcement" is used because both the response to be increased and the reinforcing stimulus are both presented in imagination via instructions. The word "reinforcement" is used because the object of the procedure is to increase response probability. The term "reinforcement" was also used to make explicit that the procedure could be enforced by taking into account vast amount of data concerning the parameters of reinforcement.

Though, in principle, COR can be used to modify a wide range of behavior, this paper will be limited to the application of COR to maladaptive behavior. COR has been used to modify both maladaptive approach and maladaptive avoidance behaviors. There are two COR procedures: covert positive reinforcement (CPR) and covert negative reinforcement(CNR). First, the CPR procedure will be described together with examples of clinical application and supportive experimental studies. Second, the covert negative reinforcement procedure will be described with clinical examples and one study providing indirect evidence of the occurrence of CNR. Another study providing supporting evidence will also be presented.

Covert Positive Reinforcement

After it has been determined from the usual behavioral analysis of a patient (Cautela, 1968) that CPR is indicated, the first step in the procedure is to discover possible reinforcing stimuli. For this goal, three possible sources are utilized. The main source for identifying reinforcing stimuli is the reinforcement survey schedule (RSS) (Cautela & Kastenbaum, 1967), which is administered as part of the behavioral analysis. A second method of determining possible reinforcers is to ask the patient to suggest other events not on the RSS which would be pleasurable to him. Further information about possible reinforcing stimuli can be derived from case histories, relatives, friends, and ward personnel (if the patient is institutionalized).

It is important to have a number of possible reinforcing stimuli available for each patient so that satiation will not occur. Ayllon and Azrin (1968, pp. 119-120) found that if a reinforcer is used too frequently, it can lose its effectiveness. For this reason, the reinforcers are often varied, even within the same session.

Description of the procedure. When CPR is used, it is not necessary formally to teach relaxation, nor is it necessary to construct a hierarchy as in the desensitization procedure.

Whereas desensitization is used to modify maladaptive avoidance behavior, and covert sensitization is employed to modify maladaptive approach, the CPR procedure can be used to modify both maladaptive approach and avoidance behaviors. A typical example of the application of the CPR procedure is presented below.

A male *S* treated for homosexuality, who had lost sexual urges toward males by the use of covert sensitization, was reluctant to call a girl for a date. He claimed he was nervous and sometimes even forgot our instructions about calling a particular girl he knew well. He was instructed then as follows:

> In a minute I'm going to ask you to try and relax and close your eyes. Then I will describe a scene to you. When you can imagine the scene as clearly as possible, raise your right index finger. I will then say the word "reinforcement." As soon as I say the word, "reinforcement," try to imagine the reinforcing scene we practiced before, the one about swimming on a hot day, feeling the refreshing water, and feeling wonderful. As soon as the reinforcing scene is clear, raise your finger. Do you understand the instruction? Remember to try to imagine everything as vividly as possible, as if you were really there. All right, now close your eyes and try to relax.

After the patient has closed his eyes and appears comfortable, the therapist presents a scene such as this one:

> I want you to imagine that you are at home in the kitchen and you say to yourself, "I think I'll call Jane for a date." When you have the scene clearly, raise your finger. [As soon as he raises his finger to signal clear imagery, the experimenter says "reinforcement."] Was the delivery of the reinforcement clear? All right, let's continue. After you've decided to call Jane, you walk toward the phone and you start to dial. Raise your finger when this is clear ["reinforcement"]. All right, you have finished dialing. Jane answers. You say, "Hello" and ask her if she is free Saturday night and tell her that you would like to take her out. Raise your finger when this is clear ["reinforcement"]. Now do the whole procedure yourself. Imagine you decide to call. Deliver the reinforcement to yourself. Imagine you are dialing. Deliver the reinforcement to yourself. Then imagine you are asking for a date and deliver the reinforcement to yourself. When you are all finished raise your index finger. Now take your time. Make sure you get clear imagery. You can see the kitchen; you can see and feel the telephone, etc. Also try to imagine that you are comfortable and confident while you are in the kitchen going through the procedure. All right. Start.

After the finger is raised, the therapist asks the following questions: "Was everything clear?"; "Did you have any trouble?" He then asks him to try it again. After the patient has practiced the entire sequence, he is told to practice twice a day at home, doing the procedure twice each practice session. He is urged to try to actually make the call and when he is about to call, he is told to deliver the reinforcement to himself at the same places as he did in imagination.

Other Scenes Employed in the Successful Use of CPR

1. Response to be increased: relaxation during an examination:

It is the day of the examination and you feel confident ["reinforcement"]. You are entering the building in which the exam is going to be given ["reinforcement"]. You remember that in all the scenes you are to try to feel confident. Now you enter the building and go to the classroom ["reinforcement"]. You sit down and kid around with another student who is taking the exam ["reinforcement"]. The proctor comes in with the exam. You feel good; you know you are ready ["reinforcement"]. The proctor hands out the exam ["reinforcement"]. You read the questions and you feel you can answer all of them ["reinforcement"].
Now let's do that again. This time you look the questions over and you are not sure about one of the questions, but you say, "Oh well, I can still pass the exam if I flunk this one question ["reinforcement"]." All right, this time you look over the exam and you see two questions about which you are in doubt, and you say, "Well, I can still pass the exam if I take my time and relax ["reinforcement"]."

2. Response to be increased: thinking pleasant thoughts about females (for male homosexuals).

I want you to imagine you see a luscious looking girl on the street and you say to yourself, "Oh boy, I'd love to feel her soft skin against my body ["reinforcement"]." Then think to yourself, "I can have more fun with girls in sex than with men if I try hard ["reinforcement"]."

3. Response to be increased: appropriate clothes folding. A woman patient who exhibited compulsive clothes-folding behavior was presented with the following scene:

Relax and imagine that you're in your living room, feeling content ["reinforcement"]. You think to yourself, "I think I'll go downstairs and fold clothes—I have a few minutes ["reinforcement"]." You casually saunter into the laundry room and look at the clothes piled up, thinking to yourself, "This will only take a few minutes ["reinforcement"]."
Imagine you're on the stairs leading to the laundry room and you're thinking that you really have to hurry with folding these clothes so you can go shopping with a friend ["reinforcement"]. You're standing in front of the table with the clothes piled up and impatiently shove them aside ["reinforcement"]. You fold one thing, for example, your daughter's pajamas, and quickly put it aside ["reinforcement"]. You take the next piece, fold it quickly and it's a little wrinkled, but you put it on top of the other things ["reinforcement"].

Experimental studies employing CPR. Since the recent publication of my article on COR, there have been four unpublished studies concerned with testing the efficacy of the COR procedure. Cautela, Steffen, and Wish (1970) performed a study to determine if covert reinforcement (CPR) could increase the frequency of an over- or underestimation of circle size. Subjects were shown slides of circles and asked to estimate the diameter of each circle. Baselines of mean estimates were established for each *S*. Some *S*s were given CPR after underestimating and others after overestimating diameter size. (No *S* was reinforced for both over- and underestimation.) This group was compared with other groups who were (a) not given CPR; (b) given noncontingent CPR (CPR was presented in a predetermined manner, not dependent on person's responses); (c) and a group which received the word "reinforcement," after an over- or underestimation. The results of the experiment indicate that the *S*s in the group given CPR gave more over- or underestimation than any other group.

Analysis of variance revealed a difference significant at the 0.01 level of significance in the amount of over- or underestimation between groups. A Duncan Multiple-Range test showed the CPR group differed from the word "reinforcement" group at the 0.05 level, and all other groups at the 0.01 level. When the non-CPR groups were compared with each other, there were no significant differences.

In another study, Cautela, Walsh, and Wish (unpublished data, 1970) employed CPR to change attitudes (self-report responses) of college students toward retardates. Forty *S*s were administered attitude questionnaires about mentally retarded individuals. The CPR group was asked to imagine a retarded person, then the *E* said "shift," and they imagined a reinforcing scene. The control group was asked to imagine the retarded person only. Both groups were asked to practice at home. Posttest questionnaires were administered 2 weeks later. A two-tailed *t* test showed a significant change ($p < .01$) of attitudes in a positive direction in the CPR group and no difference ($p < .05$) in the non-CPR group.

Kropp (unpublished data, 1970) performed an experiment to determine if overt and covert reinforcement can influence children's self-concept. Thirty-four children (mean age 10.3 years) diagnosed as having various behavior disorders (some were diagnosed as psychotic) were administered the Tennessee Department of Mental Health Self-Concept Scale (44 items were chosen). The *E* would read an item such as, "I am satisfied with the way I am." The child was instructed to answer true if it applied to him and false if it did not. Then the children were assigned to one of three groups: a covert reinforcement group, an overt reinforcement group, and a control group. One day later the *E* again read the items to the children. This time, after he read a positive item, the children in the covert reinforcement group were asked to imagine a pleasant scene. Those in the overt reinforcement group were either given candy (or a token as the children were already involved in a token economy). In the control group, the *S*s were just read the items and nothing was said. A third trial was administered 1 hr later, and was similar to the first trial in which the children had to answer true or false to the statements read. An analysis of variance showed a significant difference at the .05 level between the three groups. An analysis of variance difference test showed that the covert reinforcement group was the only group that changed significantly from the first to the third test. A 2-week follow-up revealed that the change for the covert reinforcement group was maintained, still at the .05 level.

In an excellent study, Flannery (unpublished data, 1970) compared the effectiveness of CPR when Ss were in the presence of the anxiety stimulus (a rat) to a second condition in which Ss were instructed to imagine the anxiety stimulus. By various pretests, he matched four groups of 15 female Ss on fear of rats. In one group, he had the Ss imagine the reinforcing scene while they were asked to approach the rat. In another group, the Ss were asked to imagine that they were approaching the rat and then they were presented the reinforcing stimulus (in imagination). In the third group, discussions were held concerning the fear of rats. The fourth group was a no-contact control group. Posttest scores on actual approach behavior to the rat showed a significant change ($p < .05$, one-way analysis of variance) in approach behavior for both CPR groups, but no change in the talking group or the control group. The first group (rat actually present) was not significantly different from the imagination only group.

Covert Negative Reinforcement

While the CPR procedures, in general, are applicable to various types of maladaptive approach and avoidance behaviors, there are some patients with whom the CPR procedure does not appear applicable. In a few cases, patients complain that they cannot think of anything that is pleasurable. Some of the patients are those who label themselves as depressive. No matter how much the therapist tries to insist that there must be something pleasurable in their lives, the patients persist in saying there is nothing. Also there are some patients who claim that there are very few reinforcing events in their lives and when they try to imagine them they cannot obtain clear imagery. Both these types of patients usually admit that they can clearly imagine unpleasant events because they have encountered unpleasant situations most of their lives.

In the author's experience, the desensitization procedure (Wolpe, 1958) is often too difficult to apply to both the patients who claim they cannot get clear imagery or who cannot think of anything pleasurable in their lives. These patients are often difficult to teach to relax. Also, some of these patients claim that as soon as they try to relax and imagine any scene they get anxious or tense. For patients with whom neither CPR nor desensitization is applicable, it is often possible to use CNR with some success. Covert negative reinforcement is based on the escape-conditioning paradigm. In the escape-conditioning procedure, the withdrawal of a stimulus (noxious) is contingent upon a particular predesignated response made by the organism. There is much evidence that the escape-conditioning procedure increases response probability (Dinsmoore, 1968). Covert negative reinforcement has been employed effectively to reduce both maladaptive avoidance and maladaptive approach behavior.

Description of the procedure. When employing CNR, special attention is focused on describing stimuli that are aversive to the patient. The fear survey schedule (FSS) (Wolpe & Lang, 1964) and interview questions such as, "What is the worst situation you can imagine?" are employed to obtain aversive stimuli for use in the CNR technique. The patient is also asked to indicate if there are any stimuli or situations not on the FSS that cause anxiety or discomfort. He is then asked to try to close his eyes and imagine the stimulus situation. Noxious stimuli used for the escape conditioning are chosen on the basis of S's report that he can obtain clear imagery and the image can be erased immediately on request. It is also important to determine if the anxiety responses are eliminated or greatly reduced when the therapist says, "response," in order that a noxious situation is not contiguous with the response to be increased.

The paradigm for the procedure is: The noxious scene is imagined. When the scene is clear and the patient raises his finger, the therapist says "response." The patient immediately erases the noxious scene and imagines the response to be increased. When the patient feels the response scene is clear, he raises his index finger again. The therapist then inquires as to the clarity of the scenes and the ability of the patient to quickly remove the noxious scene. The patient is asked to relax. The therapist tells the patient to repeat the whole procedure by himself. Then the therapist again asks about the clarity of the scenes and the temporal removal of scenes. A more detailed example of the procedure is as follows:

> Close your eyes and relax as best as you can. [In CNR, formal relaxation is not necessary.] Now try to imagine as clearly as possible the following scene: you can feel yourself tied down in a chair in your living room. You don't see yourself there, but you try to imagine you are actually there. Now look around you. You can see all the furniture. You can feel the chair underneath you. Suddenly you see a snake coming toward you. You try to struggle to get away, but you can't. Now when this scene is very clear, raise your right index finger.

After the patient raises his finger, the therapist says "response," then immediately the patient erases the scene with the noxious stimulus and then imagines the response to be increased, e.g. walking into a room full of people and feeling comfortable. When the response is clear, the patient raises his finger. Homework is given in a manner similar to CPR.

Clinical applications. The following are examples of successful applications of CNR.

A girl who was afraid of walking more than a block from her house or a parked car, was asked to imagine her mother-in-law shouting at her (the noxious stimulus). When she signaled that the scene was clear, the therapist said the word "response," and she immediately imagined that she started to walk an extra block.

A patient who worked for a credit agency and disliked calling clients to remind them to pay their bills was asked to imagine he was calling clients and then shifted to a scene (response to be increased) in which he was calling a girl for a date.

A juvenile offender at a training school exhibited severe temper tantrums whenever a staff member denied his requests. His noxious scene was one of being teased by other boys. His response to be increased was "calm reaction" whenever he was refused a request. Within 1 week, the staff noted a decrease in his tantrum behavior.

A female with a fear of breezes who therefore avoided places with air conditioners, was asked to imagine her usually severe arthritic pain gone and then shift to a scene in which she was sitting next to an air conditioner blowing at her.

Covert negative reinforcement has also been used to modify maladaptive approach behaviors such as alcoholism, excessive smoking, homosexuality.

The patient is asked to imagine a noxious scene such as being in a gutter covered with mud, and then shift to a scene in which he refuses to engage in maladaptive behavior, e.g., refusing a drink when offered, turning down or not smoking a cigarette, turning down a homosexual advance.

Concerning CNR, there are two anecdotal observations worth noting:

1. Some patients report that the continued use of the same noxious stimulus leads to a loss of some of its aversive properties. This could have the double-barreled therapeutic effect of reducing the maladaptive response to the noxious stimulus used in the scene and also result in an increase in the appropriate response. However, the reduction in anxiety or discomfort to the noxious scene is not always desirable (e.g., an alcoholic finding it distasteful to lie in the gutter). This reduction of the maladaptive response to the noxious stimulus may be due to either satiation or to the fact that S has learned to make an appropriate response following the noxious stimulus, even though the appropriate response is not directly related to the noxious stimulus, e.g., "mother-in-law screaming" may be the noxious stimulus and "walking another block" may be the response to be increased.

2. There may be adaptive generalization effects from the use of CNR. The patient who had a fear of walking far from home reported that when a sudden and unpleasant event occurred (e.g., her kitchen stove blew up) she did not get discouraged or depressed as she usually did in such situations. Instead, for the first time in years, she walked five blocks away from home. One must be cautious, however, to be certain that she does not learn simply to avoid all unpleasant situations, rather than dealing with them.

Supportive experimental studies. Ascher and Cautela (unpublished data, 1970) provided an indirect test for the effect of CNR. Three groups of 10 Ss were used. Subjects in the CNR group were asked to imagine the most unpleasant scene they could and then shift to imagining the sound of a bell. Each S was given 30 trials pairing the noxious scene and the bell signaling the cessation of the noxious scene. In the second (nonpaired) group, Ss were asked to imagine a noxious scene 30 consecutive times and then imagine the sound of a bell 30 consecutive times. In this group, the noxious scene was never followed by the scene of the bell. A third group was a control group, which was never asked to imagine any scenes.

After the scene presentations, all Ss were individually asked to estimate the size of circles projected on a screen in a series of four trials of 18 responses each. At no time during the experiment, were Ss given any feedback concerning their results.

The first trial was the same for all experimental Ss. Each S estimated the size of 18 circles and the mean size estimation was computed for each circle size. In the second trial, one half (randomly chosen) of the CNR and the nonpaired groups were instructed to hear a bell whenever they overestimated. In the third trial, the Ss were asked to estimate as in the first trial, and they were not asked to imagine any scene. In the fourth trial in a counterbalancing fashion (according to whether they were instructed to under- or overestimate on the second trial), one half of each group was instructed to underestimate and the other half to overestimate.

Analysis of variance showed significant differences at the .01 level among the three groups. A one-by-three analysis of variance applied to the CNR group showed significant differences at the .01 level for the amount of under- or overestimation as compared with the baseline scores, whereas the scores in the other two groups did not differ from the baseline scores. In fact, in all conditions, except when CNR was used, the scores were equivalent, including the third trial of the CNR group, in which size estimations were made without CNR being employed.

In this experiment, it appears that the bell took on the properties of a conditioned reinforcer. Though there is contradictory evidence (Rescorla, 1969) that the stimulus following the cessation of a noxious stimulus can pick up reinforcing properties, some Pavlovian studies (Rescorla & Lolordo, 1965; Moscovitz & Lolordo, 1968; Rescorla, 1969) indicate that such stimuli can be used to inhibit anxiety. If, in our experiment, the bell did pick up reinforcing properties, one can assume that, in our clinical work, the response to be increased picks up reinforcing properties and then there will tend to be an increase in the performance of that response.

A study was performed by Cautela and Wisocki (1969a) which, though not published as a direct test of CNR, appears to be relevant in supporting the CNR procedure as effective. Forty-nine undergraduate Ss received a checklist composed of 18 positive statements and 22 negative statements about elderly people. Subjects were asked to rate each item along a scale of varying response tendency according to how they felt about each item. One week later, the experimental group of Ss was asked to imagine a scene in which they were bleeding and in pain and were comforted by an elderly person. They were told to practice imagining this scene twice a day. Ten days later, the experimental and control groups of Ss were given the same questionnaire. The experimental group showed a significant positive increase in attitudes toward the aged ($p < .01$). The control group score showed a slightly negative, nonsignificant change ($p < .05$). Subjects who reported practicing the scene at home, showed a significantly higher increase in scores ($p < .01$) than did the Ss who did not report additional trials.

Summary

The anecdotal and experimental evidence presented in this chapter indicates that when Ss are asked to imagine noxious and reinforcing stimuli, behavior is affected in a manner similar to that which occurs when noxious and reinforcing stimuli are presented externally. Further investigation is needed to indicate the influence of various parameters on the effectiveness of the procedures described.

References

Anant, S. S. A note on the treatment of alcoholics by a verbal aversion technique. *Canadian Psychologist,* 1967, **1**, 19-22.
Ashem, B., & Donner, L. Covert sensitization with alcoholics: A controlled replication. *Behaviour Research & Therapy,* 1968, **6**, 7-12.
Ascher, M., & Cautela, J. R. Covert negative reinforcement: An experimental test. Unpublished test, New York State Univ. at Fredonia, 1970.
Ayllon, T., & Azrin, N. *The token economy.* New York: Appleton, 1968.
Barber, T. X. *Hypnosis: A scientific approach.* New York: Van Nostrand, 1969.
Barber, T. X., Chauncey. H. H., & Winer, R. A. Effect of hypnotic and nonhypnotic suggestions on parotid gland response to gustatory stimuli. *Psychosomatic Medicine,* 1964, **26**, 364-380.
Barber, T. X., & Hahn, K. W., Jr. Physiological and subjective responses to pain producing stimulation under hypnotically suggested and waking-imagined "analgesia." *Journal of Abnormal and Social Psychology,* 1962, **65**, 411-418.
Barlow, D., Leitenberg, H., & Agras, W. S. The effect of instructions in the use of covert sensitization. Unpublished study, Univ. of Vermont, 1969. (a)
Barlow, D. H., Leitenberg, H., & Agras, W. S. Experimental control of sexual deviation through manipulation of the noxious scene in covert sensitization. *Journal of Abnormal Psychology,* 1969, **5**, 596-601. (b)

Cautela, J. R. The problem of backward conditioning. *The Journal of Psychology*, 1965, **60**, 135-144.

Cautela, J. R. Treatment of compulsive behavior by covert sensitization. *Psychological Record*, 1966, **16**, 33-41.

Cautela, J. R. Covert Sensitization. *Psychological Record*, 1967, **20**, 459-468.

Cautela, J. R. Behavior therapy and the need for behavioral assessment. *Psychotherapy: Theory, Research and Practice*, **5**, Fall, 1968, 175-179.

Cautela, J. R. Behavior therapy and self-control: techniques and implications. In Cyril Franks (Ed.), *Behavior therapy: Appraisal and status.* New York: McGraw-Hill, 1969, pp. 323-340.

Cautela, J. R. Covert reinforcement. *Behavior Therapy*, 1970, **1**, 33-50.

Cautela, J. R., & Baron, M. G. The treatment of self-injurious behavior: a multifaceted behavior therapy approach. Unpublished paper, 1970.

Cautela, J. R., & Kastenbaum, R. A reinforcement survey schedule for use in therapy and research. *Psychological Report*, 1967, **20**, 115-130.

Cautela, J. R., Walsh, K., & Wish, P. The use of covert reinforcement to modify attitudes toward retardates. Unpublished study, Boston College, 1970.

Cautela, J. R., Steffen, J., & Wish, P. An experimental test of Covert Reinforcement. Paper presented at the American Psychological Association in Miami, September, 1970.

Cautela, J. R., & Wisocki, P. A. The use of imagery in the modification of attitudes toward the elderly: A preliminary report. *Journal of Psychology*, 1969, **73**, 193-199. (a)

Cautela, J. R., & Wisocki, P. The use of male and female therapists in the treatment of homosexual behavior. *Advances in Behavior Therapy*, 1969, 165-174. (b)

Davison, G. Elimination of a sadistic fantasy by a client-controlled counter-conditioning technique: A case study. *Journal of Abnormal Psychology*, 1968, **73**, 84-89.

Dinsmoor, J. A. Escape from shock as a conditioning technique. In M. Jones (Ed.), *Miami symposium on the prediction of behavior, 1967: Aversive stimulation.* Miami: Univ. of Miami Press, 1968.

Ferster, C. B., Nurnberger, J. I., & Levitt, E. B. The control of eating. *Journal of Mathetics*, 1962, **1**, 87-110.

Flannery, R. An investigation of differential effectiveness of office vs. *in vivo* therapy of a simple phobia: an outcome study. Unpublished doctoral dissertation, Univ. of Windsor, 1970.

Franks, C. Reflections upon the treatment of sexual disorders by the behavioral clinicians: An historical comparison with the treatment of the alcoholic. *The Journal of Sex Research*, 1967, **3**, 212, 222.

Guthrie, E. R. *The psychology of learning.* New York: Harper, 1935.

Hahn, K. W., Jr., & Barber, T. X. Hallucinations with and without hypnotic induction: An extension of the Brady and Levitt study. Harding, Massachusetts: Medfield Foundation, 1966.

Homme, L. E. Perspectives in psychology—XXIV: Control of coverants, the operants of the mind. *Psychological Record*, 1965, **15**, 501-511.

Hull, C. L. *A behavior system.* New Haven: Yale Univ. Press, 1952.

Jacobson, E. *Progressive relaxation.* Chicago: Univ. of Chicago Press, 1938.

Kanfer, F. H., & Marston, A. R. Conditioning of self-reinforcement responses: An analogue to self-confidence training. *Psychological Reports*, 1963, **13**, 63-70.

Kimble, G. A. *Hilgard & Marquis' Conditioning and learning.* New York: Appleton, 1961.

Kropp, H. The use of covert reinforcement to modify children's self-concept. Unpublished data, South Florida State Hospital, 1970.

Lazarus, A. A., & Abramovitz, A. The use of "emotive imagery" in the treatment of children's phobias. *Journal of Mental Science*, 1962, **108**, 191-195.

McGuire, N. J., & Valence, M. Aversion therapy by electric shock: A simple technique. *British Medical Journal,* 1964, **1,** 151-153.

Moskowitz, A., & Lolordo, V. M. Role of safety in the Pavlovian backward fear conditioning procedure. *Journal of Comparative and Physiological Psychology,* 1968, **66,** 673-678.

Mowrer, O. H. An experimental analysis of "regression" with incidental observations on "reaction-formation." *Journal of Abnormal and Social Psychology,* 1940, **35,** 56-87.

Mullen, F. G. The effect of covert sensitization on smoking behavior. Unpublished study, Queens College, Charlottesville, North Carolina, 1968.

Murray, E. J., & Jacobson, L. T. The nature of learning in traditional psychotherapy. In Bergin & S. L. Garfield (Eds), *Handbook of psychotherapy and behavior change.* New York: Wiley, 1969.

Pavlov, I. P. *Conditioned reflexes.* Translated by G. V. Anrep. London: Oxford Univ. Press, 1927.

Pavlov, I. P. *Selected works.* Translated by S. Belsky; J. Gobbons (Ed.). Moscow: Foreign Languages Publishing House, 1955.

Premack, D. Toward empirical behavior laws: I. Positive reinforcement. *Psychological Review,* 1959, **66,** 219-233.

Rescorla, R. A. Pavlovian conditioned inhibition. *Psychological Bulletin,* 1969, **72,** 77-94.

Rescorla, R. A., & Lolordo, V. M. Inhibition of avoidance behavior. *Journal of Comparative and Physiological Psychology,* 1965, **59,** 406-412.

Skinner, B. F. *The behavior of organisms: An experimental analysis.* New York: Appleton, 1938.

Skinner, B. *Contingencies of reinforcement.* New York: Appleton, 1969. (a)

Skinner, B. F. The machine that is man. *Psychology Today,* 1969, **2**(11), 20-25. (b)

Stampfl, T. G. Implosive therapy, Part I: The theory. In S. G. Armitage (Ed.), *Behavior modification techniques and the treatment of emotional disorders.* Battle Creek, Michigan: V. S. Publications, 1967.

Stuart, R. Behavioral control of over-eating. *Behavior Research and Therapy,* 1967, **5,** 357-365.

Viernstein, L. Evaluation of therapeutic techniques of covert sensitization. Unpublished data, Queens College, Charlottesville, North Carolina, 1968.

Wagner, M. Smokers of the world unite. *Association for the Advancement of Behavioral Therapies Newsletter,* 1969, **4,** 12.

Wagner, M. K., & Bragg, R. A. Comparing behavior modification methods for habit decrement—smoking. Unpublished data, V. A. Hospital, Salisbury, North Carolina, 1968.

Wolpe, J. *Psychotherapy by reciprocal inhibition.* Stanford: Stanford Univ. Press, 1958.

Wolpe, J., & Lang, P. J. A fear survey schedule for use in behavior therapy. *Behavior Research and Therapy,* 1964, **2,** 27-30.

Mood—Emotion—Affect: The Nature of and Manipulation of Affective States with Particular Reference to Positive Affective States and Emotional Illness

Alfred Jacobs

West Virginia University
Morgantown, West Virginia

This paper is addressed to selected aspects of the nature and modification of affective states. The material is based primarily upon studies performed in collaboration with former students and colleagues, or student research that I supervised or helped to design. Monumental amounts of data and speculation by others exist in the literature, and, although I will try to refer to that portion which is relevant to the directions of my own research interests, I do not believe that the scope of this paper is an appropriate vehicle for an attempt to integrate the amount of material that exists.

The pages that follow will describe our attempts to generate hypotheses about the nature of emotional events, and to develop instruments to enable us to do research on affect. I will summarize the results of our explorations of emotion in the "emotionally disturbed," and our attempts to modify moods, particularly to induce positive moods in mental-hospital patients by a variety of complex stimulus manipulations. Our attempts to study the development of emotions in a conditioning paradigm will be presented, and finally an attempt will be made to speculate on what avenues might be profitable for future research. I do not believe that research on mood and emotion is merely an academic exercise, rather that the alteration of emotional states has significant and practical implications.

In the material that follows, affective states will be considered as members of the general category of concepts referred to as intervening variables. Many authors have defined affective states in terms of the operations used to induce the state, others in terms of various verbal, physiological, or social responses measured. Still others have defined affective states in terms of both antecedent operations and specific responses. In general, we have considered affective states as arbitrary and hopefully convenient categories for conceptualizing certain data, in order to help us gain understanding and control over important dimensions of behavior.

On a more descriptive level, we have more recently begun to conceptualize affective states as covert hedonic responses, represented centrally and in awareness. We hypothesize that affective responses are primarily generated from experiences with reinforcing states of affairs, following somewhat the theorizing of such authors as McClelland (1951) and Mowrer (1960). The presence or absence of two major classes of reinforcements—aversive and positive—and the typical responses to each contingency create a number of classes of affective states. In studies using adjective-checklists, we have been concerned with how many such classes exist.

The first two studies to be presented address themselves to the question of the numbers and types of response classes (dimensions) that are necessary for an adequate conceptualization of the area of mood and emotion, a problem of concern to a number of authors in recent years (Jacobs, Meehan, & Capek, 1959a; Jacobs, Meehan, Dale, & Weinstein, 1964; Nowlis, 1965; Plutchick, 1962). The first study explored the type of affective dimensions existing in a 173-item adjective-checklist designed to measure emotional responses, originally developed by Nowlis (1953), to which we had added a large number of adjectives.

The adjective-checklist was administered to 347 college students who had been exposed to tape-recorded narratives designed to arouse fear, depression, and feelings of well-being (Jacobs *et al.,* 1959b, 1960, 1961) and to a neutral lecture, which served as a control condition (Jacobs *et al.,* 1964). Responses to each adjective were analyzed in addition to other variables such as personality test scores and type of experimental condition. The last 40 variables were factor-analyzed with the first 40 and then six additional factor-analyses were performed to overlap the complete set of variables. Twenty-two factors were extracted by the Varimax method of Kaiser; of these, 14 factors were specific to the adjective-checklist items and accounted for 31% of the variance. Three factors included both personality test items and other variables; these accounted for 40% of the variance.

The first two adjective-checklist factors emerging seem to be complex in nature and were therefore refactored separately to yield four factors, which were named happiness, friendliness, unhappiness, and apprehensiveness. The adjectives in these four new factors plus three other factors that had a clear meaning were temporarily eliminated from the list, and a separate factor-analysis was performed for the remaining adjectives to clarify their structure. A third factor-analysis was performed on all adjectives that had been shown by a chi-square test to differentiate between experimental condition (that is, fear- or depression-narrative and control), at better than the .05 level of significance or were contained in the factors from the first factor-analysis which loaded on experimental conditions. Five factors that appeared to be related to happiness, unhappiness, fear, unresponsiveness, and work attitudes were extracted. These "sensitive to change factors" overlapped considerably three 14-item scales named happiness, depression, and fear, which had been previously developed in an empirical–rational manner to measure changes (Jacobs *et al.*, 1959a).

Considerable overlap existed among the three sets of adjective-checklist factors thus far produced, so adjectives and factors which appeared identical were combined or eliminated until 21 scales, most of which were five items in extent, were produced. A computer program that made it possible to obtain weighted total scores for *S*s on these scales was created. The adjective-checklist was given to a second group of 157 *S*s who heard the depression tape or served as control *S*s. The responses of these *S*s to the adjective-checklist were scored according to the 21 scales described above. The scores were then intercorrelated.

The intercorrelations suggested that two major clusters of factors were derived. The first was a triad of interrelationships with what was tentatively named "energy" or "activity" as a core and with positive emotions and anger as the other two variables in this cluster. Both positive emotions, and, to a somewhat lesser extent, anger, appeared to be positively related to the energy or activity factors.

The second cluster appeared more complex and included fear, which appeared to be related to a cluster of interrelated withdrawal, inhibitory or avoidance kinds of factors. The second cluster also included depression, which was highly correlated with fear. Depression had its highest relationships to what might be called "lack of energy," "passiveness," or "sickness" kinds of factors to which we gave names like "disinterested" and "quiet." As we have found in other studies, depression had a high correlation with the anger cluster and related negatively to factors in the energy and positive emotion clusters.

The adjective-checklist that had been administered to the 157 *S*s in the second group was also independently analyzed as a quasi-replication by seven overlapping factor-analyses using the Varimax method of the Kaiser as in the first analysis. Factors that were extracted from this second set of analyses were found to overlap with the factors derived from Study 1 despite differences in experimental conditions, *S*s, type of instructions, and an independent set of *E*s performing the second factor analysis.

The two lists of factors, those derived from Study 1 and those from Study 2, plus a table of the highest correlations (greater than .35) abstracted from the table of intercorrelations of scales scores of Study 1 were given to graduate students in psychology as a class project. My judgment had been that 15 of the factors in Study 2 are identifiable with those in Study 1. An additional four were somewhat suggested. Of ten student papers, which were presented in such a way that the judgment with respect to the amount of replication could be made, the median amount of replication was 13 factors.

The results of the two studies suggest a number of hypotheses about dimensions of emotion.

(1) Emotions seem to belong to one of two major clusters characterized by either a positive or generally negative hedonic tone.

(2) Positive emotions cluster around energizing or activity factors; the negative emotions cluster around an inactivity or weakness factor.

(3) Anger does not fit well into the schema. Anger seems to be weakly related to the energizing factor, but not at all to the inactivity, although anger is related to the negative emotions.

(4) Within each cluster, qualitative differences exist between emotions and given rise to such separate factors as fear or depression within the negative cluster.

(5) The levels of intensity of affective responses appear to be phenomenologically separate, and emerge as separate factors, for example, in the anger dimension, rage, anger and annoyance.

(6) Certain types of affective social interaction emerge from the analyses as independent factors, as in fear of humans, that is, shyness, positive emotion about humans, sociability.

(7) The factors in the clusters with negative hedonic tone seem to be more complexly related than the positive. However, this may be an artifact of fewer adjectives with positive hedonic aspects in the original adjective-checklist.

(8) Lack of energy or deactivation seems to include inhibitory factors such as sluggish or quiet, impairment of function factors such as weakness or sickness. Withdrawal or avoidance also seem to be related to this complex.

(9) The data also suggest that separate factors exist for intellective and/or verbal, physical and/or physiological aspects of negative emotion. For example, in fear, the intellective factor might be called "worried," the physical factor "jittery."

(10) Depression appears to be more highly related to inactivity, weakness, and illness factors than it is to fear, or than the positive emotions are related to energy or vigor.

(11) Gratefulness, relief, and other emotions that we have identified in other studies do not appear in this analysis. Perhaps the conditions for inducing them were absent.

TABLE 1. Hypothesized Dimensions of Affect

		Positive hedonic tone		Negative hedonic tone			
		Energy	Well-being	Hostility Aggression	Depression	Anxiety	Deactivation Lack of energy
Intensity factors	I	Excited Aroused	Elated Ecstatic	Infuriated Enraged	Hopeless Despair		Exhausted Spent
	II	Vigorous Energetic	Happy Glad	Angry Mad	Discouraged Dejected		Apathetic Listless
	III	Peppy Active	Contented Pleased	Annoyed Irritated	Somber Glum		Quiet Still
Other							(Sleep) Drowsy Sleepy
							(Sickness) Sick Faint
Social		(a) Assertive Bold (b) Ambitious Diligent	(a) Sociable Friendly (b) Affectionate Kindly	Revengeful Punitive	(a) Ashamed Disgraced (b) Grief Mournful	(a) Shy Bashful (b) Seclusive Withdrawn (c) Aloof Stand-offish	Idle Lazy
Intellective verbal factors		Engrossed Intent	Witty Amusing	Sarcastic Critical	(a) Pessimistic Skeptical (b) Brooding Pensive	Worried Fretful	Disinterested Bored
Physical or physiological factors			(a) Carefree Lively (b) Relaxed At ease	Violent Destructive	Weepy Sad-faced	Shaky Jittery	

Table 1 presents a hypothesized table of emotions in terms of the dimensions of positive or negative hedonic tone, levels of intensity, and social, physical, and intellective aspects. Two adjective-responses are presented to illustrate each scale, although each of the complete scales has at least five items in the *Jacobs Survey of Mood and Affect II* (JSMA). Some of the scales are derived from our own studies, some are completely armchaired because the dimensions we believe we have already found suggest that such factors may exist. I might add that the value of such models is in their usefulness in generating hypotheses. I have taken liberties with scales reported by Nowlis (1965) in his thorough summary of his own extensive work in this area as well as that of the work of others (McNair & Lorr, 1964; Thayer, 1967), and have modified them to better test out hypotheses.

I am not satisfied with these four affect clusters and two energy clusters. The depression cluster for one seems to comprise too wide a range—that is, guilt, grief, unhappiness—a better conceptualization may be possible. The emergence of emotional-intensity levels as separate factors may be an artifact which represents some cultural restrictions in the expression of strong affect, or different habitual response tendencies associated with different levels. However, others (Maier, 1956) have also speculated that there may be phase changes at transition points between anger and rage, for example. Dimensions of the activation and deactivation clusters are unclear, and separate speed and strength dimensions may exist as well as intensity levels. I may say that so far I have a preference for considering all the factors to be unipolar, agreeing with Nowlis (1965), Nowlis and Cohen (1968), and Lorr, Daston, and Smith (1967). Concepts like ambivalence—that is, combinations of love-fear or love-hate—have a long and honorable history in psychological theories. Some of our research suggests that certain activation and deactivation factors may vary independently, as well.

The relationships between emotional factors and energy or lack of energy dimensions may be much more complicated than can be accounted for by the model. In a study of the induction of frustration, for example (Brown & Jacobs, 1967; Brown, 1966), with 120 Ss we found the correlations of low to high levels of anger on the JSMAI with energy to run .10, .35, .03, and with lack of energy to run .20, .25, .35; that is, that moderate levels of anger are correlated with energy, and higher and lower levels with lack of energy. Levels of fear and well being may also have complicated relationships to energy or lack thereof. Sociability, positive work attitudes, and humor may be strongly bound up with social approval as a common determinant. In any case, we have found it difficult to derive such separate factors except by refactoring more complex factors.

The attack of a second study (Dale, Jacobs, & Mehan, 1964) centered on the connotative meanings ascribed to emotional words. Specifically, this study was concerned with whether factor-analysis of semantic differential ratings of words purporting to represent emotional states would demonstrate that such words were indeed independent concepts. Subjects consisted of 58 experimental and 76 controls drawn from undergraduate classes. The semantic-differential rating scales of emotions were presented as a booklet consisting of an instruction sheet followed by 16 pages of scales. At the top of each page, was one of the following emotional words to be rated: angry, ashamed, depressed, disgusted, embarrassed, excited, fearful, frustrated, grateful, guilty, happy, helpless, jealous, nervous, resentful, and sad. Subjects were required to rate each word, e.g., angry, on each of 9 bipolar point scales, e.g., positive negative, where 1 was positive and 7 negative. Bipolar adjective scales were chosen from the factor analysis by Osgood, Suci & Tannenbaum (1957), to load at least .80 on the evaluative (E), potency (P), or activity (A) factors (which are the three major dimensions of the semantic-differential scales) and negligibly on the other two. Three bipolar scales were chosen per factor and were presented in fixed order.

A taped narrative of 20-min duration had been prepared with the assistance of Gordon Hughes, formerly director of CBS radio (Jacobs *et al.,* 1960). The tape described, in a stream-of-consciousness technique, the feelings of a person at the funeral of a young child for whose death he feels responsible. Subjects in the experimental group listened to this tape for 3 min in a lighted classroom. The Guilford Zimmerman Temperament Survey was also administered to *S*s, and the JSMAI.

Twenty-five meaningful factors were extracted by the Varimax method of Kaiser. Of the 25 factors, 17 are derived from primarily the semantic differential data. Seven emotions (grateful, happy, excited, fearful, helpless, disgusted, and embarrassed) showed all three evaluative potency and activity ratings to have high factor-loadings on one of the factors which was extracted. In the case of resentful, frustrated, and ashamed, two of the dimensions of the semantic differential received high loadings on one of the factors extracted. Anger, depression, and nervousness may be considered independent dimensions of affect, because one of Osgood's dimensions clearly received a high loading on one factor extracted. Therefore, for 13 of the 16 adjective descriptions of mood states, it appears plausible to conclude that the analysis of the *S*s' semantic differential ratings identified these as separate dimensions or factors of emotional states. Sadness, on the other hand, does not appear to emerge anywhere as a separate factor, and guilt and jealousy have dubious support, being confounded with general factors.

In addition, some general factors appeared to be generated. Dimension one, negative evaluation, 27% of the semantic differential variance appeared to be heavily loaded by evaluation dimension ratings of a number of negative emotions such as resentful, jealous, nervous, and guilty. A second general factor we named negative-emotions activity (outer directed) and it was loaded the most heavily on activity ratings of jealous, angry, and excited. The third general factor consisted of the activity ratings of passive or intrapunitive emotions, and was loaded with the activity ratings of guilty, sad, ashamed, embarrassed, depressed and helpless. The fourth general factor consisted of the potency of negative emotions, for example, depressed potency, guilty potency, sadness potency, fearful potency.

Positive emotions did not generate a like set of dimensions. Perhaps the inclusion of more positive emotions would generate more general dimensions similar to that of the negative emotions.

TABLE 2. D^2 (Spatial Relationship) Scores for Semantic Differential Ratings of Emotional Concepts

		$(E - P)^a$	$(E - A)$	$(P - A)$
1.	Angry	8211	17,249	5942
2.	Resentful	7082	11,436	4610
3.	Jealous	6204	16,998	8692
4.	Grateful	6026	5550	2526
5.	Disgusted	5438	6617	2755
6.	Happy	5396	3081	3073
7.	Guilty	4633	6685	4072
8.	Frustrated	4623	7100	4867
9.	Depressed	4472	3655	4617
10.	Fearful	3036	5451	4529
11.	Sad	3018	4270	3452
12.	Ashamed	2924	3995	2967
13.	Excited	2919	4204	7165
14.	Embarrassed	2368	4355	4311
15.	Nervous	2259	12,375	9974
16.	Helpless	2106	3241	2223

Spatial-relationship scores based on the differences in E, A, and P ratings given to each emotion were generated from the data by Illiac at the University of Illinois from the generalized distance formula (Osgood *et al.*, 1957). For this purpose, the raw scores were summed over the three scales used for each of the sets of evaluational, potency and activity ratings and values of D^2 were computed which are listed in Table 2. Inspection of these scores reveals that the meaning of certain emotions is divided evenly and others very unevenly among the evaluation, potency and activity dimensions. For example, angry, jealous, resentful, and nervous show very large differences between the evaluational and the activity dimensions, suggesting that activity is an essential component of the meaning. Emotions such as frustrated and helpless are evenly divided in meaning among the E, A, and P dimensions, suggesting that none of the three dimensions is outstandingly different from the others in determining the meaning of the concept.

Table 3 lists the rank, mean scores of semantic-differential dimensions, and leads to the following conclusions.

(1) Semantic space for emotions in this analysis is defined at the extremes by happy and helpless in the evaluative and potency dimensions, and excited and helpless in the activity dimension.

(2) Few positive emotions were included in the analysis.

(3) The upper limits of potency of emotions do not appear to have been tapped.

(4) Helplessness seems to be the most negatively evaluated state as well as the least potent and active.

(5) Anger seems to be the most positively evaluated of the negative emotions.

TABLE 3. Mean Scores of Semantic-Differential Ratings of Emotional Concepts

	E	P	A
Happy	18.14458	14.84739	16.75100
Grateful	17.69478	14.30522	14.81526
Excited	14.89558	13.64659	17.31325
Anger	10.59036	13.46988	16.19277
Embarrassed	10.53414	10.27711	12.10843
Disgusted	10.40562	12.79519	13.22490
Fearful	10.08434	10.36145	12.29317
Ashamed	9.82329	10.55020	11.08032
Sad	9.81928	10.51406	9.69478
Nervous	9.75904	10.27711	14.38554
Guilty	9.23695	11.20482	11.83133
Frustrated	9.20080	11.07229	12.14056
Resentful	8.60643	11.52610	12.98795
Jealous	8.46988	10.65462	14.37751
Depressed	8.04016	10.31727	8.85944
Helpless	7.69880	7.97590	8.48193

In trying to fit the results of this study to those of the study previously reported, we have found here a general factor for adjectives of a negative hedonic tone, but for the positive hedonic tone, no general factor is hypothesized. We find some evidence for adjectives that one might expect to fall in the same dimension, but to be different in degree; for example, resentful and angry, or ashamed, and embarrassed, to emerge as separate factors. Again, we find some anomalies with respect to the anger dimension. Anger and jealousy load on the negative evaluational factor, and yet, are related to activity in a somewhat different way from other negative emotions such as guilt, ashamed, or depressed.

A prior study in this area by Block (1957) employed somewhat similar methods. Fifteen emotions were rated by the semantic-differential technique against 20 scales. The Block study produced two gross bipolar dimensions or emotions—pleasantness and unpleasantness—and level of activation, and a unipolar factor—interpersonal relatedness. Differences in factor-analytic techniques and emotional concepts, and the factor matrix employed probably account for the small number of dimensions.

Two other studies that I have run across have used the semantic-differential technique to study affect. The first (Sweeney, Tinling, Eby, & Schmale, 1968), using some of Osgood's scales and some developed by themselves, had *S*s rate the filmed responses, verbal associations, and drawings of *S*s in hypnotic and nonhypnotic states to 13 emotional words. The word itself and its definition were included in the ratings. Sweeney reports that all measures loaded consistently on four factors which he named evaluation, activity-potency, object relatedness, and temporality.

A second study reported by Plutchik (1962) supports our placing of anger in the positive affects, since he finds it shares more semantic-differential scales with joy than with fear, sadness, or any other emotions. Plutchik also plotted ratings of 20 emotional words on the evaluative and activity dimensions. His data suggest that anger words are active, and depression words, passive. Contrary to factor-analytic results of the first study we reported, but more in line with the second, he found a number of fear or anxiety words to fall in an *active,* bad quadrant of his plot.

At this point, we became concerned about the lack of manipulibles in our theorizing, and proceeded to a number of studies using Mowrer's theoretical discussion on relationships between emotional phenomena and conditioning as a point of departure (Mowrer, 1960). Mowrer posits four basic conditioning paradigms for emotions.

1. The onset of a stimulus previously associated with an aversive stimulus signifies danger and elicits fear.
2. The offset of a danger signal accompanied by omission of the aversive stimulus brings relief.
3. The onset of a signal that had previously anticipated successful avoidance of danger, and therefore signifies safety, is the operation for hope.
4. Disappointment is the offset of the safety signal without removal of the danger.

In an unpublished study, Skultin & Jacobs (1967) investigated affective verbal reports given by 30 college students conditioned to associate colored lights to an aversive stimulus (white noise) or to its absence—safety. The evidence suggested that Mowrer's fourfold category did not adequately represent the data. For example, the fear stimulus was followed by verbal reports of fear only slightly more frequently than disappointment and a relief stimulus (the offset of the stimulus associated with the white noise) was followed by reports of relief only slightly more frequently than hope.

Therefore, we decided to examine the possibility that positive affective states differed from negative in the conditions under which they were generated. More specifically, we began to suspect that positive affective states were more closely associated with reward or incentive motivation conditions rather than those of aversive reinforcement. Mowrer's fourfold category of conditioned cues was extended to an eightfold category. Onsets and offsets of discriminable danger and safety cues conditioned to a noxious stimulus were hypothesized to give rise to different states of affairs than those of conditioned cues anticipating contingencies of rewards or no reward.

In the first study reported by Skultin (1969), a test was constructed which described verbally the forthcoming or not forthcoming of punishments or rewards. For example, Item 1 said:

"Imagine a situation in which:

1. You were promised a worthwhile and needed reward. You feel＿＿ ,"

and the *S*s were asked to supply four words from a 73 item checklist. Item 2 said:

2. But later that promise, not the reward, is removed. You feel＿＿ .

The items were administered to graduate students in clinical psychology and to undergraduate *S*s. It seemed clear from examination of adjectives typically chosen under each hypothetical condition, that positive affective states, for example, happy, elation, hopeful, encouraged, optimistic, were associated with conditions of reward rather than those of punishment or no punishment. Denial and deprivation of rewards did not appear to be fear related. Freedom from threat did not produce hopefulness, and elation and hopefulness seemed to be much more reward-associated and not at all punishment-associated.

The most frequently chosen word for each reinforcement contingency in the study just reported was selected to make a list of eight adjectives. The stimulus events and the predicted adjectives which were tested in the next conditioning experiment are presented in Table 4. This final list fortunately contained the four stimulus contingencies and response-categories hypothesized as being related by Mowrer.

One hundred and twenty male and female undergraduate *S*s were assigned to one of three groups of *S*s who were given rewards or an aversive white-noise

TABLE 4.   Hypothesized Relationships among
Reinforcement Contingencies and Affective States
(Modified from Skultin, 1969)

Reinforcement contingency	Predicted adjective
Danger signal onset	Fearful
Danger signal offset	Relieved
Safety signal onset	Secure
Safety signal offset	Apprehensive
Reward expectation onset	Elated
Reward expectation offset	Disappointed
No reward expectation onset	Frustrated
No reward expectation offset	Hopeful

stimulus, or a control condition (neither reward nor aversive). Two conditioned stimuli were a field of blue and a field of yellow projected on a translucent screen placed on a table in front of a *S*. A 1-sec burst of white noise was presented simultaneously with the last second of presentation of the conditioned stimulus to an aversive reinforcement group during acquisition trials. Rewards, consisting of 25¢ per reinforced trial, were cumulated and displayed visually for the positive reinforcement group. Trials during a test phase were defined by six different conditioned stimulus-operations, each presented three times as follows: presentations of the color that was reinforced during acquisition and again reinforced in the same manner, presentations of the same reinforced color but with reinforcements omitted, presentations of the other color not reinforced during acquisition and again not reinforced, dark-screen periods (offsets of conditioned stimuli), which followed each of the above color stimuli. Subjects were required to report their feelings on each trial during the acquisition and test phases by choosing from the adjective response list one or more words which best described their feelings at that moment. Along with each word, the *S* was instructed to give a rating of the feeling's intensity on a seven-point scale. Adjectives not reported on a trial received a "0" rating of intensity. Subjects were also requested to report during each dark-screen period whether they had become aware of any relationship between the colors and the reinforcements.

The overall results supported the hypothesis that categories of verbal and emotional responses elicited by conditioned stimuli associated with aversive reinforcement differed from those categories elicited by those associated with rewards. Verbal reports of fear and apprehensiveness generally occurred to stimuli conditioned to an anticipatory, aversive reinforcement, and hope and elation to stimuli anticipatory of reward. Relief was generally associated to the offset of conditioned danger signals and disappointment, but not frustration to offset of reward-anticipatory signals. However, contrary to Mowrer's theory, the offset of reward-associated conditioned stimuli did not elicit verbal responses of fear and apprehensiveness, nor were verbal responses of hope and elation given for any of the conditioned stimuli associated with aversive reinforcement that signified safety. The valence or hedonic tone of the reinforcement, whether rewarding or punishing, pleasant, or unpleasant, seemed to be fundamentally determinant of the dimension of the conditioned emotional responses elicited. However, the magnitude of the reinforcement, which was not investigated in Skultin's study, could affect results in such a manner as to cause us to modify some of our conclusions.

Extension of Skultin's findings led us to a tentative reinforcement model for emotions as seen in Table 5. It has many blank spaces and we have not been able to reconcile it with the earlier empirical model in Table 1. The model has the advantages of generating hypothesis and handling data about the acquisition of emotional states or their manipulation as a function of such variables as number of trials, magnitude of reinforcement, etc. It also led us to speculate about such questions as the affective components associated with performing as an aversive reinforcer or positive reinforcer and how these might be acquired.

For example, in the Brown and Jacobs study (Brown, 1966; Brown & Jacobs, 1967) the type, intensity, and justifiability of social antecedents to aggression were varied in 135 college students. Two levels of frustration were created by decreasing the frequency of successes achieved by *S*s in a betting situation in which it was possible to win small money rewards. Two levels of attack were created by varying the provocativeness of statements by *E* regarding the performance of *S*s. Justifiability was varied by having the *E* give a logical and reasonable basis for the frustration or attack, or by not providing such pseudoevidence. Scales from JSMAI were used as one of the criterion measures and yielded some rich data. More aggressive responses were checked under high levels of frustration or attack than low, and attack led to more aggressive responses than frustration. More anxiety was evoked in the attack group than in the frustrated group. Depression and disappointment scores were complexly related to treatments. For example, very high amounts of depression were elicited by the justified attack, and very low by the unjustified attack. The Brown study suggests that even the reinforcing properties of events which we contrive in the laboratory are rarely simple in adult humans.

Having developed an instrument to study emotional states, we next did two studies comparing mood states in normals with responses of neuropsychiatric patients (Skultin, Jacobs, Glick, & Meehan, 1966). In the first study, Glick compared 20 psychotic and neurotic depressed inpatients who were given the adjective-checklist as part of a routine battery of psychological tests to a group of 20 nonpatients solicited from various sources and matched with the patients on the basis of general educational level, social status, sex, and age. Nineteen of the patients in this study were females. Although the rate of depression is somewhat higher in females than in males, the disproportionate sex ratio

TABLE 5. Affective States Generated by Reinforcement Contingencies

Dimension	Aversive reinforcement			No + R		Positive R		No − R
General	Fear		Disappointment	Frustration		Happiness		Relief
Level	Panic Fear Uneasiness	Rage Anger Frustration	Hopeless Depression Disappointment	Rage Anger Frustration		Euphoric Happy Pleased		
Uncertainty anticipation	Apprehensive		Pessimism			Hope		Secure
From others		Shame Embarrassment	Grief				Sociable Dependent	
From self	Guilt		Inadequate			Self confidence		Resourceful
Role as a reinforcer	Hostile		Rejecting Withholding			Loving Nurturant		Succorant

144

represented a chance sampling of the Ss population at Gateways Hospital at the time. A median test was applied to each of 26 dimensions in the form of the adjective-checklist we were using at that time. A summary of the results appears in Table 6 and presents the median number of words selected by the Ss on each scale, the numbers of patients and normal Ss falling below the median on each scale, and the significance levels.

TABLE 6. Affective Responses of Depressed Patients and Controls
Depressive Patients (D) versus Normals (C)

	Scale	Median score	Ds below median	Cs below median	Significance level
A	Happiness	2.9	15	5	.01
B	Depression	1.5	14	16	.01
C	Weakness	1.3	5	15	.01
D	Confidence	4.2	13	7	(ap)
E	Task-involved	2.2	10	10	
F	Panicky	.8	6	13	(ap)
G	Friendly	5.8	12	8	
H	Sluggish	1.6	8	12	
I	Tenseness	3.2	6	14	.05
J	Cautious	1.9	10	10	
K	Indifference	1.4	7	13	(ap)
L	Irritated	.9	8	12	
M	Fearful	1.7	6	14	.05
N	Contented	1.9	14	6	.05
O	Enraged	1.0	8	12	
P	Vigorous	1.0	14	6	.05
Q	Self-contained	1.4	10	10	
R	Hostile	1.2	13	7	(ap)
S	Shy	1.6	10	10	
T	Quiet	1.8	6	14	.05
U	Anger	1.4	11	9	
V	Sick	.9	5	15	.01
W	Withdrawn	1.1	8	12	
X	Hopeful	2.9	14	6	.05
Y	Relieved	1.5	12	8	
Z	Disappointment	1.4	7	13	(ap)

Fifteen out of the 26 scales were either significant or approached significance in differentiating depressed patients from normals. Positive feelings or feelings of well-being and energy were significantly lower in depressed patients and, on the other hand, depressives showed greater amounts of sadness and depression, a greater lack of interest in activity, and also greater disturbances in the fear and tension dimensions. Depressives also checked a significantly greater number of adjectives indicating weakness, helplessness, sickness, and tended to describe themselves as being more frustrated and disappointed. Overall, it can be seen that the adjective-checklist findings correspond to the usual clinical description of symptoms of depressive patients as consisting of sadness, depression, lack of energy, etc. We were convinced that we had a rather promising instrument for the identification of states of depression, despite some overlap of the score distributions of patients and normals.

In the second part of the study, Skultin compared the adjective-checklist responses of general mental-hospital patients to college students, and used three sets of instructions. The first set of instructions simply asked all Ss to describe their present emotional state by checking the appropriate words. A second set of instructions asked the Ss to imagine a situation of hopefulness or promise of reward and to fill out the checklist again, and a third set that the patients imagine that the promise of the reward was not forthcoming and again fill out the adjective-checklist. The latter two sets of instructions somewhat simulated Mowrer's conceptualization of hope and disappointment.

Thirty-eight male diagnostically mixed neuropsychiatric patients from a VA hospital were compared to 16 male college students. Table 7 presents the number of male Ss of each group who checked one or more words of each scale for each set of instructions. Chi-squares were calculated for each experimental condition in each scale, and those which are significant or approaching significance are listed in the right-hand columns.

In describing their present states, significantly more of the NP patients feel depressed, and weak, and significantly fewer feel happy, friendly, contented, and confident. Fewer patients are task-involved and hopeful, and more are disappointed and withdrawn. These results were not inconsistent with those of the study reported prior to this one except that the female depressives showed more of the components of passivity, inactivity, fear, and tension. When asked to imagine the situation of hope, more normals were confident than patients and also more were fearful. Under the disappointment instructions, more patients were fearful, fewer vigorous, and more tended to be shy or withdrawn. The results are congruent with the hypotheses that NP patients are generally a defeated group of people who react poorly to situations of frustration and disappointment because of their history of little success with such situations.

The set to respond as if hopeful or disappointed also caused large changes in the responses of both groups of Ss on the scales X and Z which we had designed to measure hopefulness and disappointment. However, the responses of the normals were almost unanimously appropriate, whereas not as many patients responded appropriately to these two instructional sets.

In general, it was found in these studies on the adjective-checklist, exploring mood differences between NP patients and so-called normal individuals is quite promising. Mental-hospital patients have often been described as emotionally ill or emotionally disturbed, as if a crucial etiological and/or

TABLE 7. Number of Mental-Hospital Patients and Normals Checking One or More Words of Scales of Affective Responses under Three Sets of Instructions

	Scale	College students N = 16			NP patients N = 38			Chi-square test significances		
		Pres. state	Hope	Disap.	Pres. state	Hope	Disap.	Pres. state	Hope	Disap.
A	Happiness	10	15	1	13	35	3	.01		
B	Depression	0	0	14	13	5	31	.01		
C	Weak	1	3	12	13	4	26	.01		
D	Confidence	12	15	4	18	27	2	.01	.05	
E	Task-involved	11	11	4	18	23	13	(ap)		
F	Panicky	0	3	7	4	4	19			
G	Friendliness	14	12	3	19	32	4	.05		
H	Sluggish	5	0	3	14	3	13			
I	Tenseness	9	9	7	26	18	24			
J	Cautiousness	8	7	6	19	12	12			
K	Indifference	9	5	6	19	8	15			
L	Irritation	4	0	12	8	3	29			
M	Fearful	5	*8*	*2*	11	*8*	*17*	.05	.05	
N	Content	11	7	0	10	25	5	.01		
O	Enraged	2	0	13	3	2	25			
P	Vigour	5	10	5	13	23	2			.05
Q	Self-contained	6	6	·4	14	16	5			
R	Hostility	2	3	7	6	16	12			
S	Shyness	4	2	0	14	9	9			(ap)
T	Quiet	10	5	9	21	19	14			
U	Anger	7	4	7	12	10	21			
V	Sick	4	2	6	8	4	21			
W	Withdrawn	3	1	3	15	5	15			
X	Hope	12	15	3	20	30	5			
Y	Relief	8	12	1	17	32	1			
Z	Disappointment	1	0	16	10	4	32	(ap)		

symptomatic aspect of the disorder had to do with affect. We have demonstrated that patients differ systematically from normals in the affective adjectives which they select to describe their present state of mood. It seems clear also that patients differ from normals in their self descriptions on scales of positive emotions or affect.

A number of other authors have reported the effectiveness of an adjective-checklist in studying mental-hospital patients. Lubin (1965, 1966) reports considerable success in separating depressed patients from nondepressed patients and nonpatients. Kellerman and Plutchik (1968) report that severely disturbed patients are more likely to describe themselves on an adjective-checklist-like instrument as unhappy, socially withdrawn, anxious, and apathetic, whereas moderately disturbed patients describe themselves as more unhappy, aggressive, rebellious, and depressed. Stotland (1969) has also written extensively on positive emotions in hospital patients.

In our own thinking at this time, we began to add up a number of facts. One, that patients differed from normals in terms of positive mood as well as negative. Two, that positive and negative affects were perhaps associated with different reinforcement contingencies. Three, that positive affects seemed to be related to energizing states. Four, that there seemed to be little data, theorizing, or concern about positive mood states. The state of affairs is well presented in an article by Carlson (1966). Carlson analyzed 172 introductory psychology textbooks from before 1900 to the 1960s for lines, sections, terms referring to pleasant and unpleasant emotions, omitting sections on research and psychopathology. He found that of approximately 6000 terms, approximately 70% referred to unpleasant emotions that 75% of the terms coded in indices referred to unpleasant emotions. He found that if there were sections on fear and love, the fear section was first in 15/18 instances; if anger and love, the anger section was first in 14/18. The proportion had dropped from 42% references to pleasant emotions before 1900, to 23% since 1960. He found that in the first 13 volumes of the *Annual Reviews of Psychology* there were 400 references to anxiety, 43 to hostility, and none to friendliness. Carlson raised the question of what expectations this was creating in psychology students. Lindauer (1968) did a similar content analysis of 18 standard literary reference texts. He found that 73% of literary references were to positive emotions, ranging from 64% in short stories to 84% in novels.

I began to wonder about psychologists' preoccupation with negative affect. Did it derive from the medical model of psychopathology and concern itself with conditions that are wrong, or from a biological growth model that presumes that ordinarily beings function well unless there is something which inhibits or cripples their growth. In any case, professional psychology had neglected the theme of the important element of American folk psychology represented by Dale Carnegie's concern with how to make friends and influence people and Norman Vincent Peale's emphasis on feeling good about the world. I began to wonder whether it might be more effective to have people practice positive mood states rather than to attempt to extinguish or inhibit negative mood states.

At this juncture, we began the first of three attempts to modify moods in mental-hospital patients with particular focus on the augmentation of positive mood states. The first study (Glick, Jacobs, Deacon, Waldron, & Lublin, 1966) was an attempt to explore a variety of materials and techniques of psychological intervention for their potential for changing mood. We attempted to translate certain well-established and traditional, psychological concepts into operations which we could teach to comparatively naive college students. The first process, which we called focused social approval, was the expression of social approval by a group of individuals by means of gestures and facial expressions, with the purpose of increasing the occurrences of selected responses of another individual. The principle is derived from the law of effect which has demonstrated on many occasions that organisms acquire responses more readily and rapidly if such responses lead to the satisfaction of needs. That humans have a need for social approval has often been demonstrated and used effectively in laboratory and field situations.

The second process was called social feedback—again derived from a traditional psychological concept. It has been well established that people not only acquire incorrect perceptions of technical information transmitted to them (Jacobs & Deacon, 1969), but also of their own behavior, relationships with others, or effect on others. There is evidence that furnishing more objective information, for example, through playback of video-taped interactions with others (Robinson & Jacobs, 1970) or feedback via reports of performance on objective tests (Jacobs & Maas, 1969), allows the individual whose perceptions have been inaccurate, to readjust his behavior. We hypothesized that audio-taped feedback to patients of their own positive behavior might correct previous perceptions of being extremely inadequate or fragile.

A third variable was referred to as positive-response elicitation. It is possible and perhaps sometimes necessary to shape responses in the Skinnarian manner. However, unless it is absolutely necessary, the shaping of responses is probably a very inefficient and tedious procedure. Most adult, human organisms, whether hospitalized or not, represent a set of very sophisticated response systems and probably possess a great many strongly learned responses. If such positive responses could be tapped by selection of appropriate stimulus material, then feedback or social approval might serve as the agents for increasing the frequency of such positive responses.

This study was particularly interested with the elicitation of positive, affective responses. We defined the class of positive, affective responses to include confidence, happiness, pleasure, interests, sociability, and optimism. We decided to study various kinds of social-relating behavior as well, including volunteering information, asking questions, initiating topics of conversation, and relating to other people.

We chose three kinds of material which were believed to have the potential of eliciting such positive responses. The first were selections of music since a number of studies suggest that affective responses are related to or can be changed by music. The second and third kinds of material we chose were related to modeling, role-playing, and identification. We selected prose materials whose subject content was concerned with positive affective responses. We had *S*s read and discuss such materials, asking them such questions as, can you remember an earlier memory like this? How did it feel? Can you think of something that has happened to you recently that is happy or exciting or feels like this?

In a third kind of procedure we demonstrated or modeled for patients and had patients act in dramatic selections in which the characters in the plays demonstrated the positive, affective responses referred to previously. We anticipated that the knowledge of social roles combined with the ability of patients to assume complex habits and sets, such as those involved in the instructions to pretend or act like a play character, might elicit positive responses. It was assumed that we could then reinforce such responses or facilitate them through feedback and reinforcement techniques. To the extent that other behavior and attitudes may be modified by such complex verbal and symbolic sequences as role or self or mood, we hoped that we might produce generalized alterations in the behavior of patients.

In addition, as suggested earlier, we were concerned with trying to train junior and senior college students enrolled in a course in abnormal psychology as personnel whose function would be to utilize these techniques. The importance of exploring the value of minimumly trained and nonprofessional personnel was self-evident in view of the various national reports of manpower shortages in the mental health area.

The experimental design was, therefore, as follows: students in classes were divided into teams of three members each and trained for 4 hr to use the materials referred to previously by means of demonstration by the experimenters, and by role-playing. Ten teams used the response elicitation materials without either social approval or feedback to serve as a control group for social interaction and exposure to the materials. Ten teams were trained to use response elicitation materials, and also to reinforce positive responses by focused social approval. Ten teams were trained to use response elicitation materials and to tape record their sessions, and to use social feedback to attempt to increase positive mood. Ten teams met with patients in a discussion session without using the response elicitation materials or focused social approval or social feedback, and met again with the patients after a 3-week interval, as a control group for the effects of general hospital treatment.

Each of these groups worked with ten unselected patients except that patients were characterized by the absence of one or more of the positive responses referred to previously and such patients did not have diagnosis of manic psychosis or of character disorder. Diagnostic group, age, sex, and medication were not controlled, but dealt with primarily and initially by random assignments to groups. The first three groups met with each of two patients for 20 min during a 3-week period. Each group worked with the same patients every week and each patient was seen by two teams per week.

The following types of responses were assessed in order to determine the effects of experimental variables. First, the *Jacobs Survey of Mood and Affect I,* an adjective-checklist consisting of 180 descriptive adjectives in 30 scales and six clusters was administered to each patient after each session as a continuous measure of mood. Second, ratings by students: students serving in the experiments rated the patient at the beginning and the end of each session on seven-point scales of happiness, confidence, sociability, and activity. Third, behavioral observation: during each session, a student rater tallyed the number of positive, social responses observed.

Because of hospital procedure, we were not able to carry out our neatly designed study as planned. Patients sometimes had to be discharged or left the hospital and our sample of ten patients in each group being seen twice a week was considerably attenuated.

We found that self-ratings on scales of anger and weakness in the JSMA decreased after treatments in the experimental groups, but not in the control groups. However, we suspected that a tendency to mark fewer adjectives on successive repetitions of the long checklist was contaminating results. Students rated significantly more patients in the reinforcement and feedback groups as having increased in happiness, and in the feedback group as having increased in confidence, whereas no significant changes were observed in the ratings of patients in the two control groups. We were aware, however, that the students' ratings could be biased because the students were rating their own patients.

A second study was therefore designed (Konrad & Jacobs, 1967) which attempted to improve the mood of chronic, institutionalized schizophrenics. Three different materials were used in a role-playing situation. These were a prose selection written specifically for the experiment, a scene from a published play, and an emotional speech (Gettysburg Address), which required no interaction. Subjects were 38 schizophrenic patients. Groups were matched on a measure of premorbid social history using a social history questionnaire (Jacobs & Willens, 1970; Willens, 1965) because evidence showed that such measures correlate with social skills. A pair of undergraduate students met with the same *S*s on each visit once a week for four weeks in 20–30-min treatment sessions. Patient volunteers were assigned randomly to three groups: a role-play group, a companionship group, and a control group. The control *S*s simply read the role-playing materials to be used by the role-playing group that week, to control for exposure to the materials. After reading the materials, they completed the short form of the Jacobs adjective-checklist. Sessions for the companionship group were unstructured sessions where the students were free to conduct the sessions any way they felt would be best for establishing a friendly relationship with the patient, e.g., talking, walking, coffee, etc. Following these sessions, the companion-group *S*s completed the adjective-checklist after reading the applicable role-playing materials.

Patients in the role-play group, except for the first session, which was like that of the companionship group, were instructed to relax and listen as the setting of a role was read to them. Patients were told that their task was to try as best as they could to take the role of a specific character as the description was read. The main character's feeling state, one of a positive mood, was extensively described in detail. The *S* was told that he should actually put himself into the shoes of the designated character and feel the emotions which were described. The description of the person and the situation was read to the *S* and then was repeated. This time the *S* was given lines to read and one of the students interacted as another player. Subject was encouraged to read the lines with feelings appropriate to the described circumstance and also encouraged to improvise a line or two after the standard lines had been read. A short closing discussion was held in which the *S* was asked if the situation reminded him of any time in his own life when he had similar feelings, and he was urged to talk about any such memories which he could recall.

The companionship treatment produced significant decreases on adjective-checklist scales in anger and increases in energy at the .05 level of significance as compared to the control group. The role-play treatment resulted in significantly greater changes on the scale of well-being than the control group whereas the companionship treatment did not. An analysis of the trends of responses was examined and it was observed that in five out of the six adjective variables being observed (except on well-being) the role-play group marked appreciably fewer adjectives initially than either the companion or the control group. The role-play group had been assigned by chance a higher proportion of *S*s whose response set was to mark few adjectives.

Therefore, the third study was designed (Konrad & Jacobs, 1968; Konrad, 1967) which attempted to remedy the short-comings of the earlier studies. Fifty-seven male schizophrenic patients, hospitalized a minimum of 2 years, served as *S*s. Mood measures from Jacobs adjective-checklist were obtained after each of eight weekly sessions of the program. Before and after ratings of social responsiveness were obtained during the first and last sessions which consisted of 20–30 min of unstructured, social interactions between *S*s and a pair of students who were called raters. Pairs of students called treaters, who had not participated in the rating session, interacted with the two experimental groups of *S*s during the middle six treatment sessions. One experimental group of *S*s (role-play group) was also seen weekly in 20–30-min sessions by the treaters who interacted by a prearranged structure that utilized preselected role-playing materials and a second experimental group was devoted to the companionship program as described in the previous study. The control group received no social interaction or experience with the students during the six weeks of treatment, but were treated similarly to the experimental *S*s in all of the pertinent aspects. The raters did not know to which treatment condition patients had been assigned. Therefore, differences among the groups in ratings of social or emotional responses after treatment could not be attributed to an experimenter bias. The groups were also matched before the study on their productivity on the adjective-checklist.

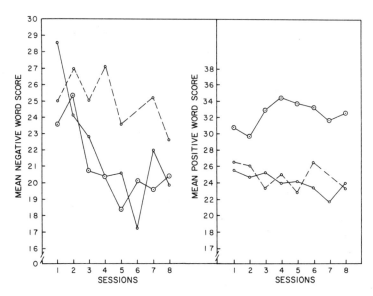

Fig. 1. Means for positive and negative word scores from the adjective-checklist.
[(○—○): Role-play Group; (○—○): Companion Group; (○– –○): Control.]

Figure 1 presents the mean positive- and negative-affect checklist scores over the eight rating and treatment sessions. It may be observed that both experimental groups decrease in negative-affect expressed over treatment, whereas the control group does not. The role-play group shows an increase in positive-affect reported as treatment progresses whereas the companionship group and control group do not. The differences are highly reliable as shown by parametric and nonparametric analyses of variance and an analysis of covariance. The role-play group maintained its superiority over the other two groups in positive-affect reported in the last rating session when no role-playing materials were employed.

Breaking down the positive- and negative-affect scores, the companionship group decreased more in fear and weakness, or lack of energy, than did the control group. The role-play group increased more in scales of energy and happiness than did both of the other groups, and decreased more in depression than the control group.

Raters also rated both companionship and role-play groups as decreasing more in fear than the control group, but no other mood ratings differentiated the groups. Ratings of social responsiveness revealed significant increases in the companionship group over the control in showing interest, openness, and total social responsiveness. Showing interest was also rated as having significantly increased in the role-playing group when compared to controls.

The Konrad and Jacobs studies provide conclusive evidence that a combination of modeling, role-playing, and reinforcement of positive responses with schizophrenics for a brief number of sessions affects their self-ratings of mood states. Patients are more likely to describe themselves as happy and energetic after such treatments. The companionship treatment, on the other hand, produced a more generalized change in social responsiveness as well as the decrease in negative-affect which was also observed in the role-play group but not the increase in positive-affect.

We have performed a number of other studies on the effect of the manipulation of complex variables on mood and emotionality. Two of these study the effect of lengthening the session in group therapy with mental-hospital patients. In the first of these (Myerhoff, Jacobs, & Stoller, 1970), emotion was contrasted in marathon and traditional psychotherapy groups. Clinicians have observed that the marathon groups generate a heightened intensity of emotions and we attempted to determine whether this observation was indeed correct. An experimental group (E) was set up to receive 18 hr of treatment in 3 days, 6 hr each day. A control group received its 18 hr of treatment in 3 weeks, three 2-hr sessions per week. The control group completed the Jacobs adjective short form checklist at the conclusion of each of the nine 2-hr sessions. The experimental group filled out the adjective-checklist after 2 and 4 hr every day and at the end of the 6-hr session. Plotted in Fig. 2 is the number of positive and

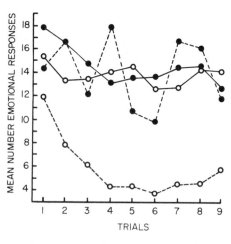

Fig. 2. Mean number of positive and negative adjectives checked by Marathon and Traditional psychotherapy group patients at each 2-hr testing period. (●——●): marathon positive emotion; (●– –●): marathon negative emotion; (○——○): control positive emotion; (○– –○): control negative emotion. [Reproduced from Myerhoff, Jacobs & Stoller, Psychotherapy: Theory, Research and Practice, 1970.]

negative emotional responses checked by traditional and marathon psychotherapy group patients at each 2-hr testing period. A rapid and rather regular decrease in the frequency of elicited negative, emotional responses can be observed in the traditional group as contrasted with the cyclical and markedly higher rate of endorsement of negative items in the marathon group. An analysis of variance showed that emotions by trials by group interaction was significant. The results suggest that in mental-hospital patients, it is not greater emotionality that differentiates marathon groups from traditional therapy groups. There is a sustained high level of negative emotional responses in the marathon group whereas the systematic decrease in negative emotions seen in the traditional group probably represents more patient comfort, and a decrease in the propensity to express more personally meaningful material of more anxiety-provoking content.

Two other studies have reported somewhat similar results. Lubin, Dupree, and Lubin (1967), found depression responses significantly higher in the middle of a week of sensitivity training than at the beginning or the end. Lubin and Zuckerman (1967) found increases in scores on the multiple-affect checklist, which measures anxiety, hostility, and depression, during a week of a T group when compared to scores obtained before the conference. A peak of negative affect seemed to occur somewhere about the middle of the week. Holmes (1967), however, found no relationship between adjective-checklist depression scores and group verbal interactions.

A second study which I planned with Nita Orlando (Orlando, 1967) studied affect elicitation as a function length of group therapy session and the effect of models. One psychotherapy group met in 1-hr sessions for an equivalent length of time to a second group which met in 2-hr sessions. All affective responses produced were given verbal reinforcement by the therapists. Subjects in 2-hr groups showed a marked and significant increase in rate of emotional responses per hour when compared to Ss in 1-hr groups. However, an examination of the behavior of the patient models, who had been selected because they had emitted a high frequency of emotional responses in other groups, revealed that the rate of affective response production of the models was lower than that of the other group-members. In other words, the models did not serve as models. The experimenters suspected that the models had taken a different set than they had in the early group, and seemed to be doing more problem-solving kinds of behavior than emitting affective responses.

A number of authors have used other strategies to try to increase or decrease the frequency of affective responses in Ss. I would like to review some of the literature with particular attention to studies dealing with positive rather than negative affects. A frequently used approach has been the verbal conditioning technique. For example, Dawson and Mastalone (1964) who were students in a psychology class I was teaching, tried verbal conditioning of the denial of anxiety responses to the Taylor manifest anxiety scale (Dawson & Mastalone, 1964). Subjects were instructed to read each statement of the 50-item manifest anxiety scale aloud and then to say true or false as to whether it applied to them personally. The first 16 statements were merely recorded on the paper by the experimenter to determine the ordinary operant level. Of the next 18 statements, denials of anxiety were followed by verbal reinforcement by the experimenter for Ss in the experimental group. Four out of five Ss in the experimental group decreased in the number of anxious responses from the pretreatment level and one Ss increased. Four of the Ss in the control group increased in the number of anxious statements and only one decreased.

Haas (1962) used verbal approval for emitting positive and negative sentence completions and found an increase in the respective categories. Ekman, Krasner, and Ulman (1964) studied the effects of positive versus negative set and awareness on operant conditioning of emotional words, using TAT stories. Only positive set-aware Ss increased whereas negative set-aware Ss decreased. Ganzer and Sarason (1964) found somewhat similar results when they treated groups in a friendly or hostile way and reinforced half of each group for negative self-references. Reinforcements did not lead to an increase in negative self-references. Portnoy and Salzinger (1964) hypothesized that affectively, negative verbal responses would be aversive and therefore would be suppressed by Ss. The opposite would be true for affective, positive responses. Contrary to the results of the two previous studies, they found all affective response classes conditionable, that is, positive and negative as well as neutral words. The Portnoy and Salinger study did not reinforce self-references, and the differences are perhaps attributable to the effect of social desirability sets in the two earlier studies reported.

Meerbaum (1963) and Meerbaum and Southwell (1965) used reflections of feeling and paraphrasing versus simple, social approval like "mm, mm." They found affective self-references increased more for reflection than for paraphrasing. Even negative affective self-references increased, but only when reflection of feeling was used. The reinforcement aspect of the reflection of feeling seems difficult to specify. Perhaps it satisfies a general need for understanding. Ullman, Krasner, and Collins (1961) had mental-hospital patients tell stories to TAT cards and reinforced emotional words. Subjects whose emotional words were reinforced by social approval showed a greater increase in adequacy in interpersonal relations in group therapy than did Ss who were not reinforced, whereas patients who were reinforced by a click did not increase in adequacy. The differential conditionability in positive and negative affective response classes under different experimental conditions, adds some support to our contention that positive responses are not equivalent to the absence of negative responses.

A number of experimenters have attempted to evoke affectively positive imagery as a context for visualization of a feared object or event in order to change behavior towards the fearful stimulus. One of the earliest of such references is that of the use of emotive imagery by Lazarus and Abramovitz (1965), as a counter conditioning technique. For example, the authors report successful treatment of a child who was fearful of the dark. He was asked to visualize a hierarchy of responses to darkness while accompanying his idols, Superman and Captain Silver.

A variation by Donaldson (1969) studies snake phobic *S*s who visualized approach behavior without a hierarchy or relaxation while *E* tried to keep anxiety to a minimum by having the *S* visualize confronting the snake and staring it down, feeding it until it is very full and becoming friendly with it. Donaldson reports that when he compares these *S*s to *S*s treated by implosive techniques, both show significant increases in approach, but do not differ from each other.

In a recent doctoral dissertation by Perloff (1970), snake phobic *S*s were assigned to a standard desensitization treatment or two groups where the same aversive items were paired with either positive or neutral imagery without relaxation. Both of the latter treatments produced greater increases in approach behavior and more positive attitudes towards snakes than did either desensitization with relaxation or the control, although the two imagery groups did not differ from each other. Perloff reports that the imagery groups also achieved more generalized benefits than the other groups.

Velten (1967) used autosuggestion to arouse elation and depression in college students. He had college students read 60 self-referent statements ranging from neutrality to elation or depression. Not only did his elation and depression groups differ on an adjective-checklist measure of mood from *S*s who read neutral statements, but also differed significantly from each other and from neutral statement groups in such performance measures as writing speed and reaction time measures. Velten's results suggest not only a slowing down of responses in depressive moods, but an activating aspect associated with elation.

Another approach to the manipulation of positive, affective states is being explored by Lovaas (1968). Lovaas refers to attempts to teach affection to autistic children by shaping techniques. Lovaas and others speculate that the failure of schizophrenic children to develop normally is a consequence of the ineffectiveness of parental stimuli such as smiles or physical closeness to have acquired reinforcing properties. Analogous to Lovaas' work with children, I am sure that in some behavior modification programs with adults, patients are being rewarded for positive, emotional responses or the overt behaviors associated with positive emotions, but I have not found any systematic research reported at this point.

The research I have summarized convinces me that the instruments which we and others have developed to measure affective states represent very useful devices particularly for the study of momentary or state changes. A number of interesting naturalistic studies (Wessman & Ricks, 1966; Nowlis & Cohen, 1968) to which I have not had space to refer, have demonstrated the value of measures of affect. Such instruments further provide an opportunity for systematically studying the relationship of positive and negative affective states to psychopathology, to deficits in adaptive behavior, and to the treatment of such conditions.

Our future research plans include the following kinds of studies: 1, affective and other behavioral consequences of variations in assertion training; 2, physical proximity in groups and personality as determinants of affective state and interaction; 3, the effect of cognitive rehearsal of positive affective experiences on mood and performance; 4, in a recently completed experiment (Schaible, 1970), we found that giving positive pseudofeedback to members of volunteer groups to be *S*s in experiments facilitated the acceptance of subsequent negative or positive feedback and increased group cohesiveness. We expect to replicate the study in a more naturalistic setting, investigating the affective consequences as well, and also the willingness in taking personal risks or self-disclosing; and 5, we have achieved some success temporarily modifying social and academic behaviors in elementary school children in rural Appalachian schools (Jacobs, 1970) by Skinnerian techniques. We suspect that, in some of our most successful cases, the success experienced by the *S*s has caused generalized increases in positive affect as well as a more positive self-concept. We plan to investigate such affective changes because we believe they may play an important role in the greater permanence and generalization of treatment effects.

References

Brown, V. Antecedents of aggression: Effects of type, intensity, and justifiability. Unpublished doctoral dissertation, Univ. of Southern California, 1966.
Brown, V., & Jacobs, A. Social antecedents of aggression. Paper read at the Western Psychological Association convention, San Francisco, 1967.
Block, J. Studies in phenomenology of emotions. *Journal of Abnormal and Social Psychology,* 1957, **54,** 358-363.
Carlson, E. R. The affective tone of psychology. *Journal of General Psychology,* 1966, **75,** 65-78.
Dale, T., Jacobs, A., & Meehan, J. A factor analysis of semantic differential ratings of emotion. Paper read at the Western Psychological Association convention, Seattle, 1964.
Dawson, M., & Mastalone, M. Verbal conditioning of the manifest anxiety scale. Unpublished manuscript, 1964.
Donaldson, D. W. Positive imagery technique and implosive therapy. Unpublished doctoral dissertation, Fuller Theological Seminary, 1969.
Ekman, P., Krasner, L., & Ullman, L. Interaction of set and awareness as determinants of response to verbal conditioning. *Journal of Abnormal and Social Psychology,* 1964, **70,** 34-323.
Ganzer, V. J., & Sarason, I. G. Interrelationships among hostility, experimental conditions and verbal behavior. *Journal of Abnormal and Social Psychology,* 1964, **68,** 79-84.
Glick, J., Jacobs, A., Deacon, S., Waldron, R., & Lublin, S. Mood modification in mental

hospital patients by undergraduate students. Paper read at the Western Psychological Association convention, 1966.

Haas, K. Verbal conditioning of affective responses. *Journal of General Psychology,* 1962, **67,** 319-322.

Holmes, J. S. Relation of depression and verbal interaction in group therapy. *Psychological Reports,* 1967, **20,** 1039-1042.

Jacobs, A., Meehan, J. P., & Capek, L. The development of an adjective checklist to measure affective states. *Psychological Newsletter,* 1959a, **10,** 115-118.

Jacobs, A., Meehan, J. P., & Capek. L. The measurement of verbal responses to experimentally induced affective states. The arousal of fear. *Journal of Psychological Studies,* 1959b, **11,** 1-6.

Jacobs, A., Meehan, J. P., & Capek. L. The measurement of verbal responses to experimentally induced affective states, II. The arousal of feelings of depression. *Journal of Psychological Studies,* 1960, **12,** 1-12.

Jacobs, A., Meehan, J. P., & Capek. L. The measurement of verbal responses to experimentally induced affective states, III. The arousal of feelings of well-being. *Journal of Psychological Studies,* 1961, **12,** 128-134.

Jacobs, A., Meehan, J., Dale, T., & Weinstein, L. Subjective dimensions of emotions. Paper read at the Western Psychological Association meeting, Seattle, 1964.

Jacobs, A., & Maas, J. Changes in self estimates of psychological attributes as a function of the direction of discrepancies between initial estimates and reported test scores. *Psychological Reports,* 1969, **25,** 359-362.

Jacobs, A., & Deacon, S. The effects of feedback on communication of medical prescription to diabetic patients. *Proceedings of APA,* 1969-1970.

Jacobs, A., & Willens, J. Training role behavior in schizophrenics. *Proceedings of APA,* 1970-1971.

Jacobs, A. Modifying social and academic behavior in the primary grades in rural Appalachia schools. Unpublished manuscript, 1970.

Kellerman, H. P., & Plutchik, R. Emotion-trait interrelations and the measurement of personality. *Psychological Reports,* 1968, **23,** 1107-1114.

Konrad, W., & Jacobs, A. Interaction of college students with schizophrenics and mood change. Unpublished manuscript, 1967.

Konrad, W., & Jacobs, A. A social therapy program with schizophrenics to change mood and social responsiveness. Paper presented at the California State Psychological Convention, 1968.

Konrad, W. The use of college students in a social therapy program with chronic schizophrenics to produce changes in mood and social responsiveness. Unpublished doctoral dissertation, Univ. of Southern California, 1967.

Lazarus, A. A., & Abramovitz. The use of "emotional imagery" in the treatment of children's phobias. In L. P. Ullman & L. Krasner (Eds), *Case studies in behavior modification.* New York: Holt, 1965. Pp. 300-304.

Lindauer, M. S. Pleasant and unpleasant emotions in literature: A comparison with the affective tone of psychology. *Journal of Psychology,* 1968, **70,** 55-67.

Lorr, M., Daston, P., & Smith, I. R. An analysis of mood states. *Educational and Psychological Measurement,* 1967, **27,** 89-96.

Lovaas, V. I. Some studies on the treatment of childhood schizophrenia. In J. M. Shlien (Ed.), *Research in psychotherapy.* Washington, American Psychological Association, 1968.

Lubin, B. Adjective checklists for measurement of depression. *Archives of General Psychiatry,* 1965, **12,** 57-62.

Lubin, B. Fourteen brief depression adjective checklists. *Archives of Genral Psychiatry,* 1966, **15,** 205-208.

Lubin, B., Dupree, V., & Lubin, A. Comparability and sensitivity of set 2 (lists E, F, and G) of the depression adjective checklists. *Psychological Reports,* 1967, **20,** 756-758.

Lubin, B., & Zuckerman, M. Affective and cognitive patterns in sensitivity training groups. *Psychological Reports,* 1967, **21,** 365-376.

Maier, N. R. F. Frustration theory: Restatement and extension. *Psychological Review,* 1956, **63,** 370-388.

McClelland, D. C. *Personality.* New York: Dryden Press, 1951.

Meerbaum, M. The conditioning of affective self reference by three classes of generalized reinforcers. *Journal of Personality,* 1963, **31,** 179-191.

Meerbaum, M., & Southwell, E. A. Conditioning of affective self reference as a function of the discriminative characteristics of experimenter intervention. *Journal of Abnormal Psychology,* 1965, **70,** 180-187.

McNair, D., & Lorr, M. An analysis of mood in neurotics. *Journal of Abnormal and Social Psychology,* 1964, **69,** 620-627.

Mowrer, O. H. *Learning theory and behavior.* New York: Wiley, 1960.

Myerhoff, H. L., Jacobs, A., & Stoller, F. Emotionality in marathon and traditional therapy. *Psychotherapy: Theory, Research, Practice,* 1970, 7(1), 33-36.

Nowlis, V. The development and modification of motivational systems in personality. In M. R. Jones (Ed.), *Current theory and research in motivation.* Lincoln: Univ. of Nebraska Press, 1953.

Nowlis, V. Research with the "mood adjective checklist." In S. S. Tomkins & C. E. Izard (Eds), *Affect, Cognition, and Personality.* New York: Springer, 1965. Pp. 352-389.

Nowlis, P. P. & Cohen, A. Y. Mood-reports and the college natural setting: A day in the lives of three roommates under academic pressure. *Psychological Reports,* 1968, **23,** 551-556.

Orlando, N. Affect elicitation as a function of massed time. Unpublished manuscript, 1967.

Osgood, C. E., Suci, G. J., & Tannenbaum, P. H. *The measurement of meaning.* Urbana: Univ. of Illinois Press, 1957.

Perloff, B. Influence of muscular relaxation, positive imagery, and neutral imagery on extinction of avoidance behavior through systematic desensitization. Unpublished doctoral dissertation, Stanford Univ. 1970.

Portnoy, S., & Salzinger, K. The conditionability of different verbal response classes: Positive, negative, and non-affect statements. *Journal of General Psychology,* 1964, **70,** 311-323.

Plutchik, R. *The emotions: Facts, theories, and a new model.* New York: Random House, 1962.

Robinson, M., & Jacobs, A. The effect of focused videotape feedback in group psychotherapy with mental hospital patients. *Psychotherapy: Theory, Research, Practice,* 1970, 7(3), 169-172.

Schaible, T. The effect of positive and negative feedback sequences on group cohesion, and feedback acceptance and desirability. Unpublished master's thesis, West Virginia Univ., 1970.

Skultin, R., Jacobs, A., Glick, J., & Meehan, J. Mood in normals versus neuropsychiatric patients. Paper read at the Western Psychological Association Convention, 1966.

Skultin, R., & Jacobs, A. Subjective emotional responses to secondary reinforcements associated with an aversive stimulus. Unpublished manuscript.

Skultin, R. Verbal-reports of emotional states and onsets and offsets of conditioned stimuli. Unpublished doctoral dissertation, Univ. of Southern California, 1969.

Stotland, E. *The psychology of hope.* San Francisco: Jossey-Bass Inc., 1969.

Sweeney, P. R., Tinling, D., Eby, L. A., & Schmale, A. H. Factor analytic studies of four expressive modes of emotion. *Proceedings 76th Annual Convention, APA,* 1968, 169-170.

Thayer, R. Measurement of activation through self report. *Psychological Reports,* 1967, **20,** 663-678.

Ullman, L., Krasner, L., & Collins, B. J. Modification of behavior through verbal conditioning: Effect on group therapy. *Journal of Abnormal and Social Psychology,* 1961, **62,** 128-132.

Velten, E. The induction of elation and depression through the reading of structural sets of mood statements. Unpublished doctoral dissertation, Univ. of Southern California, 1967.

Wessman, A. E., & Ricks, D. F. *Mood and personality.* New York: Holt, 1966.

Willens, J. Training role playing behavior in schizophrenics. Unpublished doctoral dissertation, Univ. of Southern California, 1965.

The Psychophysiology of Private Events[1]

**Ralph F. Hefferline and
Louis J. J. Bruno**
*Columbia University
New York, New York*

I shall not begin, as Socrates would require, by defining my terms. Instead, as a kind of discursive preparation for the more tightly organized material to come later, I shall recount briefly the stages by which my students and I reached our current perspective on the psychology of private events. First, though, let me say something in advance about what this perspective is. We believe that the scientific approach to private events is best made by means of electrophysiological techniques. Furthermore, we believe that feedback to the subject of what the instruments "see" may turn out to be a way to implement the ancient injunction, "know thyself," and to provide both a rationale and a method for effective training and retraining across what potentially may be the full spectrum of ontogenetic behavior.

My investigation of private events began when, as a graduate student, I tackled the problem of why a person may cling to behavior which no longer seems to serve a purpose. By this I do not mean why it is hard to break a "bad

[1] Preparation of this paper was supported in part by Grant MH-13890 from the National Institute of Mental Health to Ralph F. Hefferline, Principal Investigator.

habit." The answer there, of course, is that in the short run it is so enjoyable! What I am referring to is why a person may avoid, with utmost urgency, a situation which, to the disinterested observer, poses no threat. One answer is that it is not the situation per se which disturbs, but what it tempts the person to do, namely, what he actually did or attempted on past occasions *with dire punishment as the consequence*! Now, of course, he withdraws automatically without even remembering why.

Obviously, this answer is nothing more than a crude version of psychoanalytic trauma-theory minus the usual appeal to repression to account for the failure to remember. However, what I was looking for was not a complete explanation of avoidance; instead, I wanted some basis upon which the problem could be approached in the laboratory. Since I was at Columbia University, the inevitable choice was to start out and go as far as possible with rats.

Estes, at Indiana, had not long before completed an elaborate study of punishment using rats as subjects (Estes, 1944). He concluded:

> It is clear ... that a disturbing or traumatic stimulus arouses a changed state of the organism of the sort commonly called "emotional" and that any stimulus present simultaneously with the disturbing stimulus becomes a conditioned stimulus capable of itself arousing the state on subsequent occasions. ... When punishment is correlated with ... response, emotional reaction can ... become conditioned to the incipient movements of making the response [p. 36].

On the strength of this concordance between clinical theory and laboratory findings, I—and, later, two of my students—designed and carried through experiments on avoidance behavior in the rat (Eldridge, 1954; Hefferline, 1950; Winnick, 1956). I shall mention here only enough of this early work to show how it laid the basis for further pursuit of the problem at the human level.

An Animal Prototype of the Human Problem of Letting Go

A person with a broken arm in a sling learns quickly not to move the injured member. Even after the arm mends and the sling is removed he tends at first to hold the arm flat against his chest with elbow bent. This behavior, after it has largely disappeared, may be temporarily restored in full force if the sling is put on again and the person asked to move through a crowd. This happens despite the fact that the person "knows" that it will not hurt to move his arm or have it jostled.

In what I came to call the "holding experiment," I conditioned somewhat similar behavior in the albino rat (Hefferline, 1950). Lacking eye pigment, this animal is light sensitive, and given the chance, will turn off a bright light. For this purpose I placed a small lever switch in the cage: When the rat pressed it down, the light went out; as soon as he released it, the light returned. Under these conditions, the rat learned to hold the lever down without once releasing it for as long as 45 min. Of course, after such lengthy stretches of lever holding, it is likely that muscular strain eventually became so punishing as to override other variables. In fact, the observed behavior was that the animal would release the lever, race about the cage for a few seconds, and then fling himself once more on the lever.

Later, after the light circuit was disconnected, the rat could roam freely without penalty. Occasionally, if he happened to touch the lever, he would press it down; then, it was as if he became trapped there, unable to let go. Pressing the lever actually did, so far as he was concerned, put him back in precisely the situation in which he had been when release of the lever reinstated the light.

I assumed that the rat did not sit there reminding himself, as a person might, that if he let go the light might return. Instead, I inferred that the animal made many incipient movements of letting go; that is, it would begin to let go, but since this would, in Estes' terms, produce an "emotional" state conditioned to the proprioceptive and tactual stimuli generated by releasing, it would resume pressing to remove the state.

Since my apparatus worked on an on–off basis and could not reveal incipient lever-releasing movements, a follow-up study was done in which the animal, instead of pressing a lever, pushed against a small vertical panel hinged at the top (Winnick, 1956). The panel could be pushed beyond the point necessary to turn off the light and a pen writing on a moving paper tape indicated extent of movement. Early in conditioning, the animal wavered back and forth, frequently allowing the light to return momentarily. Later, he kept it off for long periods. The panel, however, did not remain stationary. The recording pen indicated an irregular drifting movement toward the position where the light would resume, but, before this occurred, the animal would, repeatedly, make a corrective thrust back to a "safe" position.

While Winnick's study demonstrated that the holding response is one of continuing activity, with incipient movements occurring and being corrected for, it was still merely hypothetical that the proprioceptive stimuli involved in "letting go" set up an emotional state. To test for this objectively, Eldridge (1954) designed an experimental variation which permitted respiration rate to be recorded, since breathing irregularity has long been thought to be a sensitive index of autonomic upset (Lindsley, 1951).

The rats were trained to stand on a perch several feet above the floor. Directly over the animal's head was a wooden block, counter-weighted to rise slightly if the animal pushed upward with a force of about 5 gm. Upward movement turned off the light. Lowering the head allowed it to come back. Breathing rate was measured with due observance of a number of appropriate controls. If the rate before incipient letting go was about 80 per minute, then the first two breaths after movement were likely to be more shallow, although not necessarily, and the rate invariably accelerated to anywhere from 100 per minute to—although this was rare—400 per minute.

These three experiments comprise a unit. I conditioned the holding response and gave an inferential analysis of the controlling variables. Winnick followed with a demonstration that such holding was not immobilization, but vacillation between release movement and compensatory renewals of forward thrust. Eldridge, finally, produced evidence for the presence of an emotional state of "anxiety" generated in the animal by his own proprioceptive and tactual stimuli.

While this work was in progress, I became involved also in a nonlaboratory approach to the same and related problems at the human level. This will be described in the following section.

A Phenomenological Excursion into "Somatic Psychology"

In 1951 I collaborated with Fritz Perls and Paul Goodman in a book called *Gestalt Therapy: Excitement and Growth in the Human Personality.*[2] The portion of *Gestalt Therapy* which I wrote was a kind of do-it-yourself manual, subtitled "Mobilizing the Self." It attempted to provide a means of objectively approaching, among other things, one's hand-me-downs of chronic or recurrent muscle tensions, aches, pains, and assorted subjective discomfitures. These were viewed as somatic residuals, pointless perhaps in the "here and now," but persisting from earlier life periods when they had done service with some effectiveness in holding back strong, but punishable behavior from overt expression. The theoretical and practical background was a mixed one and only partly developed, as will appear shortly, but the basic therapeutic formula for self-application was simply this: Since conflict consists of some degree of clenching of antagonistic but *voluntary* muscles, the thing to do is to cultivate awareness of just *how* one produces the physical hang-up, experiment with it, even try to make it momentarily more severe, while remaining alert to possible anxiety and bits of fearful fantasy of what might happen if one let go.

A partial statement of procedure is quoted here from a previous summary account (Hefferline, 1958):

---

[2] The term *gestalt* went into the title and was kept there at the insistance of Fritz Perls, who convinced himself and the publisher that *Gestalt Theorie* still flourished in the United States. As an adjective descriptive of the therapy, *Gestalt* was not exactly a misnomer. Figure–ground terminology did permeate the book, and in a recent chapter on "the visionary sociology of Paul Goodman," Roszak mentions "the mystical 'wholism' which the therapy inherits from Gestalt theories of perception [1968, p. 187]." However, when prepublication copies of *Gestalt Therapy* were presented to Wolfgang Köhler and Molly Harrower, they disavowed its being in any legitimate line of descent from Gestalt doctrine.

As part of his assignment the subject was encouraged to make what amounted to a systematic proprioceptive survey of his own body, conducted in private with minimum external distractions. A person neither dead nor in flaccid paralysis presumably should be able to discriminate the tonic condition of all or of any part of his skeletal musculature. The first report of a subject is likely to be that he can do this. He can feel, he says, every part of his body. When further inquiry is made, it often turns out that what he took to be proprioceptive discrimination of a particular body part was actually a visualization of the part or a verbal statement of its location. Or else, to discriminate the part, he may have had to intensify proprioception by making actual movements.

With further work, if he can be persuaded to continue, the subject may report certain parts of his body to be proprioceptively missing. Suppose it is his neck. He may discriminate a mass that is his head and a mass that is his trunk with what feels like simply some empty space between. At this stage the subject is apt to remember more important things to do and his participation in the silly business ends.

Some subjects, however, apparently made curious by blank spots and hopeful of recovering some lost degrees of freedom in their system of voluntary control, do whatever is involved in paying closer attention to and acquiring interest in this peculiar private situation. A blank spot, they say, may gradually fill in. Or it may suddenly become the locus of sharp pain, paresthesias of one sort or another, "electric" sensations, or the unmistakable ache of muscular cramp.

Then what formerly was a blank may become as demanding of attention as an aching tooth. Further and more detailed discriminations may be made. It soon becomes imperative to relax the cramp, but the subject says that he does not know how to do so; he is concerned with so-called voluntary muscles, but these are reportedly not under voluntary control. The subject is somewhat in the position of the elementary psychology student who is assured that he has the voluntary muscles needed to wiggle his ears. The difference, of course, is that in the case of ear-wiggling he has never acquired control, whereas, in the case of the cramped muscles he has somehow lost control.

As soon as the question becomes one of how to acquire or regain control, problems for investigation sprout in all directions. A host of variables, direct or indirect in their effect, become relevant. One involves merely the instruction to continue to pay sustained attention to the blocking, regardless of discomfort, and to be on the alert for subtle changes of any sort. This seems to give rise to what previously was called ideomotor action, and may in itself bring a loosening of the reported muscular clinch.

Another instruction is to increase the clinch deliberately, if possible, and then, while relaxing from this added intensity, to learn something about relaxing still further. Also relevant are procedures that make use of proprioceptive facilitation—for instance, those used in training polio victims, partial spastics, and others to make better use of whatever healthy muscle they still possess. Kabat (1950) has developed these methods systematically.

When a muscular block is definitely resolved, it is frequently claimed by the subject that there occurs vivid, spontaneous recall of typical situations, perhaps dating back to childhood, where he learned to tense in this particular manner [pp. 747-748].

The monthly reports submitted to me by over a thousand undergraduates who undertook the "experiments in self-awareness" for point credit, gave substantial basis for concluding that the experiments were deemed beneficial by those who had been able to make contact with critical aspects of their own malfunctioning and thus had discovered the manner in which they blocked or interfered with their own supposedly highly motivated efforts. However, these tended to be persons who were already in pretty good shape. Those more severely conflicted might simply drop the whole thing—as they were privileged to do at any time—or else continue it while attacking the procedures as utterly fatuous, or immoral, or else attacking me as a "concentration camp doctor" who dangerously experimented with helpless people while not assuming responsibility for what would probably be disastrous outcomes.

The criticism eventually most bothersome was one actually anticipated in the material itself (Perls, Hefferline, & Goodman, 1951):

> As you work along with us, you will be inclined from time to time to question statements that we make, and you will demand, "Where is your proof?" Our standard answer will be that we present nothing that you cannot *verify for yourself in terms of your own behavior,* but . . . this will not satisfy you and you will clamor for "objective evidence" of a verbal sort, *prior to* trying out a single non-verbal step of the procedure [p. 7] .

To meet this criticism, I shifted back to the laboratory, this time to study the "king-sized rat"—man—by *electropsychological* means. That is, I intended to apply *electro*physiological techniques to the analysis of *psychological* problems—a pursuit later called "psychophysiology": "The general goal of psychophysiology is to describe the mechanisms which *translate* between psychological and physiological systems of the organism [Ax, 1964, p. 8] ." The idea was to make public, through instrumentation, the private, physiological events which were the focus of self-awareness and self-control in *Gestalt Therapy.* Made public, these events could not only be scrutinized experimentally, but as we shall see later, they could, when fed back to the subject in visual or auditory analog, furnish a powerful method for somatic surveys and retraining.

The Electropsychological Analysis of Private Events

In shifting back to the laboratory, the presumption was, as Skinner (1953) put it, that "a private event may be distinguished by its limited accessibility but not, so far as we know, by any special structure or nature [p. 257] ." What makes a private event private is that it occurs in the region beneath the skin; what can make it public are instruments which detect the same events as do the organism's internal receptors, that is, the instruments of electrophysiology. Of course, even with electrophysiological detection, "we are still faced with events which occur at the private level and which are important to the organism without instrumental amplification [Skinner, 1953, p. 282] ," but we are now in a position to deal with these events objectively. Thus, the private events which were the object of phenomenological report in *Gestalt Therapy* became, in electropsychological analysis, the variables—dependent and independent (cf. Hefferline & Bruno, 1971)—in conditioning and psychophysical experiments.

Response Control

Our initial efforts in electropsychology, reflecting our special interest in tension patterns, dealt with covert muscular contractions. Using both negative reinforcers (Hefferline & Keenan, 1961; Hefferline, Keenan, & Harford, 1959) and positive secondary reinforcers (Hefferline & Keenan, 1963; Sasmor, 1966), we showed that a response so small as to require electromyographic techniques for its detection could, nevertheless, be controlled through instrumental conditioning procedures. Since these experiments, which we have reviewed in detail elsewhere (Hefferline, Bruno, & Davidowitz, 1971), were conducted without the *S*'s observation of the response, that is, with the variables controlling his verbal behavior rendered temporarily inoperative, they gave support both to the general position "that there is no qualitative difference between the behavior of man and that of subhuman organisms, the seeming difference being produced by the fact that man alone possesses verbal behavior [Hefferline, 1962, p. 126]," and to the particular position that private events are not distinguished "by any special structure or nature." In other words, our experiments gave reason to believe that the learning principles which apply to the public behavior of human and subhuman species would also find application in the study of private events.

Of course, there had been many earlier indications that learning principles apply to private events; these, however, had nearly all come from studies carried out under classical procedures. In a sense, this was as it should be. Since private events are by definition inaccessible to the general community, we might, on quasi-evolutionary grounds, expect to find them amenable to classical procedures, which require only that two exteroceptive stimuli be paired consistently, but intractable under instrumental procedures, which specify that the reinforcing stimulus be presented in consequence of an emitted response. At point here is the once-certain dichotomy between classical and instrumental conditioning (cf. Kimble, 1961): Classical procedures apply to elicited, involuntary, autonomic responses (most of which qualify as private events); instrumental procedures apply to emitted, voluntary, skeletal responses (most of which are clearly public). Considered in this context, our conditioning studies were somewhat enigmatic. Our procedures were surely instrumental, but the responses conditioned were hardly "voluntary": In one study, the group which had been "informed that the effective response was a tiny twitch of the left thumb ... kept so busy producing voluntary thumb-twitches that the small reinforceable type of response had little opportunity to occur [Hefferline *et al.*, 1959, pp. 1338-1339]."

The enigma, as it turned out, was as false as the dichotomy between classical and instrumental "responses." The procedures, of course, are unquestionably different—classical reinforcements are contingent upon the prior occurrence of a stimulus; instrumental reinforcements, in contrast, are response-contingent—but there are reasonably clear indications that they do not apply to different types of responses (cf. Miller, 1969). For example, there is now evidence obtained in man to show that heart rate (Engel & Chism, 1967; Engel & Hansen, 1966), systolic blood pressure (Shapiro, Tursky, Gershon, & Stern, 1969), vasoconstriction (Snyder & Noble, 1968), salivation (Brown & Katz, 1967), and electrodermal activity (Shapiro & Crider, 1967) are all susceptible to instrumental control, although each qualifies as "elicited, involuntary, and autonomic," and each has been the object of uncounted studies in classical conditioning. On the other side of the fence, there is, of course, longstanding evidence that classical procedures can be applied to the control of skeletal responses (Bekhterev, 1913), although, to our knowledge, there is only one study (Van Liere, 1953) which dealt with responses so small as to make it unlikely that their occurrence could, in instrumental fashion, modify the effects of the unconditional stimulus (cf. Rescorla & Solomon, 1967). In short, the weight of the evidence, even after taking the artifact and mediation arguments into account (cf. Katkin & Murray, 1968; Smith, 1954), leans to the position that classical and instrumental procedures apply in common to most responses, a position which suggests that there may be only one not two, varieties of learning (cf. Hefferline *et al.,* 1971; Herrnstein, 1969; Miller, 1969; Rescorla & Solomon, 1967; Schoenfeld, 1966).

The enigma of our conditioning studies has thus been handsomely resolved: Instrumental procedures do, in fact, apply to "involuntary" responses, and, it would seem, to most of the responses which might be categorized as private events, cortical activity not excepted (Fetz, 1969; Rosenfeld, Rudell, & Fox, 1969). The resolution deals us two high-valued cards—the first logical, the second methodological. Logically, it is now possible to extend to psychosomatic symptoms, that is, to symptoms of the autonomic system, the type of analysis formerly applied only to symptoms thought to be mediated by the central nervous system (cf. Dollard & Miller, 1950; Miller, 1969). Methodologically, the fact that instrumental procedures may be used to control private events means that they can be manipulated experimentally as independent variables (Hefferline & Bruno, 1971), and that they can be manipulated clinically in systematic programs of self-education and re-education.

While the logical card has only just been turned up, the methodological is now clearly in play. Hand in hand with the experiments demonstrating that instrumental control applies to one and then another private event has come another series of experiments, inaugurated in our laboratory (Hefferline, 1958), which have developed effective and public means for controlling private events in a practical way. These experiments, which have adapted the "engineering" procedures of augmented or supplementary feedback, provide the *S* with an auditory or visual analog, typically continuous, of the private event which is the object of study. The experiments, whose efficacy seems to derive from their status as a variety of discriminative instrumental conditioning (Hefferline *et al.,* 1971), have now been carried out successfully with covert muscular responses (Basmajian, 1963; Hefferline, 1958), cardiac variables (cf. Brener, Kleinman, & Goesling, 1969), salivation (Delse & Feather, 1968), electrodermal responses (Stern & Kaplan, 1967), and with the alpha frequencies of the electroencephalogram (Kamiya, 1969). An application and some of the implications of these experiments are given in later sections of this paper (see "Response Bias" and "Bio-Feedback: Controlling the 'Uncontrollable' ").

Response Discrimination

The experiments in response control made in our laboratory and in others serve, we think, to provide "objective evidence" that the self-control of private events discussed in *Gestalt Therapy* is in fact attainable. But what of self-awareness—can this too be given an experimental foundation? To answer this question, we turned again to muscular tension, first with a design modified from animal studies of response discrimination (Hefferline & Perera, 1963), and then with procedures used in the psychophysical laboratory to study sensory magnitude (Bruno, Hefferline, & Suslowitz, 1971).

In the initial study (Hefferline & Perera, 1963), "our specific objective was to train the subject, although he might remain otherwise unresponsive to an occasional minute twitch in his left thumb ... nevertheless to 'report' its occurrence ... by pressing a key with his right index finger [p. 834]". To do this, we presented a tone as quickly as possible after each thumb-twitch and asked the *S*, who was not told the specific objective, to press the key each time he heard the tone. Then, after several sessions with this procedure, we gradually reduced the intensity of the tone until it was in fact no longer presented.[3] The result was that the *S* complained that the tone was "getting hard to hear," but he continued to press the key! More exactly, 72% of the thumb-twitches were followed within 2 sec by a key-press, and 80% of the key-presses correctly reported or discriminated the prior occurrence of a thumb-twitch. Apparently, in fading out the tone, we had transferred discriminative control of the key-press from the tone to the thumb-twitch in much the same way that Terrace, in the animal laboratory, transfers control of key-pecking in pigeons from a colored stimulus to one of line orientation (1963).

---

[3] The procedure for this study was actually somewhat more complicated. A full description and the rationale are given in detail elsewhere (Hefferline *et al.,* 1971).

Our results clearly established that a private event—the covert thumb-twitch—can serve as a discriminative "stimulus" in the same sense that response-produced cues are said to provide stimuli in studies of animal learning (cf. Berryman, Wagman & Keller, 1960; Notterman & Mintz, 1965; Rilling & McDiarmid, 1965). We say "in the same sense" because we had, in effect, succeeded in teaching the *S* a discrimination at what might be called the "animal level." It was clearly not a "conscious" discrimination: Although we would say that a *S* had learned to discriminate thumb-twitches, when questioned after the experiment, the *S*—who had never been told anything other than to respond to tones—explained that he continued to press the key because he still heard the tone.

The apparent discrepancy between our account and the subject's is not, however, difficult to resolve when we recall that our instructions to the subject had explicitly equated, at least within the experimental context, the status of two responses—the overt key-press and the verbal report "I heard it." We had, in effect, told the subject to report with a key-press the same events which ordinarily he would report by saying "I heard the tone." If we assume, with Schoenfeld and Cumming (1963), that what is reported is the occurrence of a mediating event, and not the occurrence of the stimulus *per se,* then it makes sense to presume that the effect of our procedure was to enable the thumb-twitch to enter significantly into the control of those events originally evoked primarily by the tone, with the result that the twitch, via the mediating events, acquired discriminative control of *both* the key-press and the verbal report [Hefferline *et al.,* 1971].

In other words, we had, not unwittingly, demonstrated the discriminative properties of the covert thumb-twitch by conditioning an "hallucination". Of course, the drama is not necessary to the demonstration, provided one is willing to work at the "conscious" rather than at the "animal" level. Antrobus and Antrobus (1967), for example, have shown that *S*s can be taught to discriminate Stage 1 REM from Stage 2 sleep, while Kamiya (1969) demonstrated that the presence and absence of alpha rhythms in the electroencephalogram are perfectly discriminable. The wonder, in fact, is not that these private events are discriminable, but that so few others have ever been studied (cf. Hefferline, 1962).

Although basic work is still needed on a host of obvious variables—heart rate, stomach contractions, and respiration among them—our particular interest in tension patterns led us, in our second experiment on response discrimination, to investigate sustained muscular contractions. While contractions of this sort have been interpreted perceptually as a manifestation of set (Allport, 1955) and have been implicated clinically as a factor in functional disorders (Whatmore & Kohli, 1968), little is known of man's ability to report on them verbally. What is known, however, suggests that perceived tension grows as a power function of the magnitude of muscular contractions (cf. Hefferline *et al.,* 1971; J. C. Stevens & Mack, 1959). Accordingly, we chose a psychophysical method—magnitude estimation (cf. Stevens, 1956)—suitable for perceptual continua governed by the "power law" (cf. Stevens, 1961).

The method proved simple and direct. The *S* sat in a reclining chair with his right hand resting palm down on a board which held two upright bars. The tip of his little finger was placed between the bars, as shown in Fig. 1, and the *S* was asked to press his finger against the appropriate bar to produce adductive or

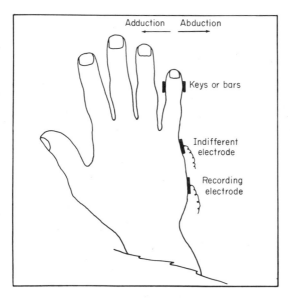

Fig. 1. Electrode placement on the hypothenar eminence and the position of the keys or bars used to define adductive and abductive tensions.

abductive tensions. An intermediate, "comfortable" tension was selected as the standard and it was assigned the value "10." On each trial the *S* was first required to reproduce the standard tension, and then, afer a 5-sec period of relaxation, was asked to produce, with verbal guidance, a preselected comparison level of tension. At this point, the *S* was told to relax and then to report a number which stood in proportion to "10" as the comparison tension stood in proportion to the standard tension.

The *S*'s numerical estimates of the comparison tensions were recorded and compared to electromyographic measurements of the same tensions, quantified in decibels relative to the energy produced by a 200-Hz sine wave at 10 μV peak-to-peak amplitude. The latter measurements were made using surface electrodes, placed as in Fig. 1, to record the electrical activity from the muscles of the hand which adduct and abduct the little finger (cf. Bruno, Davidowitz, & Hefferline, 1970). Figure 2 shows, for an experienced *S*, the relationship between perceived tension and the magnitude of abductive muscular contractions. The straight line drawn through the data points is the graph of a power function whose exponent, *t*, is approximately unity. Similar data were obtained from another *S* scaling abductive tensions and from two others who scaled adductive tensions, although naive *S*s gave somewhat less orderly data spanning a narrower range of tensions.

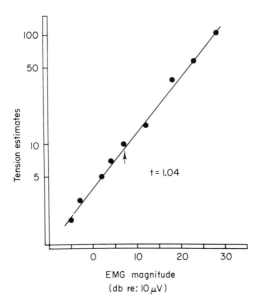

Fig. 2. Magnitude estimation of abductive tension. The function is for an individual observer giving one determination per point. The arrow marks the standard stimulus.

Several aspects of the data deserve comment. Chief among these is the fact that these are individual data taken from *S*s giving only one estimate for each tension level. These are not long-term, averaged data collected from a group of *S*s, but rather, to put it loosely, these are the data of "the here and now." They are, nevertheless, reliable—both in the sense that the same *S* gave comparable results on different measurement occasions and in the sense that different *S*s gave comparable data for the same muscle—and valid as determined by cross-modality matches (cf. Stevens, 1959) made between tension and tonal loudness (Bruno *et al.*, 1971).

The data are of particular interest in the present context because they demonstrate that tensions are perceived according to the same rule whether they be large or small, public or private. In fact, we have collected many tension functions from different observers, for different muscles, and under different procedures, but we have never found one that demonstrated a discontinuity between public and private tensions. For tension, at least, the discontinuity is not in the mind of the perceiver.

Before we turn to other matters, another word is in order about the lack of studies dealing with response discrimination. Surely the problem is not methodological: Even monkeys, who neither speak our language nor understand psychophysical procedures, can be taught to report on the visual motion (spiral) aftereffect, that is, on an "illusion" (Scott & Powell, 1963). Perhaps the lack of studies reflects a lack of interest. Here we will be the first to concede that a parade of studies demonstrating response discrimination of one private event and then another, *ad nauseam,* is not very interesting, and in any case, to paraphrase the retort of George Bernard Shaw's black girl to Pavlov after being treated to a demonstration of conditional reflexology, "we already know *that*" (Shaw, 1933). What we have in mind, however, are studies directed to problems somewhat meatier than the question of whether such-and-such a private event is discriminable. At the very least, we might ask how the perception of a private event relates to its frequency or magnitude. Or we might attempt to discover the extent to which state variables or payoff or accessory exteroceptive stimuli can influence the detection of a private event, that is, influence self-perception. Or, if the psychophysical aspects seem uninteresting, perhaps it would be worthwhile to explore conditioning approaches for new techniques to heighten self-awareness. Certainly, the possibilities are many and rich; clearly the problem is deserving of attention.

Response Bias

In the last two sections ("Response Control" and "Response Discrimination"), we dealt electropsychologically with the principles underlying the topics of self-control and self-awareness which had been examined phenomenologically in *Gestalt Therapy.* In this section, we intend to deal with a topic, response bias, whose phenomenological counterpart has been variously given as attitude, predisposition, postural organization, etc. (cf. Hefferline, 1962, p. 116ff.). The topic, which in part covers the material traditionally collated under the rubric of set, has both a long history—one which in fact is nearly as long as the history of experimental psychology itself (cf. Woodworth & Schlosberg, 1954)—and a sizeable literature, some of which was considered in an earlier paper (Hefferline, 1962). However, our present concern with the topic is not historical, but methodological and analytic; specifically, our concern is to describe first a new variety of research (Hefferline & Bruno, 1971) and then an extension of signal detection theory (Bruno & Hefferline, in preparation), both of which have important application to the study of response bias.

To see what's "new" about the new variety of research, let us look first at an example—a good example—of the old variety. Davis (1952), in one of several similar experiments, presented on each trial two tones of equal loudness, the second 5 sec after the first. He asked his *S* to close a telegraph key with the forefinger of one hand if the second tone seemed "stronger" than the first, but to close the key placed under the forefinger of the other hand if the second tone seemed "weaker". Throughout the experiment he recorded the electromyogram from electrodes placed over the extensor digitalis of each arm. He found that the proportion of "weaker" judgments, which varied in this and similar experiments from 30 to 70%, was a direct "function of the action potential difference in the two arms just prior to the second stimulus [p. 387] ". He described these results as follows:

> It is proposed that the action potentials from the two arms represent the activity state of two competing response systems; that both are excited by the first stimulus but have differing response curves and initial levels; that, other things being equal, the system which has the advantage at the time of the second stimulus will further build up its activity until enough force is generated to close a key [p. 390].

The design was indeed most ingenious: Since the two stimuli on each trial were subjectively identical, the particular outcome of a trial could only reflect the influence of "setting or biasing" factors. While ingenious, the design was nevertheless of the old or traditional variety in the sense that the private, physiological event (prestimulus tension) was, like the probability of "weaker" judgments, a dependent variable. To be sure, the design exemplifies precisely the traditional experiment in psychophysiology described by Sternbach:

> Mental or emotional behavioral activities are made to occur while physiological events are being observed; correlations between these activities and the observed physiological events are noted, and then some intervening internal event is postulated [1966, p. 2].

Of course, there is nothing intrinsically "wrong" with the traditional variety of research. On the contrary, it has brought to light many interesting correlations between private events and public behavior—witness the many correlations between reaction time and events such as heart rate, tension, alpha rhythm, respiration—and it has generated many interesting hypotheses concerning the nature of set or response bias (cf. Allport, 1955). But what of these hypotheses? How do we set about determining their validity? We might, as Davis (1952) did, replicate the originating experiment directly, by repeating it, or systematically (Sidman, 1960), by varying "nonessential" details such as the modality of the stimulus or the nature of the response. However, replication of this sort, while it may serve to support the original hypothesis, or to generate new ones if the replication "fails," cannot provide the grounds necessary to accept or reject the hypothesis. What is needed is another form of systematic replication which can provide a convergent operation with respect to the hypotheses elaborated by traditional means (cf. Garner, Hake, & Eriksen, 1956; Stoyva & Kamiya, 1968). This, in fact, is what the new variety of research does.

The new variety is distinguished from the old in that it, unlike the old, manipulates the private, physiological event as an independent variable. For example, if we were to repeat Davis' experiment using the new variety of research, we would manipulate òr vary prestimulus tension rather than simply measuring it. Of course, we would compute the same set of correlations between prestimulus tension and response probability, and we would compare these to Davis' results, but now our position would be considerably improved. Since the traditional experiment and the new variety form converging operations—they are neither identical nor orthogonal experiments, but together they converge to permit us to accept or reject a particular experimental hypothesis—if Davis' results and ours differ we can reject his notion, if they are the same we can accept the notion that "the system which has advantage at the time of the second stimulus will further build up its activity until enough force is generated to close a key."

The power for this new variety of research, which of course is not really "new" (cf. Courts, 1942; Meyer, 1953), derives from our new-found ability to control private events other than skeleto-muscular via exteroceptive feedback loops (see "Response Control" and "Bio-Feedback: Controlling the 'Uncontrollable' "). While in the past it was possible to control, and therefore manipulate as a variable, only large-scale, public events (force of handgrip, for example), it is now possible, with feedback, to manipulate events as private and subtle as cortical activity (cf. Rosenfeld *et al.,* 1969; Spilker, Kamiya, Callaway, & Yeager, 1969).

To illustrate the new variety of research, we have performed a series of studies in which covert prestimulus tension was manipulated during reaction-time, absolute-threshold, and stimulus-generalization paradigms (Hefferline & Bruno, 1971). Since all of the studies used comparable procedures, only the generalization study will be described here. This study was carried out in three phases: feedback training, discrimination training, and generalization testing.

The object of the first phase was to teach the S to control, with feedback, covert activity in the muscles of the hand which adduct and abduct the little finger. To do this, we placed the finger between the response bars, as illustrated in Fig. 1, and recorded the electromyogram from surface electrodes placed on the hypothenar eminence. Since the electromyogram taken from this placement contains, during all degrees of contraction, short waveforms during adductor activity and long waveforms during abductor activity (Bruno *et al.,* 1970), it was possible, by displaying the waveforms to the S on a triggered oscilloscope, to train him to produce adduction and abduction at covert levels. The training procedure, which was similar to that used by Basmajian (1963; 1967, p. 103ff.), has been described in detail elsewhere (Bruno *et al.,* 1971; Hefferline & Bruno, 1971). The result of the training was that the S learned to produce covert

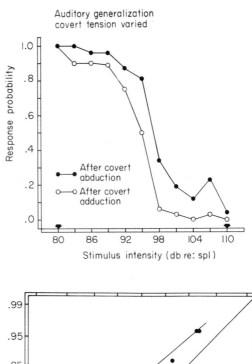

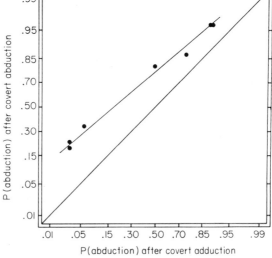

Fig. 3. Upper panel: probability of an abductive key closure to generalization stimuli presented during covert adduction or abduction, after training to respond adductively to 104-dB and abductively to 86-dB tones. Lower panel: iso-bias contour for the same data obtained by plotting, in double probability coordinates, the upper psychometric function against the lower.

adduction (50 μV peak-to-peak short waveforms) when a red pilot lamp was lit, and covert abduction (200 μV long waveforms) when a green lamp was lit.

In the second phase, discrimination training, each trial began with the presentation of the red or green light requiring covert adduction or abduction, respectively. When the tension appropriate to the light had been sustained for about .5 sec, one of two tones was presented via earphones. The S was instructed to close the adductive key (which replaced the bar in that position—see Fig. 1) whenever he heard the loud (104-dB) tone, and to close the abductive key when he heard the soft (86-dB) tone. This procedure, which was carried out for 200 trials, was adapted from one previously used by Cross and Lane (1962), as was the procedure of the next phase—generalization testing.

Generalization testing, which was carried out for 704 trials, was identical to discrimination training except that the tone intensity on each trial was chosen at random from a set of 11 intensities ranging from 80 dB to 110 dB in 3-dB steps. The S was asked to close the adductive key when the test tone resembled the loud training tone, and to close the abductive key when it resembled the soft tone.

Figure 3 shows, for an individual S, how the probability that a test tone was categorized as "soft"—i.e., the probability of an abductive key closure—varied with tone intensity and with the pretone covert tension. (The probability that a tone was called "loud" is the complement of the probability graphed.) In general, the probability of "soft" judgments was high in the region of the training stimulus for that response, decreased systematically over intermediate intensities, and was low in the region of the training stimulus for the opposite response. However, "soft" judgments were consistently more probable when the test tone was presented after appropriate rather than inappropriate covert tensions; that is, the S was more likely to call a tone "soft" if he was already "saying soft" rather than "loud" covertly.

The experiment, in effect, constitutes an eleven-fold systematic replication of Davis' 1952 study. For each of the 11 test stimuli, we have purposely given advantage on half the trials to the "soft" response system and given advantage to the "loud" system on the remainder of the trials. Like Davis, we found "that, other things being equal, the system which has the advantage . . . will further build up its activity . . . to close a key." Except that "other things," as usual, are not "equal," so that the magnitude of the effect appears to vary with the intensity of the test tone—although the prestimulus tensions were fixed in magnitude and did not vary from tone to tone. Actually, the effect of the tensions was "constant" across tone intensity, as we might intuitively expect, but to show this we must detour briefly through a signal detection analysis of the experiment.[4]

---

[4] A lucid account of signal detection concepts may be found in Green and Swets (1966).

Figure 4 depicts, in much simplified and idealized form, the hypothetical mechanisms operating in the stimulus-generalization experiment. The strong assumption is made that the physical dimension of stimulus (tone) intensity has a monotonically related correlate in psychological space. This is shown as the abscissa in Fig. 4. Along the abscissa are plotted 11 Gaussian density functions of equal variance. Since these represent the perceptual effects of the 11 test stimuli, the means of the distributions, which, quite unrealistically, are shown as

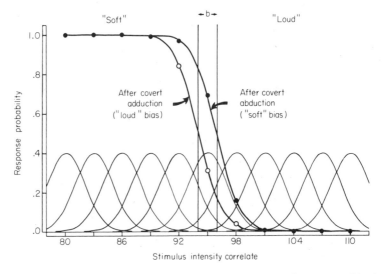

Fig. 4. Diagram of the hypothetical mechanisms correspondent to an 11-stimulus generalization experiment conducted under the method of constant stimuli. The superimposed ogives represent idealized psychometric functions plotted in psychological space.

equi-distant in psychological space, are labeled with the intensity (in decibels) of the corresponding physical stimulus. Probability density functions rather than single values along the abscissa have been used to represent the perceptual effects of the stimuli because, for organismic (cf. Corso, 1967, p. 410ff.) or for physical reasons (cf. Hecht, Schlaer, & Pirenne, 1942), the effect of a stimulus in fact varies from presentation to presentation. Consequently, different physical stimuli can give rise to the same perceptual effect, a circumstance portrayed by showing the density functions as overlapping distributions.

Because different stimuli may generate the same effect, the observer asked to categorize the test tones as either "loud" or "soft" must adopt a decision rule which will allow him to operate despite the fact that he cannot "recognize" the tones by their effects. We assume that he establishes a decision point or criterion—two such points are indicated by the vertical lines in Fig. 4—and presses the abductive key to say "soft" when he observes a perceptual effect to the left of the criterion, but "says loud" to effects to the right of the criterion. Under this rule, the probability of a "soft" judgment is given for each test stimulus by the area under its corresponding density function which falls to the left of the criterion. As shown by the ogival curves in Fig. 4, when the probability of a "soft" judgment is plotted for each stimulus above the mean of its corresponding distribution, the result, for each location of the criterion, is the usual psychometric function spread out along an axis of psychological rather than physical distance (cf. Boneau & Cole, 1967).

In Fig. 4, the idealized psychometric function labeled "after covert abduction" is the one which would be generated if the S adopted the right-hand criterion; the function labeled "after covert adduction" would come from adopting the left-hand criterion. Notice that these idealized functions are not unlike the actual functions displayed in the upper panel of Fig. 3. In fact, we assume that a S required to sustain a covert abductive tension, that is to covertly say "soft," would adopt the liberal right-hand criterion which, because more area lies to the left of it, makes "soft" judgments (abductive key closures) consistently more probable than they would be if the stricter left-hand criterion were adopted. Similarly, we assume that requiring covert adduction—saying "loud" covertly—leads to the adoption of the left-hand criterion, making "soft" judgments less probable. In short, we assume that manipulating covert prestimulus tension in the muscles about to make an overt perceptual response is equivalent, in our model, to manipulating the S's decision point or criterion.

In a sense, we have come full circle: The idealized functions in Fig. 4, like the actual functions in Fig. 3, seem to show a biasing effect whose magnitude varies with stimulus intensity. But our model, confirming our intuitions, suggests that the effect is in fact "constant" when its magnitude is judged not from the separation of the psychometric functions, but rather from the distance, "b," which separates the two criteria. What is needed now is a way to estimate this distance from actual data.

Our iso-bias contour provides the way (Bruno & Hefferline, in preparation). The lower panel in Fig. 3 shows the iso-bias contour which results when the psychometric function taken "after covert abduction" is plotted in double-probability coordinates (which "straighten out" Gaussian ogives) against the function taken "after covert adduction." Had there been no difference between the functions, the data points would lie along the major diagonal. The functions, however, were different, and what distinguished them was the psychological distance between the two decision points or criteria which were adopted to generate them. A measure of this distance, in standardized units, is reflected by calculating b', which is the difference between the two criteria divided by the standard deviation common to each of the distributions of perceptual effects. The calculation, which in this case gives a value of about 1.0 standard deviation units, is described in detail elsewhere (Bruno & Hefferline, in preparation). It is sufficient here to say that it is comparable to the d' calculation for the common iso-sensitivity contour (cf. Green & Swets, 1966, p. 58ff.), and that it, like d', depends on whether or not the equal variance assumption holds.[5] It is sufficient because the value of b' is reflected graphically by the degree to which the iso-bias contour is displaced away from the major diagonal toward the upper left-hand corner of the figure: The greater the displacement the greater is b'.

As its use here suggests, the iso-bias contour, so-called because it links points of equal bias or criterion difference, applies whenever data are taken under the method of constant stimuli (Woodworth & Schlosberg, 1954, p. 201) using operations which cause the S to adopt two or more distinct criteria (n contours result for $n + 1$ criteria). For example, we have applied the contour successfully to absolute threshold data taken with visual stimuli under the rating method (Barlow, 1956), to visual increment threshold data taken when payoff was varied (Swets, Tanner, & Birdsall, 1961), to pain and thermal thresholds taken under the rating method to examine the placebo effect (Clark, 1969), and to wavelength generalization data collected from pigeons on test trials given before and after reinforcement (Boneau, Holland, & Baker, 1965). In each case, when the psychometric function presumably taken under a liberal criterion was plotted, in double-probability coordinates, against the function presumably taken under a strict criterion, the result was a straight line—that is, an iso-bias contour—which told us immediately that the two psychometric functions were distinguished by a difference in response bias (criterion) and not a difference in sensory capacity. Here, in distinguishing bias from capacity, we see the power of the iso-bias contour (and of signal detection theory itself): It renders explicit variables which in classical psychophysics were implicit or ignored. Of course it, not incidentally, also provides the means for quantifying one of those variables, viz., response bias.

The implications of the iso-bias contour for the study of private events are, perhaps, obvious. Since it provides a way to identify changes in response bias, it allows us to hunt out those private events which influence the S's readiness or unreadiness to respond. Then, having found a biasing event, if we manipulate it—as in the new variety of research described previously—the contour provides the means to quantify the effect of our "private" independent variable.

In this part of our presentation, dealing with the electropsychological analysis of private events, we have tried to sketch in some of the methods and some of the data which provide the experimental underpinnings for an all-out study of

---

[5] Where the assumption holds, the iso-bias contour has a slope of unity. Where it does not, but variance increases with intensity, as in the present data, the slope is less than unity.

the "universe . . . enclosed within the organism's own skin [Skinner, 1953, p. 257]." In the next section, we take up in detail one of the experimental methods which seems particularly promising for the future of this private part of the universe.

Bio-Feedback: Controlling the "Uncontrollable"

In some of the studies described in previous sections, we shared with the S our "sight" or "sound" of his muscle-action potentials as electronically transduced into an oscilloscopic display or an auditory output from a speaker system. We discovered, as have many others more recently, that such an opportunity fascinates the S and that it also constitutes a powerful tool for self-training and self-control. Until recently it has been called "augmented feedback," since it supplies an external feedback loop which augments the internal loop via proprio- or interoceptors; but this term, which is often inappropriate, as when applied to signals of cortical origin, will now presumably give place to "bio-feedback," since the many workers presently joining the field are organizing under the name of the Bio-Feedback Research Society.

What has spurred this sudden rallying around a single experimental stratagem is, of course, the fact that it has effectively exploded the doctrine, widely held for so long, that autonomic activities are inaccessible to instrumental training procedures (see "Response Control"). At the present time, however, not only have they proved to be trainable in instrumental fashion, but, from the humanistic viewpoint, a host of activities previously deemed to be necessarily involuntary have come within the jurisdiction of voluntary control. A broad new vista spreads before us, with both foreseeable and unforeseeable opportunities and responsibilities. For better or worse, the internal environment has been thrown open to "civilizing" influences.

For example, "externalization" by means of bio-feedback of otherwise private events makes it possible for the first time to label and reinforce such events precisely by bringing the E and the S into common possession of the key properties of the behavior. Gardner Murphy wrote, afer a visit to our laboratory during which he learned to control three different muscles via feedback of their surface-recorded waveforms (cf. Bruno *et al.,* 1970):

> [Hefferline] and his collaborator attached electrodes to my left little finger and left ear lobe and asked me to watch an oscilloscope as I carried out small directed movements with my left little finger. Whenever I extended my finger to the left, this produced, in the midst of a shower of "noise," a well-defined peak on the oscilloscope which, as I practiced, became more and more clear—the Matterhorn, as I called it. A countermovement, flexing rather than extending the finger, produced another pattern, which I called the Jungfrau. A

third task—and a very difficult one—was to push the little finger straight out as if it slipped in a socket, producing a flat table top which I called a mesa. Soon I was producing at will the Matterhorn, Jungfrau, and mesa patterns [Murphy, 1964, p. 105].

With a little more time to spend "shaping up" his own behavior by means of the visual feedback, Murphy would have learned, as do our regular Ss, to get along without the external "crutch." He would have become able upon his own command or that of the E to produce any of the labeled responses with the same clarity and sharpness of definition that he had achieved through practice with the scope.

Our finding that bio-feedback, once it has served its purpose of permitting a selected response or sequence of responses to be sharply discriminated, and perhaps "named," can usually be "faded out" (cf. Hefferline et al., 1971), has been confirmed by Basmajian (1963, 1967), who has worked intensively on training Ss to control individual neuromuscular motor units. Basmajian states that his Ss "were provided with two modalities of 'proprioception' that they normally lack; namely, they heard their motor unit potentials and saw them on monitors [1963, p. 440]." Within 15-30 min of practice most had learned to relax the whole muscle upon command and then to recruit the activity of a single motor unit, keeping it active for as many minutes as desired. Activity at first consisted of a steady train of pulses; later, the S learned to "turn off" the unit or even to produce single firings upon request. Similar control of other units might be acquired, some Ss being able to recruit up to a fourth or fifth isolated unit. After an hour or more, a S could become so skilled, Basmajian reports, that he could produce "various gallop rhythms, drum-beat rhythms, doublets, and roll effects [p. 441]," and then might even become able to perform such tricks in the absence of the feedback necessary to establish control in the first place!

While the trained S giving "gallops" and "doublets" makes it all look easy, the voluntary singling out of an individual motor unit from the sizeable array of those that are ordinarily active in a muscle "at rest," is, presumably, not so easy. Phillips, at Oxford, comments as follows:

... The refined degree of minute localization that is evidently possible in voluntary control ... must require a marvelously subtle routing of activity in the outer cortical layers to pick up, in significant functional groupings, the required corticofugal neurons, which are scattered and intermingled with unwanted ones which may be suppressed [1966, p. 402].

It is paradoxical that what might seem to be the simplest possible response, namely, the firing of a single motor unit, should require for its production the highly selective facilitatory and inhibitory effects postulated by Phillips. Sperry in 1955 supposed that something of this sort was involved as "the neural basis of the conditioned response," and here he was speaking of something that might be as simple (?) as a particular leg movement. He argued for elaborate patterns of central nervous facilitation and/or inhibition, which he said were the neural counterparts of and derivatives from psychological expectancies and anticipatory sets. In 1958 he related the "functional settings of the brain" more intimately to the experimental psychologist's preoccupation with skeletal behavior in the following passage:

> ... Perhaps it would be more accurate and fruitful to picture the differentiation and interrelations of facilitory sets, not in terms of tree limbs and branches, but directly in terms of the potential postures and movements of the vertebrate body. The "postural sets" then have direct implication for the implicit operations of perception and thought processes, depending on the closeness or remoteness of these latter to motor adjustment [Sperry, 1958, pp. 416-417].

Today a certain expertise in bringing about subtle manipulations of the "mind–body relation" has arisen among coaches, physical therapists, psychotherapists with a somatic approach, relaxationists, and various others. We believe that much useful order could be brought to this area—and to the whole of psychology—through the systematic study of central-peripheral interactions now discernible through the use of sophisticated instrumentation for multichannel recording of patterns of bodily activity.

An ambitious but most circumspect step in this direction has been taken by George B. Whatmore, of Seattle (Whatmore & Kohli, 1968). His medical practice consists of the diagnosis and treatment of what he calls "dysponesis"—defined as misdirected effort. Daily life, he says, is made up of performing, bracing, representing and attending efforts. Performing covers the vast range of movements outwardly observable. Representing, "a form of self-signaling," is made up of the covert behaviors which produce imagery (not restricted to the visual modality). Attending is the "effort" which provides impulses from various sense organs with differential access to the nervous system, in large degree by gross or subtle eye efforts.

Bracing efforts we have met before as "holding responses," conflict, and unresolved tensions. Whatmore himself says that by bracing efforts "we hold the body, or a part of the body, rigid or 'on guard'." He states further that "often one effort is pitted against another, one muscle contracted against its antagonist", and that "these efforts can be made in any or all parts of the body such as the extremities, the breathing musculature, the neck, the back, the jaw, the tongue, and the throat [1968, p. 103]."

Whatmore quantifies dysponesis by electromyometry, allows his patient to hear his muscular effort by electromyophony and to see it by electromyoscopy. His published case studies report good results for a wide range of troublesome conditions. He avoids psychopathological terminology and describes his procedures as simply "a form of neurophysiologic engineering wherein basic principles of neurophysiology are used to carry on a retraining within the nervous system [1968, p. 102]."

In a personal communication, Whatmore (1969) reports that norms for his work were established "by measuring from persons 'relatively free of functional disturbances' and from patients and control subjects after effort training." Standard electrode positions are on the forehead, jaw, forearm, and leg. Special positions pertinent to the given patient may be on the neck, back, or other region.

It appears from Whatmore's papers that dysponesis is most frequently hyperponesis, that is, excessive muscular tension. The therapeutic goal, as in Jacobson's earlier method of progressive relaxation (1938), is to move in the direction of lowered tension, although Whatmore indicates that "some patients need more training in various forms of 'going on with the power' than they do in 'going off with the power' [1968, p. 117]." How to proceed with a given case is based, he states, as far as possible "upon laboratory and clinical evidence and not upon philosophic concepts [p. 116]." Psychoanalysis and other forms of psychotherapy "with treatment limited to interview techniques," he regards as having no correcting effect upon dysponesis. He does add, however:

> Psychotherapy can be used, when there are indications for it, along with definitive treatment of dysponesis, but it is a separate procedure that attacks [sic] a different aspect of the individual and does not alter dysponetic tendencies [p. 115].

Despite his sharp dichotomizing of the results achievable by his physiologic approach and those obtainable by "treatment limited to interview techniques", Whatmore does not take the militant stand against psychodynamics that characterizes such behavioral therapists as Eysenck (1952) or Wolpe (1962). The statement quoted above would seem to acknowledge not only a basis for co-existence, but even, on occasion, for co-function. He looks forward, of course, to the further development of his own method and asserts that "the task for the future is one of developing still better training methods of neuro-physiologic engineering wherein instrumentation and instrumented learning will undoubtedly play an increasing role [1968, p. 119]."

We, too, share wholeheartedly this interest in improved "neurophysiologic engineering." One interesting possibility in this direction involves what Walter (1964) called the "contingent negative variation"—a phenomenon better described as the "dc shift," since it consists of a shifting potential difference between, typically, an electrode at the vertex and a second one at an inactive site such as the ear lobe. The dc shift has been shown to be indicative of cerebral processes and to be controlled by a wide variety of both psychological and state variables. A parametric study is under design in our laboratory in which hopefully the dc shift will prove to be another of the private events trainable by bio-feedback and possibly useful as an index of central-peripheral interactions otherwise accessible only in a cumbersome way by multichannel recording at the periphery (Camp, 1970).

Unlike Whatmore, we see it as only a temporary state of affairs that he can talk as plausibly as he does of the independent use of "psychotherapy" and "neurophysiologic engineering". There is, to be sure, the large contingent of behavioral therapists relying heavily on the process of "desensitizing" the patient, and effecting "symptom removal" by what essentially consists of arranging a situation in which "undesirable" conditioned emotional reactions may be extinguished, or suppressed, perhaps, by conditioning stronger incompatible behavior. It can hardly be questioned that, at this level, the method is "successful" (Bandura, 1969).

On the other hand, Freudian psychoanalysis and the "depth therapies" derivative from it all take the position that the symptom is exactly that—a trait or condition symptomatic of the more comprehensive systemic malfunction— with the consequence that personality alterations of any profundity are premised upon conceptually elaborate strategies for resolving conflict. As Whatmore has said, the treatment may indeed be limited to interview techniques. This does not, however, mean per se that the effects are merely verbal ones. On the contrary, strong emotion is generated in the therapeutic situation, with consequences, inevitably, for the neurophysiologic systems with which Whatmore deals. The trouble is that one has to guess at what is going on from moment to moment in the analytic session and be continually uncertain about how and when to intervene for optimal results.

Some psychoanalysts, however, concern themselves in various degree with the physiological version of the psychological problem (Braatøy, 1954; Christiansen, 1963; Fagan & Shepherd, 1970; Lowen, 1958; Shatan, 1963). This may involve no more than encouraging the patient to experience vividly the functioning of his body; or it may include direct physical manipulations by the doctor. This combined approach has its share of partisan enthusiasts, but its superiority, if it is superior, has not been clearly established. Nevertheless, if it avails itself of bio-feedback techniques, it seems likely that its therapeutic power will increase by several orders of magnitude.[6]

Finally, in modern group therapy there is implicit a kind of crude psychophysiology of private events. Leaders of sensitivity and encounter groups set high value on various kinds of physical contact as "sensory awakeners" and

---

[6] A dramatic type of sensory feedback, made available by television technology, is now employed in many psychiatric hospitals to provide videotape self-confrontation. A patient may see and hear himself in action when he has played back for him a tape made earlier. By means of an additional closed circuit his present appearance may be shown at the same time as an insert in a corner of the monitor; in effect, he may watch himself watching himself (Berger, 1970).

"releasers." The literature to date is semipopular, but instructive (Gustaitis, 1969; Howard, 1970; Shepard & Lee, 1970; Schutz, 1967). Bio-feedback applied here could supply a new dimension. Perhaps we may close with a quotation from Mulholland which, although it comes from a most sober paper, has elements of blithe fantasy (Mulholland, 1968):

> Studies of interpersonal and group processes might achieve a new dimension using feedback methods. If the physiological response for one person were information to another, and his physiological response were information to the first, the behavior of both might be modified. For instance, if heart beat were indicated by a flashing light worn, say, on the lapel, and a man and woman were introduced, the man's light might flash more quickly. The woman, perceiving this, might be slightly embarrassed, and her light would begin flashing more quickly. The man would perceive this, and his light would flash more, etc., etc. Soon both lights may be flashing at a fast rate. I would hope that both would laugh when this occurred, restoring equilibrium [p. 436]!

References

Allport, F. H. *Theories of perception and the concept of structure.* New York: Wiley, 1955.

Antrobus, J. S., & Antrobus, J. S. Discrimination of two sleep stages by human subjects. *Psychophysiology,* 1967, **4,** 48-55.

Ax, A. F. Goals and methods of psychophysiology. *Psychophysiology,* 1964, **1,** 8-25.

Bandura, A. *Principles of behavior modification.* New York: Holt, 1969.

Barlow, H. B. Retinal noise and absolute threshold. *Journal of the Optical Society of America,* 1956, **46,** 634-639.

Basmajian, J. V. Control and training of individual motor units. *Science,* 1963, **141,** 440-441.

Basmajian, J. V. *Muscles alive: Their functions revealed by electromyography.* Baltimore: Williams & Wilkins, 1967.

Bekhterev, V. M. *Objective psychologie.* Leipzig and Berlin: Teubner, 1913.

Berger, M. M. (Ed.). *Videotape techniques in psychiatric training and treatment.* New York: Brunner/Mazel, 1970.

Berryman, R., Wagman, W., & Keller, F. S. Chlorpromazine and the discrimination of response-produced cues. In L. Uhr & J. G. Miller (Eds), *Drugs and behavior.* New York: Wiley, 1960. Pp. 243-249.

Boneau, C. A., & Cole, J. L. Decision theory, the pigeon, and the psychophysical function. *Psychological Review,* 1967, **74,** 123-135.

Boneau, C. A., Holland, M. K., & Baker, W. M. Color-discrimination performance of pigeons: Effect of reward. *Science,* 1965, **149,** 1113-1114.

Braatøy. T. *Fundamentals of psychoanalytic technique.* New York: Wiley, 1954.

Brener, J., Kleinman, R. A., & Goesling, W. J. The effects of different exposures to augmented sensory feedback on the control of heart rate. *Psychophysiology,* 1969, **5,** 510-516.

Brown, C. C., & Katz, R. A. Operant salivary conditioning in man. *Psychophysiology,* 1967, **4,** 156-160.

Bruno, L. J. J., Davidowitz, J., & Hefferline, R. F. EMG waveform duration: A validation method for the surface electromyogram. *Behavior Research Methods and Instrumentation,* 1970, **2**, 211-219.

Bruno, L. J. J., & Hefferline, R. F. An iso-bias contour for the method of constant stimuli. In preparation.

Bruno, L. J. J., Hefferline, R. F., & Suslowitz, P. D. Cross-modality matching of muscular tension to loudness. *Perception and Psychophysics.* 1971. In press.

Camp, J. A. Some factors controlling cortical dc shifts in man: A review. Electropsychology Report MH-13890-10, Columbia Univ., 1970.

Christiansen, B. Thus speaks the body. Oslo: Institute for Social Research, 1963.

Clark, W. C. Sensory-decision theory analysis of the placebo effect on the criterion for pain and thermal sensitivity (d'). *Journal of Abnormal Psychology,* 1969, **74**, 363-371.

Corso, J. F. *The experimental psychology of sensory behavior.* New York: Wiley, 1967.

Courts, F. A. Relations between muscular tension and performance. *Psychological Bulletin,* 1942, **39**, 347-367.

Cross, D. V., & Lane, H. L. On the discriminative control of concurrent responses: The relations among response frequency, latency, and topography in auditory generalization. *Journal of the Experimental Analysis of Behavior,* 1962, **5**, 487-496.

Davis, R. C. The stimulus trace in effectors and its relation to judgment responses. *Journal of Experimental Psychology,* 1952, **44**, 377-390.

Delse, F. C., & Feather, B. W. The effect of augmented sensory feedback on the control of salivation. *Psychophysiology,* 1968, **5**, 15-22.

Dollard, J., & Miller, N. E. *Personality and psychotherapy.* New York: McGraw-Hill, 1950.

Eldridge, L. Respiration rate change and its relation to avoidance behavior. Unpublished doctoral dissertation, Columbia Univ., 1954.

Engel, B. T., & Chism, R. A. Operant conditioning of heart rate speeding. *Psychophysiology,* 1967, **3**, 418-426.

Engel, B. T., & Hansen, S. P. Operant conditioning of heart rate slowing. *Psychophysiology,* 1966, **3**, 176-187.

Estes, W. K. An experimental study of punishment. *Psychological Monographs,* 1944, **57**, (3, Whole No. 263).

Eysenck, H. J. The effects of psychotherapy: An evaluation. *Journal of Consulting Psychology,* 1952, **16**, 319-324.

Fagan, J., & Shepherd, I. L. (Eds.). *Gestalt therapy now. Theory, techniques, applications.* Palo Alto: Science and Behavior Books, 1970.

Fetz, E. E. Operant conditioning of cortical unit activity. *Science,* 1969, **163**, 955-958.

Garner, W. R., Hake, H. W., & Eriksen, C. W. Operationism and the concept of perception. *Psychological Review,* 1956, **63**, 149-159.

Green, D. M., & Swets, J. A. *Signal detection theory and psychophysics.* New York: Wiley, 1966.

Gustaitis, R. *Turning on.* Toronto: Macmillan, 1969.

Hecht, S., Schlaer, S., & Pirenne, M. H. Energy, quanta, and vision. *Journal of General Physiology,* 1942, **25**, 819-840.

Hefferline, R. F. An experimental study of avoidance. *Genetic Psychology Monographs,* 1950, **42**, 231-334.

Hefferline, R. F. The role of proprioception in the control of behavior. *Transactions of the New York Academy of Sciences,* 1958, **20**, 739-764.

Hefferline, R. F. Learning theory and clinical psychology—An eventual symbiosis. In A. J. Bachrach (Ed.), *Experimental foundations of clinical psychology.* New York: Basic Books, 1962. Pp. 97-138.

Hefferline, R. F., & Bruno, L. J. J. The physiological event as an independent variable. *Psychophysiology,* 1971. In press.

Hefferline, R. F., Bruno, L. J. J., & Davidowitz, J. Feedback control of covert behavior. In K. J. Connolly (Ed.), *Mechanisms of motor skill development*. New York: Academic Press, 1971. In press.

Hefferline, R. F., & Keenan, B. Amplitude-induction gradient of a small human operant in an escape-avoidance situation. *Journal of the Experimental Analysis of Behavior,* 1961, **4**, 41-43.

Hefferline, R. F., & Keenan, B. Amplitude-induction gradient of a small-scale (covert) operant. *Journal of the Experimental Analysis of Behavior,* 1963, **6**, 307-315.

Hefferline, R. F., Keenan, B., & Harford, R. A. Escape and avoidance conditioning in human subjects without their observation of the response. *Science,* 1959, **130**, 1338-1339.

Hefferline, R. F., & Perera, T. B. Proprioceptive discrimination of a covert operant without its observation by the subject. *Science,* 1963, **139**, 834-835.

Herrnstein, R. J. Method and theory in the study of avoidance. *Psychological Review,* 1969, **76**, 49-69.

Howard, J. *Please touch: A guided tour of the human potential movement.* New York: McGraw-Hill, 1970.

Jacobson, E. *Progressive relaxation.* Chicago: Univ. of Chicago Press, 1938.

Kabat, H. Central mechanisms for recovery of neuromuscular function. *Science,* 1950, **112**, 23-24.

Kamiya, J. Operant control of the EEG alpha rhythm and some of its reported effects on consciousness. In C. T. Tart (Ed.), *Altered states of consciousness*. New York: Wiley, 1969. Pp. 507-517.

Katkin, E. S., & Murray, E. N. Instrumental conditioning of autonomically mediated behavior: Theoretical and methodological issues. *Psychological Bulletin,* 1968, **70**, 52-68.

Kimble, G. A. *Hilgard and Marquis' conditioning and learning.* 2nd ed. New York: Appleton, 1961.

Lindsley, D. B. Emotion. In S. S. Stevens (Ed.), *Handbook of experimental psychology.* New York: Wiley, 1951. Pp. 473-516.

Lowen, A. *Physical dynamics of character structure: Bodily form and movement in analytic therapy.* New York: Grune & Stratton, 1958.

Meyer, D. R. On the interaction of simultaneous responses. *Psychological Bulletin,* 1953, **50**, 204-220.

Miller, N. E. Learning of visceral and glandular responses. *Science,* 1969, **163**, 434-445.

Mulholland, T. Feedback electroencephalography. *Activitas Nervosa Superior,* 1968, **10**, 410-438.

Murphy, G. Communication and mental health. *Psychiatry,* 1964, **27**, 100-106.

Notterman, J. M., & Mintz, D. E. *Dynamics of response.* New York: Wiley, 1965.

Perls, F. S., Hefferline, R. F., & Goodman, P. *Gestalt therapy: Excitement and growth in the human personality.* New York: Julian Press, 1951.

Phillips, C. G. Precentral motor area. In J. C. Eccles (Ed.), *Brain and conscious experience.* New York: Springer-Verlag, 1966. Pp. 389-421.

Rescorla, R. A., & Solomon, R. L. Two process learning theory: Relationships between pavlovian conditioning and instrumental learning. *Psychological Review,* 1967, **74**, 151-182.

Rilling, M., & McDiarmid, C. Signal detection in fixed-ratio schedules. *Science,* 1965, **148**, 526-527.

Rosenfeld, J. P., Rudell, A. P., & Fox, S. S. Operant control of neural events in humans. *Science,* 1969, **165**, 821-823.

Roszak, T. *The making of a counter culture.* New York: Doubleday, 1968.

Sasmor, R. M. Operant conditioning of a small-scale muscle response. *Journal of the Experimental Analysis of Behavior,* 1966, **9,** 69-85.

Schoenfeld, W. N. Some old work for modern conditioning theory. *Conditional Reflex,* 1966, **1,** 219-223.

Schoenfeld, W. N., & Cumming, W. W. Behavior and perception. In S. Koch (Ed.), *Psychology: A study of a science.* Vol. 5. New York: McGraw-Hill, 1963. Pp. 213-252.

Schutz, W. C. *Joy: Expanding human awareness.* New York: Grove Press, 1967.

Scott, T. R., & Powell, D. A. Measurement of a visual motion aftereffect in the Rhesus monkey. *Science,* 1963, **140,** 57-59.

Shapiro, D., & Crider, A. Operant electrodermal conditioning under multiple schedules of reinforcement. *Psychophysiology,* 1967, **4,** 168-175.

Shapiro, D., Tursky, B., Gershon, E., & Stern, M. The effects of feedback and reinforcement on the control of human systolic blood pressure. *Science,* 1969, **163,** 588-590.

Shaw, G. B. *The adventures of the black girl in her search for God.* New York: Dodd, Mead, 1933.

Spilker, B., Kamiya, J., Callaway, E., & Yeager, C. L. Visual evoked responses in subjects trained to control alpha rhythms. *Psychophysiology,* 1969, **5,** 683-695.

Shatan, C. Unconscious motor behavior, kinesthetic awareness and psychotherapy. *American Journal of Psychotherapy,* 1963, **17,** 17-30.

Shepard, M., & Lee, M. *Marathon 16.* New York: Putnam, 1970.

Sidman, M. *Tactics of scientific research.* New York: Basic Books, 1960.

Skinner, B. F. *Science and human behavior.* New York: Macmillan, 1953.

Smith, K. Conditioning as an artifact. *Psychological Review,* 1954, **61,** 217-225.

Snyder, C., & Noble, M. Operant conditioning of vasoconstriction. *Journal of Experimental Psychology,* 1968, **77,** 263-268.

Sperry, R. W. On the neural basis of the conditioned response. *British Journal of Animal Behavior,* 1955, **3,** 41-44.

Sperry, R. W. Physiological plasticity and brain circuit theory. In H. F. Harlow & C. N. Woolsey (Eds), *Biological and biochemical bases of behavior.* Madison: Univ. of Wisconsin Press, 1958.

Stern, R. M., & Kaplan, B. E. Galvanic skin response: Voluntary control and externalization. *Journal of Psychosomatic Research,* 1967, **10,** 349-353.

Sternbach, R. A. *Principles of psychophysiology.* New York: Academic Press, 1966.

Stevens, J. C., & Mack, J. D. Scales of apparent force. *Journal of Experimental Psychology,* 1959, **58,** 405-413.

Stevens, S. S. The direct estimation of sensory magnitudes—loudness. *American Journal of Psychology,* 1956, **69,** 1-25.

Stevens, S. S. Cross-modality validation of subjective scales for loudness, vibration, and electric shock. *Journal of Experimental Psychology,* 1959, **57,** 201-209.

Stevens, S. S. The psychophysics of sensory function. In W. A. Rosenblith (Ed.), *Sensory communication.* New York: Wiley, 1961. Pp. 1-33.

Stoyva, J., & Kamiya, J. Electrophysiological studies of dreaming as the prototype of a new strategy in the study of consciousness. *Psychological Review,* 1968, **75,** 192-206.

Swets, J. A., Tanner, W. P., & Birdsall, T. G. Decision processes in perception. *Psychological Review,* 1961, **68,** 301-340.

Terrace, H. S. Errorless transfer of a discrimination across two continua. *Journal of the Experimental Analysis of Behavior,* 1963, **6,** 223-232.

Van Liere, D. W. Characteristics of the muscle tension response to paired tones. *Journal of Experimental Psychology,* 1953, **46,** 319-324.

Walter, W. G. The convergence and interaction of visual, auditory, and tactile responses in human nonspecific cortex. *Annals of the New York Academy of Sciences,* 1964, **112,** 320-361.

Whatmore, G. B. Personal communication, 1969.

Whatmore, G. B., & Kohli, D. R. A neurophysiologic factor in functional disorders. *Behavioral Science,* 1968, **13,** 102-124.

Winnick, W. A. Anxiety indicators in an avoidance response during conflict and nonconflict. *Journal of Comparative and Physiological Psychology,* 1956, **49,** 52-59.

Wolpe, J. The experimental foundations of some new psychotherapeutic methods. In A. J. Bachrach (Ed.), *Experimental foundations of clinical psychology.* New York: Basic Books, 1962. Pp. 554-575.

Woodworth, R. S. & Schlosberg, H. *Experimental psychology.* (rev. ed.). New York: Holt, 1954.

Author Index

Numbers in italics refer to the pages on which the complete references are listed.

Subject Index

68343